# Employment, Inequality and Globalization



The nature of globalization and the fallout from the international financial crisis have brought profound changes to societies and economies around the world. This book documents that, over the last two decades, the growth of nonstandard and informal employment has led to greater inequalities. This is partly explained by the fact that adjustment policies in the 1980s, market liberalization policies in the 1990s and, more recently, globalization and anti-poverty policies did not pay sufficient attention to policies for employment and income redistribution. As a response to these trends, this book recommends the development of clearer policies for employment and income redistribution. These policies should now become an integral part of national and international economic policy making. This is even more relevant in the current context of the international financial crisis as:

- several elements of globalization, especially the unfettered markets, and the growing inequality have given cause to the current crisis and,
- there is growing evidence that the employment, human and social effects of the financial crisis will be felt well after an economic recovery has taken place, especially if no corrective action is taken.

This volume will be of benefit to policymakers, scholars and practitioners alike.

This book was published as a special issue of the *Journal of Human Development and Capabilities.*

**Rolph van der Hoeven**, PhD, Free University of Amsterdam is Professor of Employment and Development Economics at the Institute of Social Studies (ISS) in The Hague and member of the Committee on Development Cooperation of the Dutch Government. Earlier he was Director of ILO's Policy Coherence Group, Manager of the Technical Secretariat of the World Commission on the Social Dimension of Globalization, Chief Economist of UNICEF and policy analyst for the ILO in Ethiopia and Zambia. His work concentrates on issues of employment, inequality and economic reform on which he is widely published.

# Employment, Inequality and Globalization

## A Continuous Concern

*Edited by*
**Rolph van der Hoeven**

Routledge
Taylor & Francis Group
LONDON AND NEW YORK

First published 2011
by Routledge
4 Park Square, Milton Park, Abingdon, Oxon OX14 4RN
605 Third Avenue, New York, NY 10017

*Routledge is an imprint of the Taylor & Francis Group, an informa business*



This book is a reproduction of the *Journal of Human Development and Capabilities*, vol. 11, issue 1. The Publisher requests to those authors who may be citing this book to state, also, the bibliographical details of the special issue on which the book was based



*British Library Cataloguing in Publication Data*
A catalogue record for this book is available from the British Library

ISBN 13: 978-0-415-59701-2 (hbk)

**Disclaimer**
The publisher would like to make readers aware that the chapters in this book are referred to as articles as they had been in the special issue. The publisher accepts responsibility for any inconsistencies that may have arisen in the course of preparing this volume for print.

Typeset in Garamond
by Taylor & Francis Books.

# Contents

# Notes on Contributors

**Alice H. Amsden** is Barton L. Weller Professor of Political Economy at the Massachusetts Institute of Technology. In 2009 she was appointed by the UN Secretary-General Ban Ki-Moon to a three-year seat on the UN Committee on Development Policy. *Scientific American Magazine* chose her as one of the Top 50 Visionaries in 2002 for her book *The Rise of the Rest: Challenges to the West from Late-Industrializing Economies* (OUP, 2001, trans. into Persian, Portuguese, Korean and Japanese). She is currently working on a book entitled *The Rational Revolution: Developing from Role Models*, which argues that, outside macro-economics, developing countries learn from each other's experiences, not theory, which argues that, outside macro-economics, developing countries learn from each other's experiences, not theory.

**Giovanni Andrea Cornia** teaches economics at the University of Florence in Italy. He has also taught courses at the European University Institute and the Universities of Bologna, Cambridge, Clermont Ferrand, Helsinki, and Pavia, and lectured in several other universities. Between 1995 and 1999 he was the Director of the UN University World Institute for Development Economics Research, and before that held research positions with UNICEF, UNECE, UNCTAD and the Economic Studies Centre of FIAT. His work has focused primarily on growth, macro-economic, inequality, poverty, human development and mortality and health issues in developing and transitional economies.

**Alex Izurieta** is Senior Economic Affairs Officer in the Development Policy and Analysis Division of UN Department of Economic and Social Affairs (DESA). His area of expertise is the analysis of global economic developments and the evaluation of policy scenarios with the help of macro-economic and global models. He has contributed to the two flagship publications of the Division, *World Economic Situation and Prospects* and *World Economic and Social Survey*, as well as to UN/DESA Policy Briefs and other official UN documents on economic and social issues. He co-authored his chapter, with Ajit Singh, for the *Journal of Human Development and Capabilities* in his capacity as Research Associate of Cambridge Endowment for Research in Finance; Judge Business School.

**Richard Jolly** is Honorary Professor and Research Associate of the Institute of Development Studies at the University of Sussex. He has just completed a book with Louis Emmerij and Thomas G Weiss, *UN Ideas That Changed the World* (Indiana University Press, 2009), the last of the 17-volume UN Intellectual History project, for which he was a co-author of three previous volumes. From 1982 to 2000, Richard Jolly was an Assistant Secretary General of the UN, first as Deputy Executive Director of UNICEF and from 1996 as Senior Coordinator of the Human Development Report and Special Adviser to the Administrator of the UNDP.

**Thandika Mkandawire** is Professor and Chair of African Development in the Department of International Development at the London School of Economics and Olop Palme Professor at the Institute for Future Studies in Stockholm. He served as Director of UNRISD for the years 1998–2009. From 1986 through 1996 he was Executive Secretary of the Council for the Development of Social Science Research in Africa (CODESRIA) based in Dakar, Senegal. Prior to taking up his appointment with UNRISD, he was Senior Research Fellow at the Centre for Development Research in Copenhagen. He has taught at the University of Stockholm and at the University of Zimbabwe.

**Ajit Singh** is Emeritus Professor of Economics at Cambridge University and Senior Research Fellow at the Judge Business School Cambridge. He also holds the Tun Ismail Ali Chair in International Economics at the University of Malaya, Kuala Lumpur. His research falls into three areas: the modern corporation and the theory of the firm, including corporate finance, and the market for corporate control; 'de-industrialization' and structural change in advanced and developing economies; and globalization and economic policy in emerging markets. He is the author of nearly 200 articles including about 100 in leading refereed academic journals. He has also authored or edited several books, and scholarly monographs. In 2004 he was elected an Academician of the British Academy of Social Sciences.

**Rolph van der Hoeven** is Professor of Employment and Development Economics at the Institute of Social Studies in The Hague and member of the Committee on Development Cooperation of the Dutch Government. Earlier he was Director of the UN International Labour Organization (ILO)'s Policy Coherence Group, Manager of the Technical Secretariat of the World Commission on the Social Dimension of Globalization, Chief Economist of UNICEF, and policy analyst for the ILO in Ethiopia and Zambia. His work concentrates on issues of employment, inequality and economic reform on which he is widely published.

**Rob Vos** is Director of the Development Policy and Analysis Division, the core economic research unit of the UN Department of Economic and Social Affairs. He is responsible for two of the UN's flagship reports, the *World Economic and Social Survey* and the *World Economic Situation and Prospects*, as well as for the Secretariat of the UN's Committee for Development Policy. He has published widely on development issues. His recent books include (with J. A. Ocampo and K. S. Jomo) *Diverging Growth* (Oriental Longman and Zed Press, 2008), (with J. A. Ocampo) *Uneven Economic Development* (Oriental Longman and Zed Press, 2008), (with J. A. Ocampo and A. Cortez) *Ageing and Development* (Oriental Longman and Zed Press, 2008), and *Public Policies for Human Development* (Palgrave/ Macmillan, 2010).

# *Introduction: Employment, Inequality and Globalization: A Continuous Concern*

ROLPH VAN DER HOEVEN
*Rolph van der Hoeven is Professor of Employment and Development Economics at the Institute of Social Studies in The Hague, The Netherlands*

This book is based on a special issue of the JHDC, which grew out of a seminar on Work, Employment and Globalization at the Institute of Social Studies.[1] Through no intent of the organizers, this seminar coincided with a crash in the financial markets, turning the USA sub-prime mortgage crisis of 2007 into a financial crisis, an economic crisis and a social crisis. A major reason for organizing the seminar was that, over the past two decades, rising non-standard and informal employment has become an important factor of personal income (International Labour Organization, 2008) and factor inequality (van der Hoeven, chapter 5). This could be partly explained by a related observation that adjustment policies in the 1980s, market liberalization policies in the 1990s and, more recently, globalization and anti-poverty policies did not pay sufficient explicit attention to policies for employment and income redistribution (Jolly, Mkandawire, and Amsden, chapters 2, 3 and 4 respectively).[2] At the seminar, arguments were presented to explain why these policies as well as policies for human development should (again) become an integral part of national and international economic policy-making.

However, given the timing of the seminar, one of the major questions that also emerged was whether analyses on employment, inequality, human development and globalization are still relevant in the current context of a large financial crisis. Most participants argued that such analyses remained highly relevant for at least two reasons.

Firstly, several elements of globalization, especially the unfettered markets (including the labour market)[3] and the growing inequality (resulting in many households having to indebt themselves in order keep up spending on basic needs),[4] have given cause to the current crisis; therefore, policy recommendations pertaining to the analysis of the structure and nature of current globalization and its impact on employment and inequality become even more relevant in times of crisis.

Secondly, there is growing evidence that the employment, human and social effects of the financial crisis will last for a while, especially if no corrective action is taken. Reinhardt and Rogoff (2009), for example, foresee that a deceleration or decline in Gross Domestic Product growth will lead to rising unemployment with a much longer duration than the deceleration or decline in Gross Domestic Product itself. Based on a sample of past crises, in the north and the south, they observe an average slump in employment lasting 4.8 years, compared with a deceleration or decline in output growth of only 1.9 years. van der Hoeven and Luebker (2007) investigated the behaviour of labour shares in national incomes during recent periods of financial crises and observed a ratchet effect: labour shares decline during crises but in many cases do not return, once the economy has picked up, to their pre crisis level. There is also evidence that indicators for human development exhibit a similar ratchet effect. Arbache and Page (2007), for example, show that in Africa child mortality increases during growth decelerations but hardly falls during growth accelerations. Further, primary school completion rates and life expectancy are and remain substantially lower in countries experiencing growth decelerations.

There are thus are strong reasons to include policies for employment, income inequality and human development as priority issues in designing short-term and longer policies to deal with the crisis. But, might there be trade-offs between policies for employment, income inequality and human development? A recent study on explanations for growing inequality over the past decade (Angeles-Castro, 2006) concludes that high employment levels reduce inequality and, especially for developing nations, high employment levels in the industrial sector reduce inequality. Targeting for employment and for reduction of income inequality can thus be combined objectives in policy-making. In a similar vein, Stewart and Ranis (2002) argued that human development and economic growth can be joint and reinforcing targets for policy-making. It thus seems more than appropriate to argue for greater attention to employment, income inequality and human development in times of crises.

Jolly (chapter 2) goes further and argues that a shift in international paradigm, or policy framework, if not a new one, is needed to meet the current crisis. For the past 30 years, the ruling paradigm has essentially been that of neo-liberal economics and the underlying philosophy has been that of neo-classical economics, directed to the goal of achieving greater economic efficiency in the allocation and use of resources on a global scale. Politically, it has been guided by the interests and priorities of the major western economic powers, with the purpose of extending markets and investment opportunities throughout the world. According to Jolly the current global economic crisis has brought home the inadequacies of this paradigm and its serious consequences for countries, rich and poor. Efficiency as the guiding principle has failed to ensure stability, and the untrammelled pursuit of market forces has allowed inequalities to increase to unprecedented levels. He calls for a framework that, in addition to economic efficiency, systematically includes objectives of sustainability, stability, equity and social justice, and human rights, and notes that many of these objectives were an integral part of the 'human development paradigm'. Globalization has neglected these objectives, leading amongst others to the current crisis. Fukada-Parr, (2009) adds that, also in the run up to the crisis, the preoccupation with the Millennium Development Goals has resulted in a distorted concept of human development: the lost in translation aspect of the Millennium Development Goals.

Stiglitz (2009) in a similar vein argues that the dominant view during the current process of globalization was that unfettered markets were judged sufficient to ensure economic efficiency. The best role for government was a limited one, and somehow the benefits of the growth that this would engender would trickle down to everybody in society. Added to that was the view of a dominant strand of economists arguing that the problem in the market economy was rigid wages, and that if it was not for wage rigidities then the economy would work in the way that classical economics predicted. According to Stiglitz, the implication of the Keynesian rigid-wage theory was very invidious but very pervasive: get rid of the rigid wages, and let labour markets be more 'flexible'. That has been the basis of a whole set of doctrines undermining job protections and labour rights. But, as he rightly observes, wages are not rigid — in the Great Depression wages fell by about one-third: the problem that Keynes recognized was that wages can be too flexible. Stiglitz observes that lack of aggregate demand was the problem with the Great Depression, just as lack of aggregate demand is the problem today. Accordingly, imposing more wage flexibility can result in exacerbating the underlying problem of lack of aggregate demand. He puts the nature of the problem that we face today as follows: 'The people in the global economy have the same skills as before the crisis, and the machines and real resources are the same as before the crisis. The problem is that there is an organizational failure, a coordination failure, and a macroeconomic failure' (Stiglitz, 2009, p. 12).

In reviewing some organizational and coordination failures, Mkandawire (chapter 3) analyses why social and employment concerns in Africa have been neglected in Africa. For Mkandawire, labour markets constitute an important arena for addressing issues of poverty and are not simply institutions for the static efficient allocation of existing labour resources; they are also sites for the realization of basic civil and social rights. Furthermore, they perform the developmental role that is often obscured by the preoccupation with market clearance. Also, labour market institutions can be sources of savings through contributory schemes such as pensions, and labour market policies cannot only ensure decent working conditions but can also create incentives for both employers and employees to improve 'human capital'. He observes that one common feature of the 'success stories' was their extensive intervention in the labour markets but also that labour markets are probably among the most politically difficult markets to manage in the process of late industrialization. He recalls that during the so-called Golden Age of capitalism (1945–1975), under Keynesian influence, full employment was prioritized as a key objective of public policy. For 'late industrializers' such as the East Asian countries, employment creation was a central aspect of their social policy. He recalls that when poverty entered the policy agenda in the 1970s under the 'Basic Needs' and 'Growth with Equity' strategies, labour markets and employment immediately assumed a central role. Social development — in the form of full employment — was thereby embedded within both macroeconomic policy agenda and development. He deplores that much of the post-World War II consensus was to unravel by the end of the 1970s. The implementation of adjustment policies has led to a massive trend worldwide towards 'flexibility' of the labour force: trade unions have been sidelined and coerced to toe the line. In many cases, employment has been deliberately casualized through sub-contracting arrangements and the like. Although important exceptions can be cited — such as China and some other East Asian countries — the employment situation has been worsening in many other parts of the developing world. Mkandawire observes that in much of the developing world the working population is being increasingly crowded into the ubiquitous 'informal economy', which cannot be a sector pulling countries out of the crisis.

One reaction to the all invading adjustment policies in the 1980s and 1990s has been a greater concern for poverty alleviation, which has now become one of the major targets for international development cooperation. Amsden (chapter 4) warns that one-sided attention to poverty issues can however misguide national policies: 'To slay the dragon of poverty, deliberate and determined investments in jobs above starvation wages must play a central role, whether for self-employment or paid-employment'. She fears that the grass roots approach to solving poverty does not go far enough, because it aims only at improving the supply side of the labour market, making job-seekers more capable, and not the demand side, making new jobs available for them. It acts as though new ways of earning a living emerge (at a positive wage) simply because the supply of job-seekers is better clothed, housed, and fed, or enjoys more human rights — which is the same fallacious reasoning behind Say's Law, to the effect that the supply of whatever an economy produces creates the demand to buy it (at a positive price). She observes that, by not strengthening the demand side, 25 years of supply-side poverty alleviation has left poverty rates for the poorest people unchanged. She argues that employment generation is different from poverty alleviation, because it has a concept behind it, 'capital'. This means that the labour market is influenced by, and influences, all flows through the savings–investment nexus, including accumulation, distribution, and innovation. This she sees at the heart of political conflict. Multi-faceted policies, therefore, are required to promote employment growth, from fiscal and monetary to industrial and trade.

In reviewing some of these political issues and the need for policy change, van der Hoeven (chapter 5) wonders why the growing income inequalities within and between countries, as well as the recent spurge of international reports on this issue, have in general not led to many changes in international development policies. One reason might be that a new strand of analysis emphasizes what it calls unashamedly 'deserved and undeserved inequalities' (Fereira, 2007, p. 20). For example, in reviewing the phenomenon of declining labour shares over the past two decades, some argue that the decline in labour share after financial crisis was, in effect, the consequence of a too high labour share before the crisis, thus partly blaming malfunctioning labour for the build-up of the crisis. However, only in a minority of cases have financial crises been caused by bidding up wages and labour shares. In most cases the crisis was caused by external events or rent-seeking behaviour of capital owners.[5] He therefore calls for a review of labour market institutions and argues that these should include explicit concern for redistribution of value added. He bases his arguments an a recent findings by Freeman (2007) that the most effective and observable function of labour market institutions is, when successful, a reduction of inequality, and that labour market institutions have varied effects on growth and employment. van der Hoeven gives a number of examples demonstrating that it is possible for economic policies to target better towards goals of employment creation and reduction of income inequality but questions whether there is yet the political will to do so. He argues that such will was present in not too remote times; for example, both in Western Europe after the Second World War and in Eastern Asian countries during the so-called Asian miracle, low levels of income inequality were combined with rapid growth. Although these two examples may at first instance look very different, they have at least one element in common: both are examples of restrained capitalism. In Europe the restraints came from social pacts and the functioning of the labour markets, while government bureaucrats and political elites provided the restraint in the East Asian countries. The current crisis and the increasing public concern for improved income equality can well provide the basis for a renewed political will to make employment creation and reasonable income distribution again major objectives for economic policy-making.

Some argue that such a change in attitudes might be in the making. Stewart (2009) reviews Polanyi's work and argues that, as was the case after the great depression in the 1930s, the pendulum is swinging again to a situation where market forces might be restrained by regulation, state takeover social protections and Keynesian macro-economics. Cornia's analysis (chapter 6) might provide some support to this. He reviews the decline in income inequality that has taken place over 2002–2007 in most Latin American countries in contrast to a steady increase between 1980 and 2002. He analyses the factors that could explain this decline in inequality, and that might raise it again during the current crisis, focusing in particular on favourable external conditions, cyclical factors, improvements in the distribution of educational achievements, the subsequent drop in skill-premiums, and changes in macroeconomic and social policies. The latter have been introduced in several countries, particularly in the increasing number of left-of-centre governments that came to power during the past decade. His results (based on an econometric test for the years 1990–2007 that included nearly all countries of the region) indicate that, in addition to a favourable business cycle and external conditions, a decline in skill premium and the new policy model of fiscally prudent social-democracy had a favourable impact on the distribution of income. He suggests that if such a policy approach will survive the current crisis, part of the recent inequality decline will be permanent rather than temporary.

However, there remain huge international challenges for countries wishing to embark on a more egalitarian and human development focused growth path. The opening of product and financial markets has made economies more integrated and, even with huge barriers to migration, labour markets have also become more integrated. As a consequence the number of workers that are now part of the global labour market has hugely increased. For various reasons this is, under the current model of globalization, leading to greater stratification and a growing inequality, which national and international policies have to face up to. Izuerta and Singh (chapter 7) discuss a hotly debated policy question; namely, whether globalization of the world's labour, capital and product markets, together with rapid economic growth in India and China, will have an adverse effect on workers in the USA and other advanced countries. In essence, they pose the question whether fast growth in developing countries needs to be at the expense of growth in advanced countries. Projections in their article indicate that, at a disaggregated regional and country level, there exist supply-side constraints that may thwart the expansionary demand effects of fast growth in India and China. These supply constraints relate to natural resources (energy and raw materials). Scenario simulations suggest that if these resource bottlenecks can be overcome by technical progress, both advanced and developing countries may continue to grow and achieve high employment. These challenges are currently exacerbated by the current crisis where the need for increase in demand has only become too obvious, but they reject the thesis that the labour market would become a binding constraint for future world growth.

In the final chapter, Vos discusses international measures necessary to deal with current globalization and the current crisis. Such measures should be seen from the backdrop that no social or economic order is secure if it fails to benefit the majority of those who live under it. Vos recalls that this demands nothing less than what European political philosophers in the seventeenth and eighteenth centuries called a 'social contract': an implicit understanding among members of a community to cooperate for mutual benefit, along with formal rules and institutional mechanisms to help build trust, balance competing interests, manage disputes and provide a fair distribution of the rewards that are generated. In today's world of increased economic and political interdependence, achieving a broad-based, rapid and sustained growth in incomes and employment involves even more complex policy challenges than in the past. Vos notices that the complexities of global interdependence in trade and finance are but one dimension of these challenges. This will require strategic vision and leadership of governments and international organizations to give substance to a new social contract that strikes a balance between achieving greater (global) horizontal equity for present generation prosperity and peace and intergenerational equity ensuring sustainable development for future (although ageing) world populations and overcoming the threat of climate change. In a world of great uncertainty, it is far from obvious how to strike such a balance, let alone what policies will work best. But as labour markets become more integrated and ever more dependent on large and more footloose multinational enterprises, Vos emphasizes a need for a 'more transparent, coherent and balanced framework' at the global level to address the employment dimensions of globalization.[6] He recalls that a more balanced pattern of domestic demand will only be achieved when rising wages (in line with productivity gains) rather than increased levels of debt provide a solid basis for expanding domestic market demand. The challenges ahead will also require economies to continuously increase their skill and knowledge base in order to successfully integrate themselves into the global production process; to ensure that the net effect of globalized production is not simply the displacement of workers; and to uphold core labour standards in order to ensure decent and productive work for all. In all cases, the benefits that global production can bring should be properly weighted against the costs, and these costs can only be minimized through active involvement of all the major actors.

The chapters in this book have all stressed that, because of unfair current globalization and because of the current crisis, greater attention need be given to policies for employment, income equality and human development both at national and international level. The challenge for international and national policy-makers to prioritize both economic and social policies bearing in mind the distributional and human development effects has only become more pressing in times of the current crisis. To pursue human development, globalization (United Nations Development Programme, 1999) (and perforce measures dealing with the current crisis) has to mean ethics, development, equity, inclusion, human security and sustainability. Fiscal stimuli and other measures to restore growth patterns should therefore be aimed specifically at key priorities of maintaining employment, reducing inequalities and all other measures to advance human development. If not, large parts of the developing world will find themselves in an even more disadvantaged position after the crisis than before.

**Acknowledgements**

Thanks go to many people in preparing the original special issue. The authors not only enthusiastically contributed but also inspired each other. Freek Schiphorst, Mansoob Murshed and Louk de la Rive Box ably chaired seminar sessions and together with Irene van Staveren, Peter Knorringa, Michael Grimm and Karel Jansen provided useful comments, as did at a later stage Sakiko Fukada-Parr, Kay Grigar, Dharam Ghai, and Stephan Klasen.

## Notes

1 Seminar on Work, Employment and Globalization, Institute of Social Studies (ISS), The Hague,18 September 2008.

2 There are of course exceptions; individuals and some international agencies have been making proposals for giving greater attention to employment policies (see, for example, World Commission on the Social Dimension of Globalization, 2004; Pollin *et al* 2006; Pollin and Heintz, 2007; Novick *et al.*, 2007).

3 Part of growing inequality can be explained by the policies undertaken during the process of liberalization and adjustment, including policies to make the labour market more efficient (van der Hoeven and Taylor, 2000).

4 '... over the past 30 years particularly, there has been an increase in inequality. In effect, we have been transferring money from the poor to the rich, from people who would spend the money to people who do not need to spend the money, and the result of that is weaker aggregate demand. The United States thought it could solve the problem: Americans who had no money were told to keep spending as if they had it. They enjoyed it for awhile. A massive debt finance bubble enabled them to continue to spend' (Stiglitz, 2009, pp. 7–8).

5 In a study of the manufacturing sector in a large sample of developing countries, Amsden and van der Hoeven (1996) argue that a decline in real wages and a fall in the wage share of value added in most non-Asian developing countries in the 1980s and the 1990s reflect a redistribution of income from labour to capital, as low wages were made to bear the burden of uncompetitive manufacturers.

6 See discussion in World Commission on the Social Dimension of Globalization (2004).

## References

Amsden, A. and van der Hoeven, R. (1996) 'Manufacturing output, employment and real wages in the 1980s: labour's loss until century's end', *Journal of Development Studies,* 32(4), pp. 506–530.

Angeles-Castro, G. (2006) 'The effects of economic liberalization on income distribution: a panel data analysis', in E. Hein, A. Heise and A. Truger (Eds), *Wages, Employment, Distribution and Growth,* Palgrave Macmillan, Basingstoke, pp. 151–180.

Arbache, J. and Page, J. (2007) More growth and fewer collapses? A New look at long run growth in Africa', *World Bank Policy Research Paper No. 4384,*World Bank, Washington, DC.

Ferreira, F.H.G. (2007) 'Inequality as cholesterol', in *International Poverty Centre (IPC) Poverty in Focus the Challenge of Inequality,* June, UNDP, Brasilia.

Freeman, R.B. (2007) 'Labourmarket institutions around the world', *Paper 13242,* National Bureau of Economic Research, Cambridge, MA.

Fukada-Parr, S. (2009) 'Human development, MDGs and the international development agenda', paper presented at the *HDRO Conference,* UNDP, New York 24 September.

International Labour Organization (2008) *World of Work Report 2008, Income Inequalities in the Age of Financial Globalization,* ILO, Geneva.
Novick, M., Tomada, C., Damill, M., Frenkel, R. and Maurizio, R. (2007) *In the Wake of the Crisis: Argentina's New Economic and Labour Policy Directions and their Impact,* IILS, Geneva.
Pollin, R. and Heintz, J. (2007) *Expanding decent Employment in Kenya: The Role of Monetary Policy, Inflation Control and the Exchange Rate,* IPC Country Report, UNDP, New York.
Pollin, R., Epstein, G., Heintz, J. and Ndikuma, L. (2006) *An Employment Targeted Economic Program for South Africa,* IPC Country Report, UNDP, New York.
Reinhart, C. and Rogoff, K. (2009) 'The aftermath of financial crises', *NBER Working Paper 14656,* National Bureau of Economic Research, Cambridge, MA.
Stewart, F. (2009) 'Relaxing the shackles: the invisible pendulum', *The Journal of International Development,* 29, pp. 765–771.
Stewart, F., Ranis, G. and Ramirez, A. (2002) 'Economic growth and human development', in S. Fukida Parr and A.K.S Kumar (Eds), *Readings in Human Development,* Oxford University Press, New Delhi, pp. 61 84.
Stiglitz, J. (2009) 'The global crisis, social protection and jobs', *International Labour Review,* 148(1–2), pp. 1–13.
United Nations Development Programme (1999) 'Globalization with a face', *Human Development Report 1999,* UNDP, New York, p. 44.
van der Hoeven, R. and Taylor, L. (2000) 'Introduction: structural adjustment, labour markets and employment: some considerations for sensible people , *Journal of Development Studies,* 36(4), pp. 57–65.
van der Hoeven, R. and Luebker, M. (2007) 'Financial openness and employment: the need for coherent international and national policies', in J.A. Occampo and K.S. Jomo (Eds), *Towards Full and Decent Employment,* Zed Books, London, chapter 2, pp. 22–53.
World Commission on the Social Dimension of Globalization (2004). *A Fair Globalization: Creating Opportunities for All,* ILO, Geneva.

# *Employment, Basic Needs and Human Development: Elements for a New International Paradigm in Response to Crisis*

RICHARD JOLLY
*Richard Jolly is Honorary Professor and Research Associate of the Institute of Development Studies at the University of Sussex, UK*

**Abstract** This article reviews various strands of development policies such as employment and basic needs policies, structural adjustment policies, human rights and human development policies, as well as policies emanating from the so-called Washington Consensus leading to current globalization practices. It argues that the present global crisis presents an important opportunity for making major changes in the objectives, directions and operations of the international system. Major efforts of financial and economic stimulus without such changes are short-sighted and dangerous. A new approach, a shift of paradigm or framework, is needed that is more flexible, less dogmatic, and is multi-disciplinary and clearly directed to long-term international goals: sustainability, stability, equity and human rights. There is also a need for more coherence in objectives and strategies across the system of international organizations. The human development paradigm, now marking its 20th anniversary, has many of the qualities required to be the basis for such an international framework, adapted to the specifics of each country. Some moves toward this should be considered.

## Introduction

A shift in international paradigm, or policy framework, if not a new one, is needed to meet the current crisis in global economic and social governance. For the past 30 years, the ruling paradigm has essentially been that of neo-liberal economics, with priorities and operational guidelines largely set by the Washington consensus, administered by the International Monetary Fund (IMF) and the World Bank and the World Trade Organization (WTO) . The underlying philosophy has been that of neo-classical economics, directed to the goal of achieving greater economic efficiency in the allocation and use of resources on a global scale. Politically, it has been guided by the interests and priorities of the major western economic powers, with the purpose of extending markets and investment opportunities throughout the world.

The current global economic crisis has brought home the inadequacies of this paradigm and its serious consequences for countries rich and poor. Efficiency as the guiding principle has failed to ensure stability, and the untrammelled pursuit of market forces has allowed inequalities to increase to unprecedented levels. The unwillingness of international pharmaceutical companies for several years to allow generic sales of anti-retrovirals against HIV/AIDS at much lower prices in South Africa became a human rights scandal. Most generally of all, the market has no controls to encourage the actions required to slow climate change and to moderate its consequences. All these are examples of priority issues that now need to find a place in a new framework for global governance. In short, we need a framework that, in addition to economic efficiency, systematically includes objectives of sustainability, stability, equity and social justice, and human rights. Whether this can be a totally new paradigm or a shift of the old paradigm is one of the issues to be considered in this paper. Either way, it is argued that the human development paradigm provides a framework for many of the elements that should be included.

## UN approaches — employment, basic needs and human development

Almost from the beginning, the United Nations made major economic contributions to ideas about international strategy for raising the living standards of people as a key international concern, especially of those living in the poorer countries of the world. Over the years, these have focused centrally on three major aspects of the human condition: employment, basic needs and human development.

At the beginning, employment was central to the United Nations' economic objectives and approaches. In three major reports during 1949 and 1951, successive expert committees of the United Nations made proposals for national and international measures for full employment, measures for economic development and measures for international economic stability. All three took full employment as the starting point and objective of their analysis, although the report on measures for economic development soon 'identified rapid creation of new employment as the main part of the solution and long-term economic development as the critical condition for achieving it'.[1]

The first report, for which Nicholas Kaldor, a distinguished economist, had the main responsibility for drafting, proposed a set of measures to maintain domestic full employment, following orthodox Keynesian lines. In addition, and more originally, the report proposed international coordinated action, to make possible the pursuit in every country of national policies for full employment. This envisaged the IMF having a key role in maintaining a full employment level of international demand: if a country's imports fell below some 'normal' level (i.e. a level consistent with full employment), the country would be required to deposit with the IMF an amount of their currency equivalent to the deflationary impulse thereby propagated. This, as John and Richard Toye describe it (Toye and Toye, 2004), was seen by critics as 'extreme Keynesianism' and the report attracted much criticism and was soon rejected. This led to the second report, in which a more general strategy of economic development was proposed and which moved the United Nations back on to safer ground. This was in any case a desirable outcome, since the original Keynesian proposals were more suited for industrial countries than to developing ones.

Since that time, mainstream development theory and policy have tended to focus on economic growth as the key objective and the major means for raising living standards. There have been two major exceptions arising from within the United Nations: Basic Needs Strategy, originating within work of the International Labour Organization (ILO) in the 1970s; and the human development approach, formulated by the United Nations Development Programme (UNDP) when it created the *Human Development Report* (HDR) in 1990. Economic growth was important to both approaches, but in each case economic growth was neither the key policy objective nor the only or main means for achieving the objectives. In both approaches, employment re-entered as a key element.

The ideas for basic needs arose from the work of the ILO World Employment Programme in two ways and at two levels. This work began, first, with a series of international missions investigating employment problems and strategy in Colombia, Sri Lanka, Kenya and other developing countries in the early 1970s. These identified three types of distinct employment problems underlying concern with the employment situation: the frustration of job-seekers unable to obtain the type of work that they expect or think is reasonable; the low level of incomes obtained by many workers and their families: and the under-utilization and low productivity of the labour force, both male and female.[2]

Second, the ILO established a research programme to examine a wider range of issues related to employment and development strategy, including those such as income distribution, technology, rural development, and population. The ideas emerging from both initiatives were later brought together coherently and comprehensively into a development strategy, presented in *Employment, Growth and Basic Needs: a One-World Problem*, a major document prepared for the World Employment conference in 1976.

For several years, *Basic Needs* (BN) gathered increasing support within the development community. After endorsement by the OECD in the late 1970s, BN became the consensus on development thinking among donors. However, BN was dramatically sidelined in the 1980s with the rise of Thatcher and Reagan to power, a move to the right in economic policy and the shifting of development attention and priorities to the problems of world recession and rising debt. Led by the IMF and the World Bank, policies of stabilization and structural adjustment rapidly became orthodoxy over the 1980s. More than 50 developing countries, primarily in sub-Saharan Africa and Latin America, adopted these policies – usually as a condition of receiving Bretton Woods support. Many parts of the United Nations raised objections to the severity of the cutbacks and human neglects of structural adjustment, notably United Nations Children's Fund (UNICEF), the United Nations Economic Commission for Africa (ECA) and the ILO.

Towards the end of the 1980s, structural adjustment policies were increasingly directed to the goals of what became known as the Washington Consensus (W-C). This set of 10 conditions went far beyond a simple focus on domestic strategy. Rather, most elements were designed to open economies to developed country investments and influence. These 10 included: fiscal discipline; abolition of subsidies; tax reform; market determined interest rates; competitive exchange rates; trade liberalization; liberalization of inward foreign direct investment and inflows of capital flows; privatization of state enterprises; deregulation and minimal oversight of financial institutions; and legal security for property rights. All of these were consistent with a neo-liberal view of the world, but did not necessarily flow from it. Rather, they represented the interests and policies of the industrial countries, more particularly the United States, the United Kingdom, Germany and Japan.

Human development was first presented by the UNDP in 1990. Although the UNDP had often spoken of the need for human development approaches in the 1980s, it was the initiative of the UNDP Administrator, Bill Draper, to ask Mahbub ul Haq, the distinguished and innovative Pakistani economist, to create an annual HDR. This gave the idea of human development intellectual substance, institutional support and worldwide promotion and publicity. Human development has followed a different trajectory from BN. For almost two decades, annual HDRs have been a focus of intellectual creativity and evolution in applying the human development paradigm to many issues and new areas: security, gender, consumption, globalization, care, culture, climate change, technology and democracy have been key examples. The human development approach has gained increasing attention and interest, academically and within developing countries.

Meanwhile, however, mainstream development policy, at least until the recent crisis, has remained locked internationally into neo-liberal approaches, influenced considerably by the Bretton Woods institutions, especially and increasingly by the IMF. Although new approaches have shifted the focus on poverty reduction and action towards the Millennium Development Goals (MDGs) and much interesting empirical material has been developed by the Bretton Woods Institutions, this has largely been done within the neo-classical economic paradigm, not outside it.

The global financial and economic crisis of 2008/09 has raised possibilities of change. In the short run, the crisis has already led to the adoption of massive programmes of Keynesian stimulus within the developed countries, in an effort to stave off depression and restore economic growth. Internationally, a number of actions to coordinate national policies among the richer countries have also been agreed, together with a major expansion of IMF resources of unprecedented magnitude, at least in principle. The crisis has also caused many to question the Washington consensus and raised serious doubts about the current neo-liberal economic paradigm. Although it is by no means clear that the international community is ready for any significant shift from the previous approaches by the Bretton Woods Institutions and donors towards developing countries, there is now a strong case for exploring possibilities. But if there is to be a shift, it is the argument of this paper that it must involve an explicit shift of framework and approach, not merely a few pragmatic adaptations. Further to this argument is the belief that human development could form the core of a new approach.

## Human development and basic needs

The formal definition of human development was presented on the first page of the HDR 1990, as follows:

> Human development is a process of enlarging people's choices. The most critical of these wide-ranging choices are to live a long and healthy life, to be educated and to have access to resources needed for a decent standard of living. Additional choices include political freedom, guaranteed human rights and personal self-respect. (UNDP 1990, p. 1)

The report continued by saying that 'development enables people to have these choices' (UNDP, 1990, p. 1). Later HDRs, and much of the human development literature, have elaborated how national and international development policy can strengthen the capabilities of people to have and exercise these choices. All of the HDRs have adopted a critical approach to neo-liberal orthodoxy in varying degrees and have presented, in contrast, strategies for national and international advance in which human development objectives are central to the analysis and recommendations.

The closest links between human development and earlier development strategies are with strategies for BN, strongly promoted in the 1970s, initially by ILO. The origins of BN in the 1970s are found in the ILO Employment Missions — especially the one to Kenya in 1972 — and in the ILO's research programme — particularly its Bachue model.[3] The elements and recommendations of these activities were later synthesized by ILO into a BN development strategy for the World Employment Conference of 1976. The BN approach put the focus on ensuring that the poorest group of each country should achieve a minimum standard of living within a defined time horizon — originally taken to be the end of the twentieth century, which was about 25 years. Basic needs included two elements: certain minimum requirements of individual households for private consumption, such as adequate food, shelter and clothing; and, secondly, essential services provided by and for the community at large, such as safe drinking water, sanitation, public transport, health and education. Employment and participation entered as strategic elements for achieving BN: each person available for and willing to work should have adequately remunerated employment and there should be popular participation in the making of decisions that affect the lives and livelihood of the people and individual freedoms.

There were two further points, sometimes forgotten in later writings about BN:

> The satisfaction of an absolute level of basic needs should be placed within a broader framework, namely the fulfilment of basic human rights, which are not only ends in themselves but also contribute to the attainment of other goals.
>
> The concept of basic needs is of universal applicability. The objectives to be set will naturally vary according to the levels of development, climatic conditions, social and cultural values. Basic needs are therefore in large part a relative concept; but there are also certain minimum levels of personal consumption and access to social services which should be universally regarded as essential to a decent life, and which should therefore be looked upon as minimum targets for raising the living standards of the very poor for the entire international community. (ILO, 1976, p. 7)

One of the virtues of ILO's BN approach was that it set out a clear and specific macro-economic strategy for national and international action. These macro-strategies combined economic growth with an explicit strategy of redistribution, involving a pattern of growth 'leading to more equitable distribution of the gains from growth' and to 'increasing growth rates as well' (ILO, 1976, p. 8). The projections in the report suggested that minimum income and standards of living for the poor could not be achieved, even by the year 2000, without some acceleration of average rates of growth *and by some measures of redistribution*, thus requiring 'both redistribution and growth together' (ILO, 1976, p. 43).

As earlier mentioned, BN strategies received increasing international attention over the later years of the 1970s, including in the World Bank (although, not it seems, in the IMF).[4] Within the World Bank, the BN 'concept was put forward as a significant escalation, even radical redefinition, of the poverty strategy and it excited debate over several years' (Kapur *et al.*, 1997, p. 265). McNamara, the World Bank's President over this period, was personally very supportive of the concept and even suggested that 'meeting basic needs or eliminating absolute poverty by the end of the century' could be proposed as an approach to the Third Development Decade (Kapur *et al.*, 1997, p. 266).

Many were cautious, however, and some were far from convinced — including Ernest (Ernie) Stern, the Bank's senior Vice President. Debate within the Bank continued for several years, focusing on such issues as the underlying ideology of BN, whether basic needs implied more government intervention in production and distribution, and whether or not there were trade-offs between growth and meeting BNs. On the latter point, McNamara insisted that he wanted both growth and BN and cut off 'any discussion of acceptable trade-offs' (Kapur *et al.*, 1997, p. 267). But the World Bank historians concluded that the majority of Bank staff was opposed, even at times describing BN as 'haircurling', 'a mistake', 'a slogan', 'dirigisme' -in short, 'a superfluous new idea'. Hollis Chenery, Vice President for research at the Bank, was basically in favour, but insisted that there was a trade-off between BN and growth (Kapur *et al.*, 1997, p. 267). This debate is revealing of the 'two Banks' that existed, and still exist, within the World Bank: on the one hand, the Bank of the President, the research department, and the *World Development Report*; and on the other, the Bank of the bankers who shovel out the money.[5] (Perhaps there should even be reference to three Banks, since important differences were also evident between the research department and the President).

By 1981, as the World Bank history records, the option of a large-scale lending programme for BN 'had been closed out by mounting economic instability, political conservatism and McNamara's departure' (Kapur *et al.*, 1997, p. 267). But it adds, BN research and advocacy during the 1970s had prepared the ground for making basic education and primary health the Bank's 'new and principal vehicles for direct poverty alleviation during the 1990s' (Kapur *et al.*, 1997, p. 268), even though these fell far short of the original BN proposal.

Almost as a final fling, an afterword, the World Bank issued in 1982 an insightful and analytical publication, *First Things First: Meeting Basic Human Needs in Developing Countries.* This was written by Paul Streeten with the support of Mahbub ul Haq and several others, including Javed Burki, Norman Hicks and Frances Stewart. Not surprisingly, the links between BN and HD are therefore close, indeed closer than has often been recognized.

Although Paul Streeten summarized the essence of the BN strategy as incomes + public services + participation (Streeten, 2003), *First Things First* brings out a range of subtle analyses and clarifications over the various meanings of BN. This document presented BN as an 'integrating concept' and linked it to earlier thinking on a Minimum Level of Living in India (Pant, 1974) as well as to the roles and work of other parts of the United Nations, including the World Health Organization (WHO), United Nations Educational, Scientific and Cultural Organization (UNESCO), Food and Agriculture Organization of the United Nations (FAO) and UNICEF, especially following the launch of the ILO BN strategy.

Equally insightful and analytical was the ILO's own publication on BN methodologies, published in 1977 and written by Dharam Ghai, A. R.

Khan, E. L. H. Lee and T. Alfthan (Ghai *et al.*, 1977). After a careful analysis of the BN Approach to Development, this elaborated the principles of quantifying and satisfying BN, considered some of the ethical and philosophical premises, and then illustrated how development planning could use BN methodology for setting quantitative targets and making plans for production.

In *First Things First*, Streeten foreshadows the later focus on choices and capabilities in the UNDP's work on human development. He notes that better education, nutrition and health are beneficial in 'enhancing people's adaptability and capacity for change' as well as for creating a political environment for stable development (Streeten, 1982). He also explains that 'the basic needs concept is a reminder that the objective of the development effort is to provide all human beings with the *opportunity* for a full life' (1982; original emphasis). And he notes that a wide-ranging interpretation 'verges on the notion that the satisfaction of basic needs is a human right' (Streeten, 1982 ).

Nonetheless, as explained, the Bank moved from debate over BN to embracing a neo-liberal approach to development in the early 1980s. By then, the Bank and the IMF had been accorded the dominant place in donor leadership and a dominant economic place *vis-a vis* the United Nations. Not surprisingly, BN concerns became almost totally marginalized, if not forgotten, within the international organizations, although interest in many developing countries and in the academic community lingered on.

## Contrasts and similarities between human development, basic needs and neo-liberal approaches

There are both important differences and important similarities between human development and BN and Neo-Liberal analysis and strategy. It is helpful to clarify the differences. But it is also useful to note the similarities, especially as they may indicate the possibility of some coming together of the different approaches. These relate to goals, underlying philosophies, methodologies, national and international priorities and the indicators used by which to judge success.

As regards goals and objectives, the fundamental difference is that human development focuses on people and the expansion of human choices and their capabilities as the core of development. BN gives an overwhelming priority to employment and meeting the basic human needs of households for consumption and for ensuring their access to essential services. NL focuses on the maximization of economic welfare, with market efficiency and economic growth the centre of analysis.[6]

The underlying philosophy also is an area of differences and similarities. There is common ground between human development and NL philosophies in several areas — but for different reasons, as indicated in Table 1. If one is searching for common ground, some might argue, why stress the

TABLE 1. Common ground — but for different reasons

| Human development | Neo-liberalism |
|---|---|
| Underlying philosophy | |
| Freedom of choice — but by developing and strengthening human capabilities and functionings | Freedom of choice — but by increasing utilities and satisfaction of preferences |
| — Emphasizes all human rights | Emphasizes mainly political and civil rights |
| — Concern for equity and justice | |
| Education, health and nutrition | |
| Important in themselves | Important as investments in human capital |
| As a means of empowerment | |
| As human rights | |
| Ending discrimination | |
| A human right | A human right |
| — For fairness | For efficiency |
| Governance | |
| Democratic and inclusive | Democratic |
| Important state functions | Minimal state |
| Focus on all human rights | — Focus on political and civil rights |

different reasons? Yet they are important since in some areas or contexts, the different reasons lead to different conclusions for policy and action, as the table makes clear. BN never really elaborated a comprehensive philosophy, although its values are clearly those that give highest priority to the elimination of poverty.

Democratic governance is a further example of both similarities and differences. Both human development and NL emphasize the need for human rights and for a democratic state as key elements of governance. But NL — and the W-C — have tended to propound a *minimal* state while human development and BN stress the importance of a core of state functions. Even on this, the neo-Washington consensus appears to be have shifted from its strictly minimalist view of the state in the 1980s to a somewhat more expansive outlook in the late 1990s and shifted even further midst the present crisis, especially to emphasize the need for tougher financial regulation and for elements of Keynesian stimulus.

As regards BN and human rights, the fulfilment of basic human rights was identified as part of the broader framework within which BN should be pursued. This was in the Director General's introduction, and no doubt he was thinking particularly of labour rights. The issue of human rights was given little attention in the later parts of this publication. One should note, however, that the publication was prepared in 1976 and attention to human rights as an operational part of development strategy only really gained momentum in later years, especially with the adoption in the 1990s of 'the rights-based approach' to development. The connection between human development and human rights has always been both stronger and more elaborated than between basic needs and human rights.

These differences in philosophy indicate important areas of common ground to build upon — while recognizing important differences in priorities. As explained, BN puts meeting the basic needs of the poorest as the highest priority. Human development puts broadening choices and opportunities at the head of the list, with strengthening human capabilities, participation and moderating inequalities close behind. There are close links between these two. In contrast, NL emphasizes freeing markets and getting prices right at the top, all as means to promoting efficiency. Although all three give an important place for education and health, for BN these are core elements of essential services, for human development they are essentials of strengthening human capabilities, while for NL they are priorities if and when the rates of return indicate they are good investments (which rate-of-return analysis normally suggests they are).

Internationally, there are also important differences in priorities. The NL approach stresses the virtues of opening international markets and removing barriers to trade and capital flows, while offering aid to the poorest countries for a limited period. In contrast, human development and BN follow a more structuralist economic view, emphasizing the need internationally for more democratic governance and for actions to strengthen the bargaining position of poorer and weaker countries, including their right to adopt policies that enabled them to withstand the gales of global competition in order to build up their industrial base. The BN strategy also stresses — or at least in the 1970s stressed — the importance of migration policies, the brain drain and the need for trade-adjustment policies to moderate the social and economic costs of unemployment as the structure of industrial production changes. In the longer run, the human development approach seeks ways to incorporate human principles into the rules and regulations governing the global market.

The HDRs, beginning in 1994, also broadened attention to issues of security, presented as the concept of human security and linked to conflict prevention and disarmament. Almost three-quarters of the HDRs have included some analysis of the benefits of disarmament or some policy recommendations towards this. In 30 years of the World Bank's *World Development Reports*, the topic has hardly been mentioned; nor was it made an element of the BN documents. Conflict prevention has been given some attention in the *World Development Reports*, although mostly in relation to the problem of failed states.

Finally, there are significant disciplinary contrasts. As paradigms, human development is multi-disciplinary and pragmatic, emphasizing decentralized approaches and ends rather than means. Here there are important parallels with BN. In contrast, NL is mostly economic, tending to dogmatism, aspiring to general equilibrium and emphasizing means rather then ends. This gives NL some important strengths — especially in being strong in mainstream economic theory and analysis, and robust in careful and often econometric analysis of recent good quality data. Human development, although focusing on fundamentals, is often casual in its analysis and weak in the data it uses, although it shares this with NL analysis when the latter turns to — or simply neglects — non-economic issues.

## Inequality and redistribution

Extremes of income inequalities have soared over the past two or three decades, within developed and developing countries and between the richest and poorest countries. Although in theory there is no reason for neoliberal analysis to ignore inequality — and, indeed, several reasons why it should be considered — in practice it has been sidelined during the heyday of NL dominance.[7] Achieving greater economic efficiency has been presented as the central objective, with the underlying assumption that greater efficiency and economic growth will lead to the 'lifting of all boats' by a combination of rising incomes and trickle-down. The World Bank historians, for example, acknowledged this as the position of the Bank in the 1960s, when they described McNamara's arrival as president and wrote that 'McNamara's contention that trickle-down was not working had been novel for mainstream academics and international agencies in 1968' (Kapur *et al.*, 1997, p. 221).

Much of this pre-occupation with economic growth and assumptions of trickle-down continues today, especially among donors in the international community and in spite of the priority given to poverty reduction focused on the MDGs. Economic growth is treated as the first and most important condition for achieving the MDGs, both to generate higher incomes for the poorest — Goal Number 1 — and for generating higher government revenues for government, to enable their support for expanding education, health and other basic services, key elements of Goals Numbers 2-6. The need for some redistribution is rarely, if ever, raised. Trickle-down is still used to defend against the need for specific redistributive actions, together with the argument that redistribution is in any case a matter for national policy (as if priorities for growth and the MDGs were not also matters of national policy.) The very word redistribution is seen as unnecessarily provocative, raising risks of blunting economic incentives and creating political divisions that could threaten stability and growth.

All this is in sharp contrast to both BN and human development. As explained earlier, BN explicitly made redistribution with growth part of the macro-strategy for reaching the goals within 25 years. In contrast, and in spite of levels of national inequality being mostly higher today than in the 1970s, growth alone, without reference to redistribution, has been consistently presented as the orthodox condition for halving poverty rates within the 15 years available for meeting the MDGs.[8]

At times, BN has been subject to the same criticism, also misleadingly. Paul Streeten summarized the essence of the BN strategy as incomes + public services + participation. He went on to stress that it was an integrating strategy — and as such, like human development, it went far beyond being simply a strategy for ensuring education and health for all. And Redistribution with Growth was a key focus of its macro strategy of BN as devised by the ILO.

## Reactions to human development and HDRs from policy-makers and economists

Over two decades, the human development paradigm has been widely presented and promoted. Some 20 HDRs have been produced, many making intellectual innovations and applying the paradigm to major issues and contemporary concerns such as gender, globalization, technology and climate change. These HDRs have been issued in English, French and Spanish, and often in other languages too. HDR 2007/08, for instance, was issued in 12 languages and with its statistical annexe, downloaded 400 000 times, more than any other UN report. Press launches and distribution in some 100 000 copies each year have ensured widespread coverage in the media of most countries. Country rankings using the Human Development Index have been used in a number of economic and development textbooks. The Human Development Index has also ensured headlines in the main press of most countries. There have been over 8000 news articles published on the Human Development Index and other indices since 1990.[9]

In parallel, over 600 National HDRs have been produced applying the methodology of human development to problems and issues in over 130 individual countries There have also been regional reports on the comparative human development situation in all the main regions of the world, most notably several outspoken human development reports in the Arab region. Many of these reports have been of high analytical quality.

A further indication of growing interest is the increasing number of academic courses that have been launched on human development, at least 20 at latest counting. This has been reinforced by a growing volume of academic research on human development, much of it published in the peer-reviewed *Journal of Human Development and Capabilities* that has been published three or four times a year since 2000 and has been deepening the theoretical underpinnings of human development and carrying the paradigm into an increasing diversity of areas.

So why has there not been a more positive response internationally, in action and in a shift of global paradigm? There are several reasons. First, the economics profession have mostly operated within a neo-classical paradigm of economic analysis. Mainstream economists have stuck more rigidly to this one paradigm than have other social scientists adopted any single paradigm. Mainstream economists often defend their approach by arguing that the neo-liberal paradigm is more robust than other paradigms, that it is essentially value-free and that their analysis of problems is increasingly evidence-based and scientific. This view underlies their claim that economics is the Queen of the Social Sciences.

This confidence is, of course, not without merits but it can be and has been challenged. From within the economics profession, there were strong attacks from Keynesian economists over the first three decades after the Second World War, although more weakly in the 1980s and 1990s. But recently, there has been a remarkable resurgence of criticism, at least operationally. In development studies, doubts about using neo-classical economics and the dominant mode of analysis have also been expressed, especially by those sensitive to the approaches and findings of other social sciences. Even within the economics profession, many distinguished economists have questioned the idea that economics is a value free science, perhaps the Nobel Laureate, Gunnar Myrdal, most notably. More radical development theorists — structuralists, dependency theorists and Marxists (in increasing order of radicalism) — have long challenged the limitations of neo-liberal economics and neo-liberalism, along with the W-C. And in terms of international development policy, there have been many analyses pointing to the contradictions between the main conclusions of neo-liberal analysis with respect to the benefits of free trade — its neglect of market imperfections and income distribution in reaching policy conclusions. The fact that most developed countries have major areas of their economies where the principles of free trade and market liberalism, for all their alleged benefits, are simply not applied ought to introduce questions about second-best options, but this is rarely considered.

There is a second reason why human development ideas have not gained more traction in development policy-making. Criticisms of economic orthodoxy in the 1980s and 1990s had some impact, but largely in persuading policy-makers to adopt broader goals, much less in rethinking the means by which they were to be pursued. The old means and strategies were thus largely maintained. UNICEF in the 1980s, for instance, had called for Adjustment with a Human Face; and the ECA for a succession of programmes of African-led economic recovery and development. The HDR had argued along similar lines, captured in the memorable phrase of the HDR 1990: 'It is short-sighted to balance budgets by unbalancing the lives or people' (UNDP, 1990, p. 34).

These criticisms and calls for new action, reinforced by the positive experience of UNICEF, the WHO and other institutions in accelerating actions towards goals for the reduction of child mortality and towards other human advances, led over the 1990s to donors and the rest of the international community accepting that human goals needed to be an important part of development strategies. Such goals were adopted in the final resolutions of the World Summit for Children in 1990, the International Conference on Population and Development in 1994, and the World Summit for Social Development in 1995. Goals and other actions focused on human development were also brought into virtually all the other international conferences of the 1990s, culminating in the adoption of the MDGs at the Millennium Summit.

Although some increases in funding went directly to UN agencies and to some countries for the support of these goals, the bulk of funding continued to be channelled to the Bretton Woods Institutions. The power structure and dominating paradigm of the international system was therefore little changed. Thus the main strategy for the achievement of the MDGs became an acceleration of Gross National Product growth — with the requirements for acceleration set within the orthodoxy of neo-liberalism and the Washington consensus. It is true that after Wolfensohn became president and following the '50 years is enough' protests, the World Bank became more flexible in its analysis and policy, although even then, its macro policy — which had to be coordinated with the IMF — continued largely along neo-liberal lines and those of the W-C, with the key elements set by the IMF.

In all these respects, the adoption of a human development approach and global strategy might have represented a new beginning. Human development unashamedly approaches analysis from a multi-disciplinary perspective, as clearly set out in the HDRs and in much of the writing by such analytical giants as Amartya Sen. It puts a high value on distribution and equity, along many dimensions including gender inequality. These goals and values, as already explained, differ from those of neo-liberal analysis, although there are areas of overlap.

The politics underlying these developments must be made clear, although the point has been made earlier and analysed many times before. Neo-liberal policy and conclusions match the interests of countries dominant in wealth and economic power. This is most clearly shown by the specifics elements of the W-C, underlying the policies of the Bretton Woods Institutions over the past two or three decades. It is no secret that the key elements of this consensus have been dictated by the interests of the United States, and to a lesser extent of Europe and Japan. It is hardly surprising, therefore, that when human development has reached conclusions differing from this consensus, its messages for international policy are not adopted, even if lip-service is often paid to its human goals and even to its broad messages.

This neglect has been encouraged by a tendency to view the HDR approach as little more than a strategy for ensuring education, health and other basic services for all. This is a major misunderstanding and misreading of the HDRs. Every single report from the beginning has emphasized that human development is conceptually and operationally distinct from a narrow preoccupation with education and health and goes far beyond them in the policies they recommend. This confusion is reinforced by the way the Bretton Woods Institutions generally use the term human development to mean investment in education and health as key actions to increase human resources.

## The Washington Consensus and its problems

The W-C has been excessively narrow, economistic, reductionist and ideological. It has primarily served the economic interests of the industrial countries. It has never received strong support from within the United Nations, and its narrowness and neglect of human factors has often been criticized by individual UN agencies and non-governmental organizations. And in terms of its impact on economic growth and development in the poorest countries, many would argue that it has had disastrous consequences.

One of the great defences of the W-C is that it would bring economic growth to poorer developing countries and that growth, in turn, would bring — or at least make possible — a wide range of other benefits, from rising living standards, stronger public services like education and health, and wider national development, and even produce the additional resources required to tackle environmental problems.[10]

Recent evidence has shown otherwise. A range of careful econometric studies of the application of the W-C orthodoxy to developing countries has shown that, in general, the W-C has been 'anti-growth' (Vreeland, 2007). This finding is based on increasingly sophisticated econometric studies, covering a large number of 'adjustment episodes' and allowing for such critical issues as the extent of each country's compliance with the conditions laid down by the IMF. Recent studies have been by Barro and Jong Wha-Lee (2005) and Dreher (2006) . These analytical results are borne out by experience. Many of the poorer developing countries and many transition countries have laboured under BW conditionalities for long periods many to achieve slow economic growth at best. Even before the current crisis, some 55 countries were poorer in terms of per-capita income than they were 10 or 20 years before — and some for even longer periods (UNDP, 2007).

In sharp contrast, many Asian countries — Korea, Taiwan, Malaysia, Singapore, Thailand, and of course China and India — have over the same period reached high per-capita growth rates by following strategies that were often in sharp contrast to the orthodoxies of the W-C and the Bretton Woods Institutions. This is the case both of national strategies for development over the long run and of strategies for short-term recovery from crisis. Following the Asian financial crisis of 1997–1999, countries like Malaysia consciously and successfully followed policies at variance with those being promoted by the IMF and the World Bank. Moreover, the Asian region successfully developed financial mechanisms of regional support so as to escape what they saw as restrictive measures of the Bretton Woods Institutions.

## The need for broader international approaches

So what needs to be done, especially in relation to the economic and financial crisis of 2008/09 and the longer term challenges that the world faces? This is not the place for a full review of all such actions. Instead the paper focuses on the issues largely neglected so far, the structural changes needed globally in relation to long term problems and the changes required to respond to the poorer countries. Even with this more limited frame, a number of key issues can be identified.

The more dogmatic elements of the W-C need to be dropped, especially those that have failed to deliver. There also needs to be new elements to deal with long-run issues such as climate change and other environmental problems, as well as actions to avoid recurrence of crises. Objectives such as diminishing poverty and narrowing extremes of national and international income distribution also need to be made part of new approaches as well as mechanisms to offset extreme asymmetries in bargaining power and participation in the global economy.

In short, a broader international approach is needed, one which includes four new objectives:

- Sustainability — especially rapid action to slow and offset climate change and other environmental problems.
- Stability — not just for developed countries but especially for developing countries that have suffered the consequences of instability more seriously and for much longer periods.
- Economic justice and greater equality — especially after recent decades when inequalities have risen rapidly in most countries as well as between the richest and poorest countries internationally.
- Human rights — in line with global priorities.

Also, measures to encourage economic efficiency in the use of resources.

Such broader objectives are by no means new to the international community. They have already been adopted formally by votes or by consensus in many parts of the UN system, including in meetings and organizations dealing directly with international economic issues and relationships. These broader objectives have not, of course, been totally neglected or even just accepted in words but not in deeds. There has been action in almost every area, but typically in separate silos of decision and action rather than across the board.

This raises two major issues, both of which need attention: greater coherence is needed across the international system; and, secondly, the sharp disjunction needs to be ended between conditionalities in the mainstream financial and economic areas of action and the lack of mechanisms for follow-up and support in much of the rest. In large part, both needs reflect the fact that the mainstream financial and economic issues have been the responsibilities of the Bretton Woods system, with international action and resources largely channelled through them. Other economic and social issues have generally been the responsibility of other organizations of the United Nations. Although many forces have been at work, this has generally reflected the power and interests of the major economic powers that have consciously used their influence to ensure economic and financial matters remain in the hands of the Bretton Woods Institutions (and the WTO), leaving the United Nations with the non-economic issues and often with declarations rather than decisions.

## Need for a shift in international paradigm

A shift in paradigm or a new framework for international action will not be easy to establish, for the reasons already elaborated. Yet there is perhaps some room for manoeuvre. Crisis brings opportunity — and already many leading voices, political and economic, have recognized the need for major change. At the end of the G-20 meeting in April 2009, Gordon Brown, the British Prime Minister and chair, stated that 'the old Washington Consensus was over'. In the run up to the meeting, Dr Ngozi, Managing Director of the World Bank, said that 'we need a shift of paradigm'. Many commentators have stated the need for new approaches.

So far, most of the policy changes have been within the developed countries. International support for the developing countries has concentrated on increasing finance for economic stimulus, with the vast bulk of this channelled through the IMF. At the time of writing, there are reports that for countries which have built up their reserves, such as Tanzania and Mozambique, the IMF has explicitly advocated fiscal stimuli.[11] This is a welcome change, although far from sufficient.

There are other points of hope for a shift in paradigm or for new approach. In the first place, and most important of all, the global crisis and recession beginning in 2008 has stirred widespread awareness that the pursuit of narrow economic orthodoxy over the past two decades has set the stage for much of the current crisis. A failure of regulation in the developed countries allowed housing and debt bubbles to grow. In the poorer countries, growth rates were pathetically low. In contrast, many Asian countries operating outside neo-liberal orthodoxy achieved spectacular success.

In the industrial countries, Keynesian solutions, unimaginable in the hay days of market fundamentalism, have been rapidly applied to rescue the system. The question now is whether the process of recovery can be sustained — and whether it can be combined with a process of restructuring, globally and nationally, to tackle the longer terms challenges of sustainability, stability, poverty reduction, global inequality and human rights.

A second point of hope are the 130 or so developing countries that have already produced reports analysing the human development situation in their own context, usually with recommendations for policy and action to improve it. These reports have often already served as a focus for lively national debate on priorities for change. In the new context of the global crisis, many of these reports may provide a frame for recovery and broader change.

In the mid-1990s, Mahbub ul Haq wrote 'If the human dimension is to show up fully in development policy decisions, the first and biggest battle lies within the corridors of power of developing countries'. But he added that 'full awareness of the issue must also be woven into international decision making and the programmes and practices of bilateral and multilateral donors' (ul Haq, 1995, p. 10). Does the current economic crisis present the opportunity when this change, or at least something of it, might be possible?

A third point of hope is that Dominique Strauss-Kahn, the Managing Director for the IMF, has himself set out objectives for reform and change in the institution. He has explicitly stated that countries receiving IMF loans will no longer be required to sign up to a lengthy list of policy conditions. An IMF policy paper has explained that countries would be given additional leeway, to ensure that they are not forced to cut back on social spending to meet 'arbitrary macro-economic targets' — although what exactly was meant by arbitrary was not defined. Some reforms have also been formally agreed: a doubling of the limit that each country is able to borrow in bail-out loans and a dramatic increase of $250 billion of special drawing rights, financed by the sale of the IMF's gold reserves.

It is, however, far from clear that this will add up to a serious shift of paradigm, let alone that the dogma of the old paradigm will die. It is more likely that there will minor modifications — perhaps less dogma about opening developing country markets to capital flows and less about minimizing regulation. But crisis presents the opportunity for more serious rethinking and international reform. So far, most of the discussion of international reform has focused on changes in the representation and voting structure of the Bretton Woods Institutions. Although this is important, and in the very long run is likely to lead to some changes in operations, earlier and more direct action is needed.

## Precedents for broadening concerns and objectives

There are interesting examples of broader concerns being brought into international governance. The ILO, for instance, was founded as part of the Versailles Peace Conference in 1919, and mostly at the initiative of the three great powers of the time — the United States, the United Kingdom and France. It was given a mandate recognizing that 'lasting peace can be established only if is based on social justice'. This bold declaration was used to define a range of economic measures requiring international and national actions to improve labour conditions round the world, including such specifics as collective bargaining, equal pay for men and women for work of equal value and the abolition of child labour. But notwithstanding mixed motivations,[12] major steps were taken in international labour legislation and in setting up the ILO itself as an institution to carry them forward. And over subsequent years, the broader principles of social justice were further elaborated in the international system and slowly but significantly carried into action.

Since the founding of the United Nations, governments have agreed further elements for international economic and social relations, each bringing in principles of social justice well beyond those of basic economics. These include the following:

- 1945 — The Charter of the United Nations, which enshrined four key principles: peace through negotiation rather than war and conflict; sovereign independence for all countries; economic and social development to raise living standards everywhere; and human rights for all.
- 1944-1946 — the Articles of Agreement of the IMF, which called upon the Fund to provide support to enable countries 'to correct maladjustments in

their balance of payments *without resorting to measures destructive of national or international prosperity*'. The report to the First Annual meeting of Governors was even more explicit in explaining how this should 'promote the balanced expansion of international trade and investment and in this way *contribute to the maintenance of high level of employment and real income*' (Vreeland, 2007, p. 88; emphasis added).

- 1948 — The Universal Declaration of Human Rights, followed in 1968 with binding Conventions on Civil and Political Rights and on Economic, Social and Cultural Rights, now ratified by 160 and 156 countries, respectively.
- 1975-1995 — The four World Conferences on Women, the first of which agreed to create a Convention for the Elimination of All Forms of Discrimination against Women, which was adopted in 1981.
- 1990 — The World Summit for Children, the first of the world summits of the 1990s, which encouraged all countries to ratify the Convention on the Rights of the Child and agreed many follow-up actions including goals for the 1990s, which were later broadened and extended into the MDGs.
- 1992 — The Earth Summit, which agreed an Agenda 21 of actions in relation to sustainable development and the environment, including climate change, preservation of the earth's bio-diversity, forests and other.
- 1995 — The World Summit for Social Development, which adopted goals for the eradication of poverty, full employment and secure, stable, inclusive and just societies, to be achieved through 10 commitments.
- 2000 — The Millennium Summit, which ended with the Millennium Declaration and agreement on the MDGs. The Declaration identified many elements required for strengthening global governance, including actions on poverty reduction.
- 2005 — World Summit, which was a follow-up meeting to the Millennium Summit, to take stock of progress, consider additional actions needed and to consider how to strengthen the United Nations in relation to development, security and human rights for all.

All of these landmark events have defined further principles and policies of global governance. They are ready to be drawn upon for a new paradigm or framework to guide international relations, economic, social and political.

## The challenge of moving beyond the Washington Consensus

The current crisis presents an important opportunity and need to move towards a new international framework. Any attempt to shift from the W-C will need to grapple with several difficult challenges, political, disciplinary and institutional.

A first issue is whether it is desirable or even possible to have a single paradigm for the economic operations of all international organizations. The W-C has been the paradigm of the Bretton Woods Institutions, not of the UN institutions — and even then, over much of the past three decades, more the paradigm of the IMF rather than the World Bank. After the mid-1990s, the World Bank became more eclectic and more flexible in its concerns and policies, the result of strong leadership at the top of the Bank and the sustained calls for change from many groups outside, especially many non-governmental organizations. All this was possible in spite of economic interests of the powerful economies and the ruling paradigm of development theory. If nothing else, this shows a certain freedom of manoeuvre, which may well be increased if and when the emerging powers of the developing world begun to use their economic weight.

Clearly, a new paradigm must be responsive to the experience and thinking of the new economic powers. The world is changing rapidly, with the economic centre of gravity moving away from the West and towards the emerging economic powers of the East, China and India most obviously, including Japan but also including other countries. Hopefully, this will make possible a shift from a paradigm that served the dominant interests of the major western economic powers to one that is more internationalist and, in many respects, more open to the thinking and positive experience of a much wider group of countries. In place of principles given by the dominant neo-liberal economic paradigm, a more flexible paradigm will need to be adopted, more directed to a wider range of objectives and based on a wider range of development experience. This will open up more issues for debate and negotiation — much as in national politics where elements of ideology and paradigm are less clear and the specifics of the case in point more often becomes the focus of debate and decision.

If a new paradigm is to reflect this much broader experience and diverse set of views and interests, it must itself be an open, more diverse and more flexible paradigm. In particular, it must be able to embrace the experiences of the Asian economies that have followed paths outside neo-classical orthodoxy over their successful development trajectory of the past several decades.

Such considerations suggest that the most appropriate way forward is to have a broader and more flexible framework within which specific guidelines can be found or developed for the operations of individual international agencies. In a sense, this was the case for the W-C. The paradigm was largely given by neo-liberal economics. The 10 specific guidelines were broadly and publicly justified by the neo-liberal paradigm but in fact went far beyond what could logically be deduced from the neo-liberal paradigm itself. In its very phrase, it was the W-C, not the neo-liberal consensus. Although the Bretton Woods Institutions and the General Agreement on Tariffs and Trade (GATT) — and later the World Trade Organization (WTO) — operated by this paradigm, most of the rest of the United Nations never did.

If the main international economic institutions become more flexible, it will make it possible for them to be more responsive to broader issues, especially those pioneered or traditionally promoted by the United Nations, like human rights and climate change. Over the past decade, something of this has happened with the adoption of the MDGs and in other areas where the United Nations has taken the lead like debt relief.

## Building blocks for a broader approach

As regards the future, several building blocks are available for constructing a more coherent international framework and guidelines.

1. The broader principles of human rights and social justice listed earlier have already been formulated and are ready to be drawn upon. It will be much easier to start with those that have already been agreed than to start afresh on negotiations about which principles should be included.
2. The human development approach is also available to be used as a broader frame of reference, or even adopted as an all-embracing frame for all the international agencies. This would be a way to shift the international focus to people and human advance, linked to human rights and social justice. The multi-disciplinary approach would also make it possible to embrace the objectives and concerns of all the international agencies, such as the specialized agencies like the WHO. Such an approach at country level could also build on the national strategies which have been mapped out in the more than 600 National HDRs. A human development approach would also bring in issues of cross-generational equity, thus providing a frame for tackling climate change and other environmental issues as key dimensions of sustainable strategies.

But, some might ask, does human development add up to a development strategy? In terms of objectives, the human development approach would represent an advance, certainly over the W-C. Its objectives are more comprehensive and its human concerns are more explicit and readily understandable. It also embraces human rights and other ethical and philosophical issues, relating to individuals and also to communities and nations, economic and social sectors, national and international. The fact that human development is defined in terms of broadening choices and strengthening capabilities, in ways that are linked also to human rights, gives its objectives a breadth and flexibility, more so than narrower economic strategies which concentrate on economic objectives.

Perhaps more debatable are questions about the adequacy of human development as a strategy for policy and action. Certainly, the succession of annual HDRs have explored strategies in relation to contemporary problems and issues — growth, consumption, globalization, human security, technology, climate change, water and sanitation, human rights and gender equality. These have explored an agenda of policy concerns and a demonstration of applying human development analysis in relation to a great diversity of issues. National HDRs have done the same, and produced policy conclusions more directly related to national or regional level issues.[13] Monitoring progress is also an area where the human development approach brings a wider set of concerns than is typical with neo-liberal economic analysis.

This said, human development analysis is rarely as decisive as is the neo-liberal approach. With human development there is rarely a certain answer, more an emphasis that shows a direction for advance, but with trade-offs in relation to its various concerns. There is no one solution given by a methodology of maximization. To some, this may seem a clear objection. To others, however, this may see an opening to the real world of differing perspectives, judgement and political bargaining.

It is a mistake to pose these differences too starkly. There are overlaps between neo-liberal and human development analyses of issues of similar issues, even though generally human development analysis embraces a broader area of concerns. As mentioned earlier in this paper, NL analysis values and assumes concern for rights, although usually in the political and civil area. In a human development approach, rights are brought into the analysis of means and outcomes more explicitly. As another example, human development analysis will often find useful many tools of neo-liberal economic analysis — to clarify issues such as cost-effectiveness, opportunity cost and to make critical assessments of factors inhibiting the efficient operations of the market. However, the imperatives of using market signals in most situations or striving to move towards some situation of general equilibrium are not of central concern for human development, if relevant at all.

3. Human development can serve as a framework to bring greater coherence between the operations of individual agencies. Guidelines already exist for all the international agencies and funds, given in their original mandates and periodically updated by resolutions of their Boards. Further updating and adjustments may well be needed. But the major need is for UN reform to focus on the need for achieving greater coherence between the mandates and objectives of organizations and funds working in similar areas. A start on this has already been made through the MDGs. But this is only a beginning, and often too much of the emphasis has been on bureaucratic coordination rather than fine-tuning of operations towards common objectives, based on experience and the ability of different agencies to contribute. A human development framework could provide this in a way that was beyond neo-liberal economics, especially because of its narrower objectives and disciplinary boundaries.
4. Recent resolutions on priorities for expanding and strengthening global action are where additional international action is clearly needed. Climate change and efforts to diminish inequalities, international and national, are two of the most obvious priorities. So is tougher and more coordinated international regulation of banks and financial institutions. Here the key point is that priorities for action need to be identified from research and experience, and adapted to a diversity of country contexts — rich and poor, small or large, agricultural and dependent on a few commodity exports or with a more diverse semi-industrialized economy. In many cases, such issues have been the subject of representative conference or meetings, from which clear resolutions have already emerged. For the most part, they have not been a logical deduction from an all-embracing paradigm. But they do have implications for the construction of such a

paradigm for the future. In short, other words, an issue-specific or problem-specific approach, drawing on well-analysed country experiences that can be adapted to the context of each country, should be followed in formulating a broader paradigm. The application of this paradigm will need to be flexible, closely adapted to the context and issues of specific countries.

## Implications for the IMF and the World Bank

This brings us to the IMF and the World Bank. Can their operations be adapted to a more flexible paradigm and their operations made more sensitive to country situations? Can their operations be linked more closely with others of the international community, especially those of the United Nations? Which elements of the W-C ought to be replaced?

As emphasized above, the W-C represented the economic interests of the dominant western powers. One must therefore ask whether any such overall consensus is either appropriate or even possible in a more pluralistic world, with a centre of economic gravity shifting to China and the East and with different views and experiences of what is necessary for robust and sustained development.

Two points already suggest there is some room for manoeuvre. As emphasized above, the latest evidence now shows that the W-C has had, on the whole, a negative effect on economic growth in the developing countries. Tough-minded realists may attempt to argue that this does not matter to the main economic powers, since free trade and capital flows from were always the real objectives, not growth. It is, however, hard to sustain this argument. Were the interests of the developed countries in trade or capital investment opportunities adequately served by such a miserable performance on growth? In sharp contrast stands the dramatic success in terms of economic growth (and many other indicators of development) of many Asian economies that did not follow orthodox western strategies. They are now much more robust economic partners with the developed countries than countries where growth was a failure. All these provide strong arguments for suggesting that there can be a *real politik* in making major shifts from the old W-C and to making major changes in the lending operations of the Bretton Woods Institutions.

A more desirable position might be that the Bretton Woods Institutions should provide resources in response to well-crafted national strategies without pre-conceptions as to the form of development strategy proposed. There would of course need to be conditions relating to repayments and repayment schedules for loans or other financial support. But these would be of the same sort as required by commercial banks making loans to the country as part of their normal operations. Indeed, many developing countries have increasingly turned to commercial banks for loans, finding that loans on this basis are preferable, even at slightly higher interest rates.

Although it may seem bold to propose that the Bretton Woods Institutions respond to national requests without pre conditions as to the form and content of national strategy, this was of course a major focus of debate when the Bretton Woods Institutions were first created. The British held the view that anything beyond this would mean interference in domestic policy-making, and thus of national sovereignty. Indeed, Keynes initially reported back to the UK Foreign Office that, after long debate, he had convinced the Americans to drop this dimension of the Articles. He was wrong and the United States got their way with a more intrusive policy.

A more flexible and pragmatic approach must be adopted in relation to the specifics and stage of development of each country. It must also be sensitive to the positive lessons of Asian experience, allowing more time for adjusting to the challenges of the world economy and less commitment to the rapid pursuit of global integration with global markets.

A new framework must be directed towards the long-run objectives of sustainability, stability, equity and human rights. They must also allow for action towards a wider range of national objectives, including fuller employment, rising living standards, pursuit of the MDGs and greater equity. And any new paradigm must also be multi-disciplinary.

## Conclusions

The present global crisis presents an important opportunity for making major changes in the objectives, directions and operations of the international system. Major efforts of financial and economic stimulus without such changes are short-sighted and dangerous.

A new approach, a shift of paradigm or framework, is needed to one that is more flexible, less dogmatic, multi-disciplinary and clearly directed towards long-term challenges and international goals: sustainability, stability, equity and human rights.

There is also a need for more coherence in objectives and strategies across the system of international organizations, drawing on the resolutions and decisions already adopted at many international meetings over the past few decades.

The human development paradigm, now marking its 20th anniversary, has many of the qualities required to be the basis for such an international framework, adapted to the specifics of each country. Some moves toward this should be considered.

## Acknowledgements

This paper grew out of lively debate and discussion with Louis Emmerij, who subsequently provided many helpful comments and additions. The ideas were presented at the special symposium in the Institute of Social Studies (ISS) marking the inauguration of Rolph van der Hoeven as professor. Rolph subsequently helped to produce a coherent presentation of a revised and much longer draft. I am grateful to them both, as well as for the comments from an anonymous reviewer on an earlier draft.

## Notes

1 For references to the three reports and fuller analysis, see Emmerij *et al.* (2001) and also Jolly *et al.* (2009).
2 See, for instance, *Employment, Incomes and Equality: A Strategy for Increasing Productive Employment in Kenya* (ILO, 1972, p. 1).
3 See Hopkins *et al.* (1976). In Colombian mythology, Bachue is the Goddess of Love and Fertility.
4 Boughton (2001) makes no mention of basic needs, at least none referred to in its index.
5 On the two banks, see Emmerij (1995).
6 I have set out the contrasts between human development and NL at length elsewhere — (see Jolly, 2003) so here I simply summarize the core differences, including also comparisons with BN.
7 One important exception has been the World Bank's (2005) *World Development Report 2006*, which contained a strong, innovative and comprehensive analysis of inequality.
8 For example, there is no explicit reference to the need for income distribution in Sachs (2005).
9 Data from the UNDP, Human Development Report Office.
10 This was a central argument of the World Bank's 1992*World Development Report*, issued at the time of the Earth Summit in Rio.
11 *The Economist*, 30 May-5 June 2009, p. 62.
12 Of course there were mixed motivations in the creation of the ILO — as can be seen in its mandate and underlying concerns. A particular motivation of the time was to avoid the threats to social stability from the Bolshevik Revolution and pressures from trade interests to prevent imports from poorer countries undercutting domestic production in the more developed countries
13 Human development analysis has also been applied to international trade. See the UNDP Asia-Pacific Human Development Report 2006, 'Trade on Human Terms: Transforming Trade for Human Development in Asia and the Pacific', and two background papers for the Asia-Pacific HDRs (for the same study) by Kamal Malhotra, 'National Trade and Development Strategies: Suggested Policy Directions', and by Chantal Blouin, 'Trade and Health in Asia: Challenges of Globalization' — published by the HDRUnit, UNDP Regional Centre in Colombo.

## References

Barro, Robert J. and Lee, Jong-Wha. (2005) 'IMF programmes: who is chosen and what are the effects?', *Journal of Monetary Economics*, 52(7), pp. 1245-1269.

Boughton, James M. (2001) *Silent Revolution: The International Monetary Fund 1979-89*, IMF, Washington, DC.

Emmerij, Louis (1995) 'A critical review of the World Bank's approach to social sector lending and poverty alleviation', in *International Monetary and Financial Issues for the 1990s*, Volume V, United Nations Conference on Trade and Development, New York and Geneva, pp. 15-33.

Dreher, Axel (2006) 'IMF and economic growth: the effects of programs, loans, and compliance with conditionality', *World Development*, 34(5), pp. 769-788.

Emmerij, Louis, Jolly, Richard and Weiss, Thomas G. (2001) *Ahead of the Curve: UN Idea and Global Challenges*, Indiana University Press, Bloomington, IN.

Ghai, D.P, Khan, A.R., Lee E.L.H. and Alfthan, T. (1977) *The Basic-needs Approach to Development: Some Issues Regarding Concepts and Methodology*, ILO, Geneva.
ul Haq, M. (1995) *Reflections on Human Development*, Oxford University Press, New York.
Hopkins, M.J., Rodgers, G.B. and Wery, R. (1976) 'Evaluating a basic needs strategy and population policies', *International Labour Review*, November–December, pp. 261–279.
International Labour Office (1972) *Employment, Incomes and Equality: A Strategy for Increasing Productive Employment in Kenya*, ILO, Geneva.
International Labour Office (1976) *Employment, Growth and Basic Needs: A One-World Problem*, ILO, Geneva.
Jolly, Richard (2003) 'Human development and neo-liberalism: paradigms compared', in S. Fukuda-Parr and A.K. Shiva Kumar (Eds), *Readings in Human Development*, Dehli, Oxford University Press, pp. 80–92.
Jolly, Richard, Emmerij, Louis and Weiss, Thomas G. (2009) *UN Ideas that Changed the World*, Indiana University Press, Bloomington, IN.
Kapur, D., Lewis, J.P. and Webb, R. (1997) *The World Bank: Its First Half Century, Volume 1: History*, Brookings Institution Press, Washington, DC.
Pant, P. (1974) 'Perspective of development, India 1960–61 to 1975–76: implications of planning for a minimum level of living', in T.N. Srinivasan and P. K Bardhan (Eds), *Poverty and Income Distribution in India*, Statistics Publishing Society, Calcutta.
Sachs, Jeffrey D. (Ed.) (2005) *Investing in Development: A Practical Plan to Achieve the Millennium Development Goals*, London, Earthscan (for the UNDP).
Streeten, P. (1982) *First Things First: Meeting Basic Human Needs in Developing Countries*, Oxford University Press (for the World Bank), New York.
Streeten, P. (2003) 'Shifting fashions in development dialogue', in S. Fukuda-Parr and A.K. Shiva Kumar (Eds), *Readings in Human Development: Concepts, Measures and Policies for a Development Paradigm*, 2nd edn, Oxford University Press, New Delhi.
Toye, J. and Toye, R. (2004) *The UN and Global Political Economy: Trade, Finance and Development*, Indiana University Press, Bloomington, IN.
United Nations Development Programme (UNDP) (1990) *Human Development Report 1990*, Oxford University Press, New York.
United Nations Development Programme (UNDP) (2007), *Human Development Report 2007/8*, Palgrave Macmillan, New York, Table 14, pp. 277–280.
Vreeland, J.R. (2007), *The International Monetary Fund: Politics of Conditional Lending*, Routledge, Abingdon.
World Bank (2005) *World Development Report 2006, Equity and Development*, New York, Oxford University Press.

# *How the New Poverty Agenda Neglected Social and Employment Policies in Africa*

THANDIKA MKANDAWIRE
*Thandika Mkandawire is Professor and Chair of African Development in the Development Studies Institute (DESTIN) at the London School of Economics, UK*

**Abstract** This article argues that a shift towards issues of poverty is a welcome antidote to policy-making that had expunged poverty from the central agenda to focus on stabilization, debt management and static allocative efficiency. Unfortunately, in correcting a narrow policy agenda the new focus pushes a good point too far when it focuses attention only on the proximate causes of poverty and narrows the development agenda. Development was aimed at more than poverty and, significantly in countries that have successfully combated poverty, the most important policy measures were not explicitly directed at poverty. Indeed in many cases, other objectives — pre-empting social unrest, nation-building, 'human capital' developmental considerations — lay behind the policies that, *ex post*, can be read as poverty reducing. Eradication of poverty is always embedded in social and economic development. The determinants of human development goals are multiple and cut across sectors. The new challenge in Africa is to bring back development, but now one that is democratically anchored and socially inclusive.

## Introduction

For most African countries the single most important cause for the deepening of poverty has been the combination of 'maladjustment' (Mkandawire, 2005), highly truncated social policies and the persistence of unrepresentative and authoritarian regimes that have either stubbornly refused to address the obvious crises confronting their countries or have idiosyncratically complied to external diktat without engaging in national debates to address the crisis. Politically underpinning this has been the social differentiation since independence and the accompanying ideological shifts that have contributed to the shift in focus of state policies away from social and employment policies.

Today Africa has one-third of the persons below the poverty line — 300 million out of one billion worldwide — an increase of 150 million during the

TABLE 1. Populations living on less than US$1 per day, 1987–1998 (millions of people)

| Region | 1981 | 1990 | 2001 | Annual % change (1981–2001) | Absolute change (1981–2001) |
|---|---|---|---|---|---|
| East Asia & Pacific | 796.2 | 472.7 | 271.6 | −4.67 | −524.53 |
| Europe & Central Asia | 3.0 | 2.3 | 17.1 | 7.54 | 14.07 |
| Latin America & Caribbean | 35.4 | 49.1 | 49.2 | 1.43 | 13.84 |
| Middle East & North Africa | 9.1 | 5.5 | 7.2 | −1.04 | −1.94 |
| South Asia | 474.0 | 462.7 | 431.3 | −0.42 | −43.48 |
| Sub-Saharan Africa (SSA) | 163.1 | 227.6 | 312.6 | 2.82 | 149.49 |
| Total | 1482 | 1220 | 1089 | | |
| SSA as percentage of total | 11.0 | 18.7 | 28.7 | | |

*Source*: Calculated by author from World Bank CD-Rom, 2005.

past two decades at a time when poverty in other major regions of the world is declining (Table 1). The rising proportion of global poverty attributable to Africa has led the World Bank to talk about the 'Africanisation of world poverty' (White and Killick, 2001, p. 5).

The countryside remains the home of the majority of the poor in Africa. Seventy per cent of the poor live in the rural areas. It was with respect to agriculture more than anything else that liberalization made its most lavish promises. First, it was asserted that to the extent that structural adjustment programmes (SAP) would do away with the arsenal of policies that produced an 'urban bias' in state policies (price controls, marketing boards, food subsidies, overvalued exchange rates, protection of inefficient industries, etc.), it would favour the rural producers by tilting the terms of trade in their favour. This would lead to increased production and increased income for the poor. Second, it was assumed that the withdrawal of the state from a number of social activities would not be harmful to the rural poor since the poor had limited access to the subsidized goods and services anyway. Growth in agriculture production has turned out anaemic and rural communities have suffered major reversals in state provision of services.

Urban poverty is also growing rapidly in Africa. Two factors have conspired to increase urban poverty: the declining real wages, and declining employment opportunities. Real wages in manufacturing fell sharply throughout the 1980s. This was not only an expected outcome but also a designed and recommended one. In its axiomatic statement it is assumed that liberalization of markets will not only increase growth but will increase it in a labour-intensive manner that will create employment that will reduce poverty. In the event, this has not taken place in Africa. Declining real wages have instead been associated with declining employment. For 12 countries for which relevant data are available, the annual growth rate in formal sector employment fell from 2.8% in the 1975–1980 period to less 1% in the 1980s and 1990s (see Tables 2 and 3). The lack of employment opportunities and the dismantling of many protective labour laws have led to greater informalization of labour in urban areas. On average, the informal sector is now believed to employ over 60% of the urban

TABLE 2. Employment growth in selected countries

| | 1980-1990 | 1990-2000 | 2000-latest | 1980-latest |
|---|---|---|---|---|
| China | 1.77 | 2.59 | 0.91 | 1.76 |
| India | 1.21 | 1.61 | 0.59 | 1.14 |
| South Africa | −0.71 | −0.47 | 0.20 | −0.32 |
| Egypt | 1.04 | 0.42 | 0.01 | 0.49 |
| Algeria | −0.66 | −1.03 | 0.09 | −0.53 |
| Morocco | 0.54 | −0.08 | 0.31 | 0.26 |
| Côte d'Ivoire | −1.70 | 0.00 | −0.44 | −0.71 |
| Sudan | −0.70 | 0.98 | 0.40 | 0.23 |
| Ghana | −0.32 | 0.61 | 0.29 | 0.19 |
| Nigeria | −0.71 | −0.32 | 0.30 | −0.24 |
| Kenya | 0.32 | −0.68 | −0.13 | −0.16 |
| Ethiopia | −0.51 | 0.30 | −0.01 | −0.07 |
| Tanzania | −0.47 | 0.02 | 0.57 | 0.04 |
| Congo | −0.47 | −3.44 | −0.07 | −1.33 |

*Source*: ILO (2005).

labour force. There is no doubt that those who make their living in those sectors exhibit enormous ingenuity and resilience. And there can be no doubt that state repression and harassment in the past has often made the task of survival and self-reproduction difficult. However, for the majority of the population in that sector, such 'survival strategies' are not only temporary but permanent features of a life of hard work, self-exploitation and poor remuneration. Evidence from casual observation and some solid empirical material suggests that the informal sector has been adversely affected by the fall in demand from urban households, increasing input costs and increasing competition from new entrants consisting of people resorting to the informal sector for survival or to supplement dwindling incomes in the formal sector.

## *Inequality*

During the 'Golden Age' of post-World War II capitalism there was no relationship between inequality and growth, leading some economists to consider the unchanging wage-profits share as one of the stylized facts of modern-day capitalism. This assumption was extended to developing countries and was used by various authors, such as Dollar and Kraay (2001), to downplay the question of inequality when they argued that 'growth is good

TABLE 3. African employment elasticities to gross domestic product growth

| | 1992-1996 | 1996-2000 | 2000-2004 |
|---|---|---|---|
| North Africa | 0.78 | 0.74 | 0.77 |
| Sub-Saharan Africa | 0.74 | 0.57 | 0.48 |

*Source*: ILO (2006).

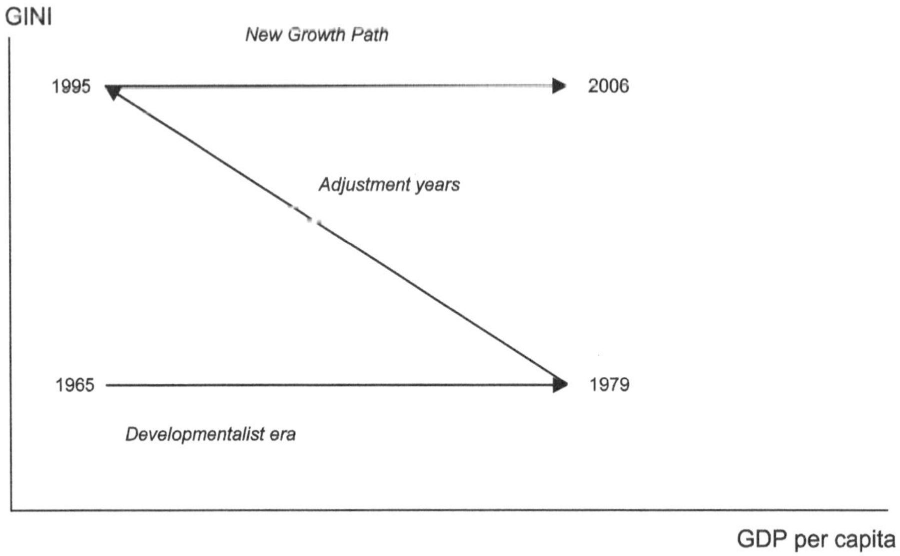


FIGURE 1. The ratchet effect of growing inequality.

for the poor'. In both the rich and poor countries that have changed, SAP has produced a new dynamic in which the inequality and growth are positively related (Piketty and Saez, 2006). Thus, using the same data as those used by Dollar and Kraaj, Lopez (2006) found that growth under adjustment (in the 1990s) was associated with inequality, although not in the 1970s and 1980s. The data on inequality in Africa are quite startling and now compare with the notorious Latin American levels (see Table 4). Ominously, while growth did not reduce inequality, recession increased it.[1] This asymmetry produces a ratchet effect so that once inequality is worsened in a phase of recession, it is maintained in the phase of recovery (as in Figure 1). The new growth rates are not sufficient to reduce inequality from stagnation of the 1980s and 1990s.

In retrospect, we can see that initiatives against poverty in the 1960s and 1970s failed. This can largely be attributed to the lack of a comprehensive

TABLE 4. Some indicators of personal income distribution

| | Share of total income | | | |
|---|---|---|---|---|
| | Poorest 20% | Richest 20% | Ratio or richest to poorest | Gini coefficient |
| Sub-Saharan Africa | 5 | 52 | 10.2 | 0.51 |
| East Asia | 4 | 44 | 6.5 | 0.38 |
| South Asia | 9 | 40 | 4.6 | 0.32 |
| Latin America and Caribbean | 4.5 | 53 | 11.7 | 0.49 |
| Industrial countries | 6 | 40 | 6.4 | 0.34 |

*Source*: Calculated by author from World Bank CD-Rom, 2005.

social policy framework that would have tied together the various aspects of social policy and translated the significant growth rates into improved welfare for the majority of the people. The earlier initiatives failed because of the waning of the 'nation-building' élan that was focused on national cohesion, the greater social differentiation that negated the egalitarian ethos of the nationalist movements and the crisis of the economic model and the end of strategic thinking about the economy spawned by the failure This prompted new strategies — the International Labour Organization's (ILO's) basic needs strategy, which was predominantly focused on employment and technological choice; and the World bank's 'growth with equity', focused on rural development. These strategies brought the issue of poverty and equality on the policy agenda. However, both lacked the social policy scaffolding that would have simultaneously addressed the challenges of distribution, production, protection and reproduction that are key aspects of social policy. In any case, they were soon to be set aside with the rise of neoliberalism.

## The new poverty agenda

By the 1990s poverty came back to the international agenda, first in the form of social funds to address the pauperization of sections of the middle class and later as Poverty Reduction Strategy Papers (PRSPs) and Millennium Development Goals (MDGs). The new poverty agenda is repeating the same mistakes, although for different conceptual and ideological reasons. In the following section we discuss some of the blind spots of the new poverty agenda.

### *Neglect of lessons of history*

The first blind spot relates to the neglect of history. The history of poverty, especially its on-and-off appearances on national and international agenda, has been one of the central preoccupations of modern social science. However, the current discourse on poverty seems totally oblivious to the earlier appearances of poverty on the social agenda and thus rarely bothers to ask why things that have not worked in the past will worker better now. In the four decades since Africa's modal year of independence, 'poverty' as a concern has strutted and fretted on the policy stage only to be rudely shorn off and then dragged back on again without much explanation. 'Late industrializers' such as the Nordic countries, and the more recent cases of the East Asian 'developmental states', provide useful lessons for current initiatives against poverty but are rarely drawn upon.[2] If current poverty reduction approaches have any historical antecedents, they resemble features of the Poor Laws under the Anglo-Saxon model — a not remarkably successful way of rapidly combating poverty despite its apparent preoccupation with the issue of poverty (Esping-Andersen, 1990; Huber, 2002; Rothstein, 2001; Stephens, 2002). And yet it is precisely this model that shapes the agenda of poverty today.

## *The technocratic thrust of policy*

One important lesson of history is that ideas matter. The pursuit of poverty reduction or eradication is always about norms. Poverty and the response to it — development — featured prominently in the nationalist political discourse. By political commitment and social origins, most of the first-generation African leaders were deeply committed to the eradication of poverty. Indeed in many countries' manifestos of the nationalist movements, poverty was explicitly identified among the factors that the attainment of independence would address . The other two factors were ignorance and disease. Together they formed an 'unholy trinity' against which nationalist swords were drawn in the post-colonial era (Adesina, 2007; Mkandawire, 1999b). In addition, the exigencies of 'nation-building' and social cohesion were such that social polices became a central aspect of the early years of 'development plan ning', as Tade Aina (2004) notes. In particular, education became a 'moral imperative' in overcoming the legacy of colonialism and in the human resource needs of a modern economy. Many social policies and schemes, such as community development, rural credit systems, pan-territorial pricing, adult literacy campaigns, free health and education programmes, were instituted. Levels of literacy increased dramatically after the attainment of independence. Other social indicators such as infant mortality and life expectancy showed some progress (Sender, 1999).

The point of evoking this period is not to suggest that there were some halcyons days of resounding victories against poverty. After all, the relative good growth performance in the post-colonial period had many problems and was highly contested at the time. Within Africa, the model of development was the subject of severe criticism. For one, its gains were unevenly distributed and the overall development strategies did not seem to address issues of poverty and the growing inequality despite the relatively more extensive social policies of the time. Many of the modern welfare measures such as pensions and health plans remained segmented and exclusive, and there were no signs that the segmented social policy regime was moving towards unification as happened in some of the more advanced welfare states. The benefits accruing to the 'Labour aristocracy' seemed too well entrenched and ring-fenced to allow for spill over (Arrighi, 1973; Waterman, 1975). On the international level, the ILO's famous report on Kenya (ILO, 1972) was among the first international organizations to openly point to the negative effects of growth without equity and to recommend 'Basic Needs Strategies' that would simultaneously and purposefully address issues of growth and equity. The World Bank also produced its own variant of 'redistribution with growth' strategies (Chenery *et al.*, 1974). Aid was to shift away from the heavy infrastructural and often 'urban-biased' projects towards rural development projects designed to benefit 'the poorest 40 percent'. 'Rural integrated development schemes' were the main vehicle for delivering development to the rural poor.

By the end of the 1970s, poverty and development were unceremoniously pushed off the scene as policy shifted towards macro-economic issues of stabilization and debt repayment. The inspiration for the change came partly from the failure of the post-colonial development strategies to deal with the new crisis induced by declining terms of trade and high interest rates and partly from the poor performance of MacNamara's big integrated rural development projects. However, the fundamental and decisive driver of the shift was the ideological turn in the key industrial countries, leading to the ascendance of ideologies that were 'anti-statist' while placing enormous faith in rather reified markets. The crisis and the ideological shifts conspired to dethrone developmental concerns and to place stabilization at the core of economic policy. In this new assault on the development agenda there was a notion of causation, which insisted that the growing poverty in Africa was due to poor economic performance produced by internal policy mistakes.

The new poverty agenda generally eschews the identification of social and political actors that could form broad 'reform-mongering coalitions' (Hirschman, 1971) that would underpin the implementation of the desired strategies. In much of the analysis, the discussions ends with laments about 'lack of political will' or the assertion that in African conditions such coalitions will not emerge anyway, with the implication that donors will drive the political agenda through conditionalities and selective empowerment of 'change teams'. To understand the political battles on poverty it is important to also bear in mind the numbers of social actors driving the current poverty agenda. These actors are driven by different motivations, interests, understanding of poverty and power. These diverse drivers partly account for the state of disarray in policy debates and the gravitation towards the lowest common denominators in the poverty discourse. We need to revive these debates in Africa to identify what are the political agenda of the different social actor, be they foreign or domestic, class, gender, ethnic, public or private.

Almost from the very beginning, structural adjustment was obsessed with circumventing the elites so that donors could proceed with their humanitarian tasks or with 'bribing' the elites into doing what they did not want. However, as John Toye (1999) reminds us, in the real world, anti-poverty policies are rarely an expression of pure humanitarian impulse. National elites tend to take some action either under duress or because they are convinced it is in their interest to do. This might be because some aspect of poverty has a 'public bad' character with negative externalities that can affect the rich (i.e. public health, crime, etc.), or because it might advance national security objectives or because it might facilitate economic growth by improving the health and education of the populace.[3]

When the new poverty agenda has sought to identify social actors that might support, it has leaned on social organizations that are sharply different from those that have played the historical role in shaping the welfare state in the developed countries. During the past two decades, new social movements have arisen that have forced the poverty on the international agenda. Many of these movements belong to what is now referred to as non-governmental organizations (NGOs) and were inspired by ideologies or perspectives that avoid the 'grand narratives' of development, and concentrated instead on small-scale micro-levels projects in which personal engagement and testimony was important. One of most highlighted features of current poverty eradication strategies is the prominent role given to civil society (in the form of NGOs). The participation of non-governmental actors is intrinsic to both the design and implementation of national anti-poverty programmes. Yet the new approach ought to be viewed in light of two historical observations. The first is that in none of the successful cases of mass poverty eradication have NGOs played a central role. Even in the more recent accounts of successful policies, the same is true[4] (on this, see Mehrotra and Jolly, 1997). Second, the kinds of social movements that constructed the 'social pacts' or were the backbone for poverty eradication in the past differ substantially in both form and programmatic focus from today's NGOs. The old movements were movements that were strategically related to the production process and therefore able to make consequential demands on the social order. And in the elite-led version of social policy, the elite were domestic and not international bureaucracies.

Virtually all countries now agree that the private sector and the market will assume a central role in the development process. Historically, the role of the private sector was viewed as contributing to accumulation, employment and technological change while pursuing private gain. Where these private gains diverged from social gains, the state was expected to intervene through various incentives, taxes and regulatory measures. The state was also expected to provide certain goods — both merit and public goods. In recent years these traditional roles of business and the state have changed considerably, with the rolling back of the state and the increasing engagement of the private sector in social provisioning through the privatization of public services, in social protection and 'self-regulation' through corporate social responsibility, and in poverty reduction through various public–private partnership projects and other initiatives. One new innovation in the fight against poverty has been the notion of public–private partnership that draws on three discourses: the role of the state in creating an 'enabling environment' for the private sector, the notion of civil society and the notion of corporate social responsibility. In recent years, there has been greater stress on corporate self-regulation, voluntary initiatives, non-governmental systems of labour regulation and multi-stakeholder institutions as ways of regulating business and bridging the gap between private and social gains. Concerns have arisen regarding both the capacity and legitimacy of these new regulatory approaches. They also have political implications.

Finally is the role of the poor themselves as social actors. Much has been said about empowerment. At its best, the PRSP process basically builds on empowerment at the micro-level and disempowerment or exclusion at the macro-level. The weak are never empowered by the powerful. The rich have many ways of restricting the policy agenda This they do through various practices, such as limiting the agenda, selectively leaving out social actors (such as unions) likely to make claims that have significant macro-level effects, and through the right of veto that is built into these processes. The poor have to grab power themselves. And this brings us to the question of the political cohesion of the poor themselves and their organizational capacities and political ideologies. If they cohere, what do they cohere around and with what organizational capacity do they act in the political arena? And so a number of questions arise: Why are democracies pursuing economic policies that are known to be deflationary, seemingly backed by their supporters? Why are new democracies more orthodox in this respect than older ones? Why have the poor not used their voting power to push for policies that are pro-poor and lead to sustainable improvements in the lives of the poor?

### *Too narrow a focus on poverty*

Another lesson of history is that pro-poor programmes are not necessarily pro-poor, and if badly designed and dogmatically insisted upon they can even undermine the long-term development prospects of poor countries. Combating the proximate causes of poverty does not always mean combating the underlying structural causes of poverty. Indeed, some of the most successful cases of combating poverty were not expressly designed to do that. Social policy in developing countries that is only about poverty eradication is too narrow. Historically, it has other objectives such as national or social cohesion, and equity. Indeed, in a number of countries that have successfully dealt with poverty within a relatively short period of time, the relief of poverty was not even the most important motive for the introduction of social policies. Often the fall in poverty has had much less to do with policies aimed at poverty *per se* than with those aimed at much wider social objectives of improving social welfare based on a wide range of considerations, including citizenship, nation-building, judgements on who constitutes the poor, ideological predisposition with respect to the efficacy of free markets, theories of human behaviour, bureaucratic capacities, overall economic strategies, and international pressures and norms. In the Nordic or East Asian countries, for example, 'poverty reduction' *per se* did not play a significant role,[5] and was subordinate to other social objectives — 'catching up', equality, full employment, solidarity, nation-building, and so forth — that were to have far-reaching implications on poverty more than those that may have been deliberately aimed at. Even the choice of instruments that have had the most dramatic effect may not be guided by poverty *per se*.[6]

### *Lack of development strategy*

On the assumption that the appropriate structures to emerge will be dictated by market forces, the contemporary strategy of poverty reduction is usually silent on sectoral policies. The model that has dominated economic policy during the past two decades has tended to treat any specific sectoral policies that are not axiomatically derived from the core model as 'distortions'. Up until recently, 'industrial policy', 'social policy' and 'labour market policies' were only acceptable if they involved self-negation and meant the extension of the reign of the market to these spheres.

Most strikingly, there is silence on industrialization and technological innovations in agriculture. These are sectors that have historically played an important role in the alleviation of poverty, and they have always required quite explicit policy measures. How policy regimes have addressed the 'agrarian question' has been an important aspect of their stance on poverty. According to Chen and Ravallion (2004) , growth in the primary sector has had approximately four times more impact on poverty reduction than growth in the secondary and tertiary sectors. For many countries, the immediate impact of economic growth on poverty will be transmitted through agriculture. Increasing productivity and access to assets by the majority of the population in rural areas must still be a central concern of policies against poverty. In addition, it is important to consider special social policies that would protect rural populations from vulnerability to the vagaries of climate and markets, which are major components of poverty. In the past, many social policies such as stabilization funds and pan-territorial pricing played such protective and redistributive roles. However, in the era of liberalization these institutions and policies were dismantled or reversed. In the spirit of the current emphasis, strategies for managing the negative consequences of volatile rural incomes are emerging that rely more heavily on markets to supplement the many ways governments and households manage risks. In most cases, they are premised on the existence of financial markets and other institutions that do not exist in developing countries, 'because the costs of risk avoidance to households and businesses can be high; the capacity for self-insurance by households, groups, and even governments can be limited; and markets that support risk sharing are incomplete' (Larson *et al.*, 2004, p. 225).

One consequence of the lack of a development strategy is that although the strategy relied for its poverty alleviation on 'trickle down' and although it proclaimed 'Growth is Good for the Poor' (Dollar and Kraay, 2001), it actually had no growth strategy other than the belief that it would logically follow from stabilization and liberalization policies. Not surprisingly, the strategy failed to produce levels of growth that would reduce poverty so that the number of rural poor increased during the adjustment period (Mkandawire, 2005; Vreeland, 2007). In more recent years, African countries have enjoyed higher growth rates. Contrary to the claims that this is evidence of the lagged effects of adjustment programmes, the high growth rates are due to such 'exogenous factors' as improved terms of trade, technologically driven investments in telecommunications, debt relief, and improved governance and end of conflicts in a number of countries (Mkandawire, 2005).

## *Socially and employment blind macro-economics*

Macro-economics matters for poverty through three channels: economic growth, redistribution and stabilization of employment and output. In its original formulation the normative foundations of macro-economics were provided by social policy objectives of full employment. In its developmental form, macro-economics paid special attention to economic growth and structural transformation as instruments for the social objective of eradicating poverty and improving social welfare. More significantly, stability was not focused on growth targets that met employment or income growth targets, but around a deflationary growth path to meet financial targets such as the rate of inflation. In the 1980s the new macro-economic policy was basically deemed as self-restraining and so unlike the earlier post-World War II macro-economics, which was constrained by the social objectives of 'full employment'. On the contrary, macro-economic policy is now focused exclusively on financial variables. Their main function was to re-establish the preconditions for growth; growth itself and safety nets were to take care of poverty.

The new macro-economics was informed by a view in the developed countries that the fiscal crisis of the late 1970s had somehow been caused by welfare states and social expenditure. With the 'crisis of the welfare state' in the developed countries and the rise of neo-liberalism, the rupture of the link between macro-economic and social policy and new understanding of poverty was bound to spill over to the developing countries largely through aid agencies. From this followed the view that, under conditions of stringent budget conditions, it was necessary to 'target' assistance towards the 'deserving poor' by dismantling the existing universalistic programmes (Ali, 2003; Besley and Kanbur, 1990; Brady, 2005).[7] The 'micro-economic foundations' of the new macro-economists, especially its 'supply side' version, supported the related view about welfare and incentives and the obsession with avoiding 'welfare dependency' that was feared would be the likely outcome of many welfare measures. This in turn created the need for policies to wean the poor from such welfare dependency through targeting and onerous selection processes where there were welfare measures or to pre-empt such dependency by simply blocking the emergence of the welfare state. Macro-economics was detached from these social and developmental moorings, becoming increasingly socially blind. Economic policies and the instruments chosen to implement them were no longer restrained by social objectives, such as protecting people's incomes or eradicating poverty.

## *Neglect of labour markets*

Another factor was the marginal role of labour markets in the adjustment models. Labour markets constitute an important arena for addressing issues of poverty. Labour markets are not simply institutions for the static efficient allocation of existing labour resources; they are also sites for the realization of basic civil and social rights through what the ILO calls 'Decent Work'. Furthermore, they perform the developmental role that is often obscured by the preoccupation with market clearance. Labour market institutions can be sources of savings through contributory schemes such as pensions. Labour market policies cannot only ensure decent working conditions, but can also create incentives for both employers and employees to improve 'human capital'. One common feature of the 'success stories' was their extensive intervention in the labour markets.

Labour markets are also probably among the most politically difficult markets to manage in the process of late industrialization. When poverty entered the policy agenda in the 1970s under the 'Basic Needs' and 'Growth with Equity' strategies, labour markets and employment immediately assumed a central role. The past two decades have witnessed significant shifts in the international policy agenda, one of the most contested elements of which has been in relation to employment. During the so-called Golden Age of capitalism (1945–1975) under Keynesian influence, full employment was prioritized as a key objective of public policy. For 'late industrializers' such as the East Asian countries, employment creation was a central aspect of their social policy. Social development — in the form of full employment — was thereby embedded within both macro-economic policy agenda and development. While the Golden Age was marked by a respectable employment record for many of the advanced industrialized countries as well as significant progress in substantiating social rights, as far as developing countries were concerned the picture was far more complex. For developing countries the policies to increase employment included trade policies, technological choices, policies on local sourcing sources, and so forth.

Much of the post-World War II consensus, however, was to unravel by the end of the 1970s. The implementation of adjustment policies has led to a massive trend worldwide towards 'flexibility' of the labour force: trade unions have been sidelined and coerced to toe the line. In many cases, employment has been deliberately casualized through sub-contracting arrangements and the like. Although important exceptions can be cited — such as China and some other East Asian countries — the employment situation has been worsening in many other parts of the developing world. In much of the developing world the working population is, as we indicated earlier, being increasingly crowded into the ubiquitous 'informal economy'.

### *Trade-off between growth and equity argument*

One major factor behind the truncation of the remit of social policy was the systematic excision of equality concerns from the core policy agenda of the 1980s and 1990s. This can partly be attributed to neoliberal thinking, which has never prided itself for promoting economic equality. Its two central arguments have been 'freedom of choice' and efficiency produced by the 'invisible hand' that took the distribution of 'initial endowments' as given. It has also posited a trade-off between equity and efficiency, and in the Hayekian form between freedom and equity. Inequality would, in the classical and neo-Keynesian manner, stimulate growth by shifting income in favour of profit-earners who presumably had higher levels of savings. In the more neoclassical formulation, inequality would also serve as a spur to upward mobility for low-income groups who would exert themselves to climb the ladder while encouraging the capitalist to invest more. There was always the view that the rich were not investing enough because they were not rich enough, and the poor were not working hard enough because they were not poor enough. The World Bank downplayed the importance of inequality on growth and poverty by arguing that growth is good for the poor — the 'rising tide raises all boats' argument — and that inequality has no effect on growth (Bruno *et al.*, 1996; Dollar and Kraay, 2001). One suspects that the ready acceptance of this set of results was due to the fact that it fitted in well with the macro-economic models that the Bretton Woods Institutions (BWIs) have pushed. Furthermore, structural adjustment policies tended to reduce the instruments available to government. It is also important to recall that around this time inequality was shorn of its sociological or, more appropriately, its class basis. Economists distinguish between functional and personal income distributions The former examines the distribution of income among owners of 'factors of production' — wages for labour, profit for capital, rents for land and interest for finance — while the latter clauses incomes accruing to individuals without specifying the source of income. The dominant focus today is on personal income distribution, dividing incomes along percentiles. One major criticism levelled at this approach is that it concealed and obscures the crucial social categories of class that are still a fundamental cause factor inequality in capitalist economies. Secondly, it tends to focus attention on inequality among the lower strata or on such things as wage dispersion; third, it has a tendency to excessively focus the issue of equality on micro-level presumably on grounds that this was much less controversial and would not raise serious questions about the causal relationship between macro-economic policies pursued and the observed growing inequality in virtually all liberalization economies; and finally, it is associate with a political economy (the Median Voter) whose elegance and parsimony fails to conceal its empirical vacuity even in these countries that are democratic.

Much of classical economists, however, were concerned with functional income distribution, which produced a distinct political economy by pointing, almost naturally, to problems of class. One advantage of looking at functional income distribution is that one is reminded: of the capitalistic nature of the economies being discussed; that investment by capitalists is crucial; and that any redistributive measures that disfavour profit-earners will lead to an 'investor' strike. In addition, macro-economic reforms while eschewing any discussion on functional distribution have in fact had significant effects on it. McKinley (2001) observes that such macro-economics has had the following regressive shifts: from workers to owners of capital; from petty producers and small business people to owners of large businesses; from domestically owned businesses to foreign-owned enterprises; and from businesses engaged in productive activity to financial resources. In order to attract foreign investment and promote growth, developing countries have tended to foster policies that are favourable to capital and increase its return. This tends to reduce the labour share and may call for corrective policies in order to offset their distributional implications (Daudey and García-Peñalosa, 2007).

## *Weakened state capacity*

In all of the successful cases of fighting poverty under both democratic and authoritarian regimes, the state has assumed a 'developmental' role. One quite remarkable feature of the new social policy focused on MDGs or PRSPs is that the status and the requisite capacity of the state differ radically from the historical 'success stories'. Thus far, these policies are tethered to the demise of the 'developmental state', both as a reality and as an aspiration. Consequently, they are to be implemented by 'regulatory states' that are stripped of many of the instruments available to developmental states and whose main task is to ensure a 'level playing field' and the protection of property rights. However, in the era of adjustment, many of these of institutions were deemed guilty by association to the putatively failed strategies of industrialization and were condemned as 'market distorting', 'interventionist', clientalistic and fiscally unsustainable. Indeed, in many cases, dismantling these institutions was considered the *sine qua non* of effective policy reform and adjustment. The failure of the simplistic message of 'getting prices right', the neo-institutionalist infusion of institutions into the neoclassical theoretical framework by pointing out that markets were embedded in institutional arrangements that reduced transaction costs in various ways, and the debacle of the transition to capitalism in the former Soviet bloc, all pointed to the complexity of institutions that undergird the capitalist system and led to calls for 'getting institutions right'. As it turns out, even the narrowest social agenda that comes along with neoliberalism — targeting the poor and provision of basic health and education — has institutional prerequisites that demand much more than what has been left after 'reining in' the state. In addition, calls for 'Comprehensive Policy Frameworks' and the new broader agenda against poverty have revived interest in institutions and good governance. However, the new focus is marred by the tethering of institutions to a 'one-size-fits-all' policy perspective in which good policies are known, or what has been referred to as 'institutional mono-cropping' (Evans, 2004), in which institutions are reduced to servicing this set of 'good policies' or what has been referred to as 'institutional mono-tasking' (Mkandawire, 2009). The lessons from history, however, are that similar economic and social outcomes have been achieved by a wide range of institutional arrangements.

## *Disempowering democracies*

The revival of interest in poverty has corresponded with Huntington's (1991) *Third wave* of democratization, during which a number of developing countries have adopted democratic governance structure. Indeed in many of these countries it was the protests against impoverishment wrought by structural adjustment programmes that led to the collapse of authoritarian movement.

It is perhaps not surprising that we have a broad definition of poverty that draws on 'rights-based' development and includes 'empowerment' as one of its guiding principles. Empowerment relates to both 'participation' and 'national ownership'. Although the current insistence on human rights suggests that the desirable political regime would be democratic, it is often premised on institutional arrangements that severely restrict the remit of elected bodies (Mkandawire, 1999a, 2004). The PRSP process basically builds on empowerment at the micro-level and disempowerment or exclusion at the macro-level. And yet, although poverty is often lived at the micro-level, its reproduction, intensification or amelioration depends crucially on macro-level policies that, through omission or commission, are intended to address macro-level problems. One consequence of this is that only until recently have the new democracies placed the substantive issues on their agenda.

## Conclusion

This shift towards greater attention to issues of poverty is a welcome antidote to policy-making that had expunged poverty from the central agenda to focus on stabilization, debt management and static allocative efficiency. The new focus on poverty was a reminder of what was a central objective of development and nationalist aspirations. Unfortunately, in correcting a narrow policy agenda the new focus pushes a good point too far when it focuses attention only on the proximate causes of poverty and narrows the development agenda. Development was aimed at more than poverty, and significantly in countries that have successfully combated poverty the most important policy measures were not explicitly directed at poverty. Indeed, in many cases, other objectives — pre-empting social unrest, nation-building, 'human capital' developmental considerations — lay behind the policies that, *ex post*, can be read as poverty-reducing.

The message above, as well as the multidimensional nature of poverty, underscores the point that the eradication of poverty is always embedded in social and economic development. The determinants of human development goals are multiple and cut across sectors. The theoretical literature and official policy pronouncements recognize this multi-dimensionality and are replete with statements about the synergies among the various initiatives on the various aspects of poverty. There is no one-to-one link between the MDG relating to a sector and policies relating solely to that sector. The outcome in a given sector depends importantly on factors outside that sector. One implication is that, in order to be useful tools, the MDGs (for example) must not be seen as narrow objectives with one-dimensional interventions. However, in the urgency to meet individual targets, the development community runs the risk of losing sight of the multi-sectoral nature of interventions and development outcomes such as the MDGs. African countries have had the worst of both sides in terms of distribution of growth. They were made to sacrifice equality in the name of stabilization and the promise of growth. In the event, they got neither sustainable growth nor equality. The new challenge in Africa is to bring back development but now one that is democratically anchored and socially anchored. One of the factors driving the equity agenda has been the process of democratization. While in the early phases the new democracies pursued essentially orthodox policies, with the passage of time the politics of democracy tend to push towards more heterodox responses (Mkandawire, 2004). In Latin America there are clear intimations of a return to some of the 'populist' and social-democratic traditions of Latin American. In the older democracy of India, voters clearly suggested that the new growth of India ('India Shining') was producing inequalities that they found an anathema. One can hope that, as democracy is consolidated in Africa, the issues of poverty and inequality will receive the full attention they deserve as part of a truly transformative set of social and economic policies.

## Acknowledgments

I would like to thank Rolph van der Hoeven for substantial comments on an earlier draft and an anonymous referee for useful comments. The usual caveats about authorial responsibility hold.

## Notes

1 SAP did, however, achieve in some cases some rather perverse forms of equalization. Available data suggest that, following SAP, the urban–rural income gap was reduced by a process of 'equalising downward' while intrasectoral inequality grew (Cornia, 2007, p. 53). The perverse redistribution was the consequence of a number of structural features of the adjustment model that included de-industrialization and liberalization of labour markets, the deliberate inducements of low wage and redistributive economic policy in favour of the well-off, and the dismantling of a number of post-colonial social pacts. While change in the share of wages may not tell us much about overall distribution, it definitely has a clear bearing on urban inequality and poverty. We should not be led to believe that the perverse redistribution was unintended. Among some of advocates of adjustment this was good news. Sahn (1992) could argue that the collapse of sources in the urban areas was salutary since poor people do not take part in the formal economy and did not make much use of government services, and hence are less (either negatively or positively) affected by stabilization policies than non-poor groups that used to profit much more from public services. In the event, continued rural–urban migration and the salience of the poor in African urban politics undermine both positions.

2 For the semi-official Japanese position, Ohno (2002, p. 21) notes: 'While most of the Japanese aid officials and experts endorse the basic principles of PRSP, including national ownership and aid partnership, they express concern about its uniformity of approach, shortage of strategic contents, and increased budgetary and human resource burden on both donors and recipients. While the advocates of PRSP readily admit the crucial linkage between economic growth and poverty reduction at the general level, they tend to focus exclusively on pro-poor measures (e.g., education, health, environment, gender, rural infrastructure, etc.) in actual implementation. Serious discussion on the generation of economic growth is desperately lacking'.

3 In this respect, Mick Moore and Stephen Devereux have suggested some rather specific questions that we need to answer in relating national elites to the poverty question: 'What do they think about the national causes and solutions to poverty? Which of the potential poverty do they see as meriting public attention? Which sections of the elite are most

sympathetic to doing something about poverty? What instruments to they believe will be effective?' (Moore and Devereux, 1999, p. 4).

4 In addition there is the question of accountability and representativeness of NGOS, or as Elisabeth Jelin suggests: 'The fact is that NGOs and "private-yet-public" organizations do not have a built-in mechanism of accountability. They do not have a constituency or membership composed of their "sovereign citizens".' They are fundamentally accountable to those who provide funds and to their own ideology and consciousness, hopefully (but only hopefully) based on 'good values, solidarity, compassion, and commitment. Given the relative absence of institutional and societal accountability, there is always the danger of arbitrary action, of manipulation, of lack of transparency in objectives and practices' (Jelin, 1997, p. 412).

5 A United Nations Development Programme report on China points in the same direction when it notes: 'The poverty incidence fell most rapidly before there were specific poverty alleviation programs in existence. When these programs were flourishing, on the other hand, poverty reduction at times stagnated and even suffered reversal. This is not because China's poverty reduction policies and programs have been useless or counter-productive; on the contrary, there is reason to believe they have made a difference in the localities where they were carried out. Rather, it is because much larger forces have determined the shape and speed of poverty reduction, namely, macroeconomic and other general economic policies and trends. These include, inter alia, policies concerning farm prices, factor prices, state investments, fiscal structure, financial reform and the social safety net and social insurance regimes. When the constellation of such policies was strongly pro-poor, poverty reduction occurred at a breathtaking speed, despite the absence of explicit poverty-reduction institutions. Yet when the general policy constellation was not pro-poor, then the course of poverty reduction was much less rapid. A key conclusion from a review of this history is that there are many ways in which China's macroeconomic policies and economic institutional set-up could be made more pro-poor than they have generally been' (Bouché *et al.*, n.d., p. 12).

6 For example, the introduction of pension schemes by both Mauritius and Norway were made at very low levels of economic development, which goes against the World Bank arguments that such schemes are unaffordable in low-income countries such as those in Africa.

7 On the affinity between orthodox macro-economics and targeting, Besley and Kanbur note that it 'is in the wake of macroeconomic and structural adjustment that targeting seems to have attained a special significance in developing countries, as more and more governments have come under pressure to reduce expenditure. Indeed, targeting has come to be seen as a panacea in poverty alleviation' (Besley and Kanbur, 1990, p. 67).

## References


Adesina, J.O. (2007) *In Search of Inclusive Development: Social Policy in the Sub-Saharan African Context,* Palgrave/UNRISD, Basingstoke.

Aina, Tade Akin (2004) 'Introduction: how do we understand Globalisation and social policy in Africa?', in T.A. Aina, C.S.L. Chachage and E. Annan-Yao (Eds), *Globalization and Social Policy in Africa,* CODESRIA, Dakar, pp. viii, 339.

Ali, Abdel Gadir Ali (2003) 'Structural adjustment programs and poverty in sub-Saharan Africa: 1985–1995', in T. Mkandawire and C. Soludo (Eds), *African Voices on Structural Adjustment,* CODESRIA (IDRC) and African World Publishers, Dakar and Trenton, NJ, pp. 189–228.

Arrighi, Giovanni (1973) 'International corporations, labour aristocracies, and economic development in tropical Africa', in G. Arrighi and J. Saul (Eds), *Essays on The Political Economy of Africa,* Monthly Review Press, New York, pp. 105–151.

Besley, Timothy and Kanbur, Ravi (1990) *The Principles of Targeting,* World Bank, Washington, DC.

Bouché, Nathalie, Riskin, Carl, Shantong Li, Saith, Ashwani, Guobao, Wu and Huijiong, Wang (n.d.) *The Macroeconomic of Povrty Reduction. The Case of China*, UNDP, New York.

Brady, D. (2005) 'The welfare state and relative poverty in rich western democracies, 1967-1997', *Social Forces*, 83(4), pp. 1329–1364.

Bruno, Michael, Ravaillion, Martin and Squire, Lynne (1996) *Equity and Growth in Developing Countries: Old and New Perspectives on the Policy Issues*, World Bank, Washington, DC.

Chen, Shaohua and Ravallion, Martin (2004) 'How have the world's poorest fared since the early 1980s?', *The World Bank Research Observer*, 19(2), p. 141–169.

Chenery, Hollis B., Ahluwalia, C., Bell, J., Foluy, J. and Jolly, Richard (1974) *Redistribution with Growth*, Oxford University Press for the World Bank, London.

Cornia, Giovanni Andrea (2007) 'Policy reform and income distribution', in Jose Antonio Ocampo, Jomo K. Sundaram and Sarbuland Khan (Eds), *Policy Matters: Economic and Social policies to Sustain Equitable Development*, Zeb Books, London, pp. 53–75.

Daudey, E. and García-Peñalosa, C. (2007) 'The personal and the factor distributions of income in a cross-section of countries', *Journal of Development Studies*, 43(5), pp. 812–829.

Dollar, David and Kraay, Aart (2001) *Growth is Good for the Poor*, World Bank, Washington, DC.

Esping-Andersen, Gøsta (1990) *The Three Worlds of Welfare Capitalism*, Princeton University Press, Princeton, N.J.

Evans, Peter (2004) 'Development as institutional change: the pitfalls of monocropping and potentials of deliberation', *Studies in Comparative International Development*, 38(4), pp. 30–52.

Hirschman, Albert O. (1971) *A Bias for Hope: Essays on Development and Latin America*, Yale University Press, New Haven, CT.

Huber, Evelyne (2002) *Models of Capitalism: Lessons for Latin America*, Pennsylvania State University Press, University Park, PA.

Huntington, Samuel P. (1991) *The Third Wave: Democratization in the Late Twentieth Century*, University of Oklahoma Press, Norman, OK.

International Labour Organization (1972) *Employment, Incomes and Equality: A Strategy for Increasing Productive Employment in Kenya*, ILO, Geneva.

International Labour Organization (2005) *Key Indicators of the Labour Market*, 4th edn, ILO, Geneva.

International Labour Organization (2006) *Global Employment Trends Model 2006*, Employment Trends Team, ILO, Geneva.

Jelin, Elisabeth (1997) 'Emergent citizenship or exclusion? Social movements and non-governmental organizations in the 1990s', in William C. Smith and Roberto Patricio Korzeniewicz (Eds), *Politics, Social Change, and Economic Restructuring in Latin America* North-South Center, Miami, FL, pp. 79–101.

Larson, Donald F., Anderson, Jock R. and Varangis, Panos (2004) 'Policies on managing risk in agricultural markets', *The World Bank Research Observer*, 19(2), p. 199–230.

Lopez, Humberto (2006) *Did Growth become Less Pro-poor in the 1990s?*, World Bank, Washington, DC.

McKinley, Terry (2001) 'The macroeconomic implications of focusing on poverty reduction', in Terry McKinley (Ed.), *Macroeconomic Policy, Growth, and Poverty Reduction*, Palgrave, New York, pp. 201–226.

Mehrotra, Santosh and Jolly, Richard (Eds) (1997) *Development with a Human Face: Experiences in Social Achievement and Economic Growth*, Clarendon Press, Oxford.

Mkandawire, Thandika (1999a) 'Crisis management and the making of "choiceless democracies" in Africa', in Richard Joseph (Ed.), *The State, Conflict and Democracy in Africa*, Lynne Rienner, Boulder, CO, pp. 119–136.

Mkandawire, Thandika (1999b) 'Shifting commitments and national cohesion in African countries', in Lennart Wohlegemuth, Samantha Gibson, Stephan Klasen and Emma Rothchild

(Eds), *Common Security and Civil Society in Africa,* Nordiska Afrikainstitutet, Uppsala, pp. 14-41.

Mkandawire, Thandika (2004) 'Disempowering new democracies and the persistence of poverty', in Max Spoor (Ed.), *Globalisation, Poverty and Conflict,* Kluwer Academic Publishers, Dordrecht, pp. 117-153.

Mkandawire, Thandika (2005) 'Maladjusted African economies and globalisation', *Africa Development,* XXX(1&2), pp. 1-33.

Mkandawire, Thandika (2009) *Institutional Monocroping and Monotasking in Africa,* UNRISD, Geneva.

Moore, Mick and Devereux, Stephen (1999) 'Introduction: nationalising the anti-poverty agenda?', *IDS Bulletin,* 30(2), pp. 1-5.

Ohno, Kenichi (2002) 'Development with alternative strategic options: a Japanese view on the poverty reduction drive and beyond', in Kenichi Ohno (Ed.), *East Asian Growth and Japanese Aid,* Grips Development Forum, National Graduation Institute for Policy Studies, Tokyo, pp. 19-27.

Piketty, Thomas and Saez, Emmanuel (2006) *The Evolution of Top Incomes: A Historical and International Perspective.,* National Bureau of Economic Reasearch, Cambridge, MA.

Rothstein, Bo (2001) 'The universial welfare state as a social dilemma', *Rationality and Society,* 13(2), pp. 213-233.

Sahn, D.E. (1992) 'Public expenditures in sub-Saharan Africa during a period of economic reforms', *World Development,* 20(5), pp. 673-693.

Sender, John (1999) 'Africa's economic performance: limitations of the current consensus', *Journal of Economic Perspectives,* 13(3), pp. 89-114.

Stephens, John D. (2002) 'European welfare state regimes: configuration, outcomes, transformations', in Evelyne Huber (Ed.), *Models of Capitalism: Lessons for Latin America,* Pennsylvania State University Press, University Park, PA, pp. 303-338.

Toye, John (1999) 'Nationalising the anti-poverty agenda', *IDS Bulletin,* 30(2), pp. 6-12.

Vreeland, James (2007) *The International Monetary Fund: Politics of ConditionalLending,* Routledge, Oxford.

Waterman, Peter (1975) 'The "labour aristocracy" in Africa: introduction to a debate', *Development and Change,* 6(3), pp. 57-74.

White, Howard and Killick, Tony (2001) *African Poverty at the Millennium: Causes, Complexities, and Challenges,* World Bank, Washington, DC.

# *Say's Law, Poverty Persistence, and Employment Neglect*

ALICE H. AMSDEN
*Alice H. Amsden is Barton L. Weller Professor of Political Economy at the Massachusetts Institute of Technology, USA*

**Abstract** Grass roots methods of poverty alleviation will fail unless jobs are created or stimulated by governments (whether central or local). In the presence of high unemployment at all levels, improving the capabilities of job seekers (making them better fed and housed and educated) will only lead to more unemployment and not to more paid employment or self-employment above the subsistence level (call this the 'Kerala Effect'). To believe that improving only the supply side of the labor market is enough to reduce poverty without also improving the demand side, and investing in jobs, is logically flawed and subject to the same error as Say's Law — that 'supply creates its own demand'. Healthcare and other benefits provided through grass roots anti-poverty programs may improve the quality of life (measured by rising life expectancy). But as population growth rises, diminishing returns sets in, in Malthusian fashion, and poverty does not fall, as shown by the data provided in the article.

## Introduction

Despite championing the cause of poor people around the world, and dramatizing the 'human condition,' the United Nation's Millennium Development Goals make not the slightest mention of employment generation as a means to battle poverty; there is silence on using economic policies — employment, fiscal industrial, monetary and trade — to create more industries that could provide additional jobs above the starvation level.[1] A World Bank history that starts in 1944 and covers over half a century (Kapur *et al.*, 1997) mentions employment only seven times in a total of 1234 pages! A popular book on poverty by Paul Collier (2007), while highly praised by Larry Summers, George Soros and the *Economist* magazine, *The Bottom Billion* fails in its nine-page, small print index to make *any* reference to employment, unemployment, self-employment, jobs, or work. Even China elicits silence, no matter how fast employment has grown:

> What have been the effects of China's rapid industrialization and economic growth on employment in the country? No widely accepted answer to this question is available from the existing literature. Indeed, there are not many studies that even ask the question. (Ghose, 2005, p. 42)

These omissions exist despite the fierce global competition over jobs that will probably define the twenty-first century! Will Africa and other poor countries get any of the pie?

## *Breaking into the circle*

A steady, well-paid job is regarded as a treasure in the developing world because unemployment and under-employment are typically rampant, and a job is a ticket out of misery and into the middle class. In a country like Mexico, it allows a worker to save, buy a house, and pay for schooling. In all of India's manufacturing industries except one ('machine repair'), the 'formal' sector, where paid employment predominates, is almost three times more productive than the 'informal' sector, where most anti-poverty money goes.[2] To be self-employed in informal services like auto-rickshaws, transport porters, and ready-food stalls, is to earn less in India than an agricultural worker (Banerjee, 2005). While poverty alleviation programs tend to rely heavily on volunteers, paid employment acts as a stimulus to economic activity from greater expenditures, as Keynes argued — he called for more jobs, not poverty alleviation to combat the Great Depression. Yet despite all this, while the fight against poverty since 1980 has boomed, job growth in developing countries has stagnated, along with explanations for why this is so.[3]

This paper looks at two startling facts and then gives a general answer to why there is dementia over jobs (as well as over population planning, which is also off stage). The answer lies in the misapplication of 'Say's Law' at the grass-roots level and in US State Department politics, both biased against employment expansion.

The first fact, based on World Bank statistics, is that between 1981 and 2005, when statist employment policies were being scuttled and the poverty movement was at its prime, poverty in most developing regions did *not* decline (see Figures 1 and 2). The bottom-up approach that field-activists and foundations swear by cannot be said to be working effectively, and there is nothing to suggest the data are wrong, at least in terms of measuring how much the poorest people consume, with health improvements and water sanitation enhancing consumption and raising productivity. Whether regional poverty is measured by the population share living on less than US$1.25 a day (measured in goods and services), or as a gap between acceptable and unacceptable living standards, regional poverty rates for over 25

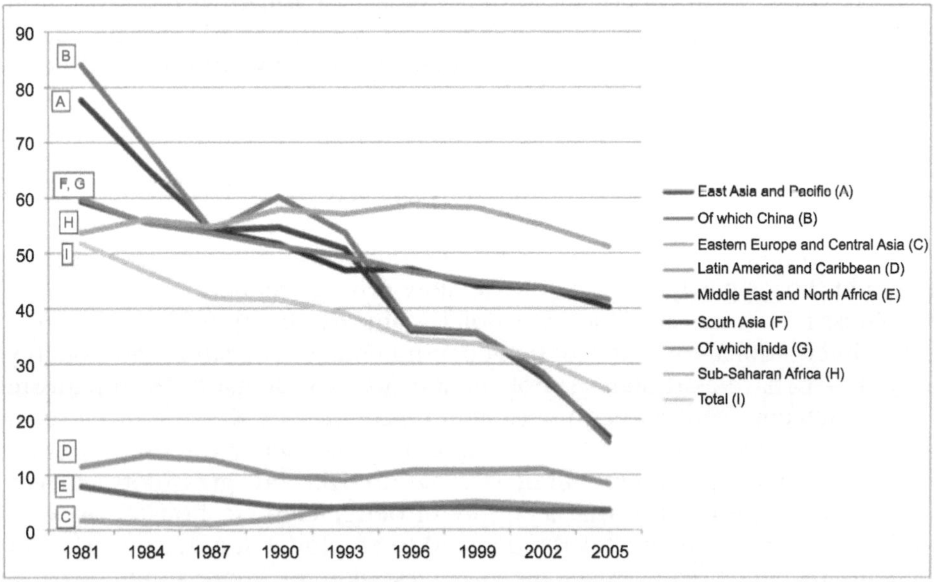


FIGURE 1. Percentage below US$1.25 per day by region.
*Source*: All data are adapted and taken from Chen and Ravallion (2008).

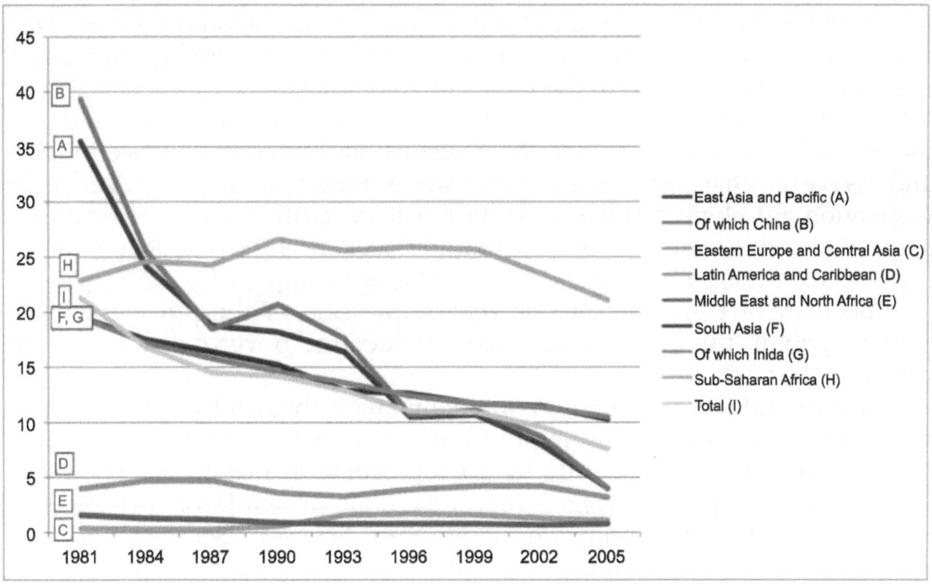


FIGURE 2. Poverty gap index (x100) by region.
*Note*: Poverty gap index = mean distance below the poverty line as a proportion of the line where the mean is taken over the whole population, counting the non-poor as having zero poverty gaps.
*Source*: All data are taken from Chen and Ravallion (2008).

years in Africa, Latin America and the Middle East *failed to fall*. The most shocking case is Africa, because attention has been focused there and absolute standards of welfare remain low. Ironically, poverty rates fell furthest in East Asia (especially China), where the ratio of employment to population in 2003 was as high as 76.6, compared with only 62.5 in the rest of the world (International Labour Organization, 2005).

While the stickiness of regional poverty rates may have other causes besides a bottom-up approach (such as HIV/AIDs and population growth), this approach gives short shrift to the use of demand side policies to create jobs, and thus is partly accountable for slow poverty reduction.

Grass roots ideas about job creation became dysfunctional because activists — international estimates of non-governmental organizations are roughly 40 000 — behave as though 'supply creates its own demand' (Jean Baptiste Say, a nineteenth-century economist later discredited by Keynes, proposed a law — now called Say's Law — to the effect that under full employment, what an economy produces will be purchased). Like Say, grassroots activists hold as an article of faith that a supply of better clothed, housed, and fed workers automatically creates the demand to employ it at a living wage. Yet if unemployment already exists, then to invest more in workers' human capabilities, whether in the form of healthcare, housing, and schooling, or of political freedom, democracy, and transparency (as the Nobel laureate Amartya Sen suggests), may create more perturbed unemployed job-seekers, rather than more plentiful jobs (Sen, 2000). To believe otherwise is a leap of faith. With slow-growing demand for new job seekers, further investments in skills may simply force people to 'hire' themselves at starvation wages, as in many micro-enterprises. If more money is poured into tertiary education, graduates are likely to add to the educated unemployed or to migrate abroad (educated unemployment in Indonesia is estimated to have exceeded 787 800 in 2007).[4] If a child is inoculated against an infectious disease but her landless parents have no livelihood and she is hungry, then the effects of the inoculation are blunted. Thus, jobs do not necessarily make an appearance simply because the supply of qualified job seekers improves as a result of grassroots activism. The demand side must also be improved.

Job dementia, or focusing on the supply side of the job market and forgetting about the demand side, may produce the poverty data presented in Figures 1 and 2.

The second fact pertaining to job dementia is that US foreign economic policy since the Pax Americana does not put 'jobs first'; to the contrary, it gives job formation low priority by leaving capital formation to create jobs *exclusively to private (foreign) investors*. This principle of 'private-only' was formulated after World War II by Dean Acheson, Secretary of State under President Harry Truman, and holds that American aid should not be given if it puts American jobs at risk, or competes for a project with American industry. If it does, it has low priority for Congressional funding (Acheson, 1969). The World Bank, whose President is appointed by the USA, also never lends to the private sector (except for loans from one small Bank subsidiary); the World Bank lends only to the governments of member states. Lending to the private sector in developing countries is left to private lenders, mostly in developed countries, which helps multinational companies expand abroad. In the 1960s and 1970s the World Bank lent heavily for infrastructure, which may have laid the foundations for steel mills, for example, which in turn created jobs. But the Bank, in the case of South Korea and India, refused to lend to the steel industry directly (even the government-owned segment). Washington opposed, in the belief that more steel mills would create global excess capacity, and thus more competition for steel mills in the USA (see Amsden, 1989; Kapur *et al.*, 1997). What the World Bank now favors are loans for privatizing government enterprises, to increase 'for-profit' opportunities. In practice, then, American foreign policy is biased against Third World employment because neither foreign aid nor World Bank loans nor Third World industrial policies can be used to promote it in a flexible way.[5]

Job dementia that is due to conflicting aims on the part of foreign donors and lenders, therefore, may also influence the desultory results presented in Figures 1 and 2.

If all governments in the developing world are corrupt, as the grass-roots generally believe, then governments may be hypothesized to become *less* corrupt with reverse brain-drain of the highest talent. This talent faces the greatest personal opportunities for economic gain through *legitimate channels* — in business, finance, and services — and does not need to be corrupt, or does not care to be corrupt given its culture. The difficult task of attracting talent back home, and into the government, requires incentives. As reverse brain-drain in fast-growing East Asia and Middle Eastern oil-producing countries suggest, governments tempt talented 'brain *gain*' back home by offering it public-sector jobs with high pay and heavy responsibility, from starting a public venture-capital fund to running a national oil company (as many as 40 developing countries now produce at least one million barrels of oil a day). With this elite in place, joined by home-educated top talent, governments can strengthen their anti-poverty programs by introducing new technologies (for energy, Brazil's sugar ethanol), by accumulating expertise (for rural electrification, China's state power companies) or by forming small and medium-size enterprises in poor regions for profit.[6] With reverse brain-drain gathering momentum, there are likely to be enough qualified professionals around to strengthen the capabilities of private companies, using a *top-down* approach that draws on government money and expertise (national and provincial). Taiwan is a role-model for this because it has always had hundreds of private small factories operating in rural regions and towns, supported by government research centers.[7] Its neighbor, China, is a paragon for collectively owned 'town and village enterprises.'

Countries like Taiwan and China, which excelled in developing after World War II, all started with prewar manufacturing experience, either from foreign émigrés or colonial firms (Amsden, 2001). A focus on poverty alleviation of professionally managed small and medium-size firms — more professional and more likely to survive than the typical micro-enterprise — might provide a way for the poorest countries to break into this circle.

### *No substitute for a good job*

To increase low incomes, a society can either invest directly in factories that provide employment, or invest in a public good like transportation that supports the rise of factories. The two are complementary, but not perfect, substitutes. A rise in paid employment has a greater absolute advantage than a rise in poverty alleviation in advancing the institutions of economic development. Falling population growth rates — a plus for development — tend to respond more to changes in paid employment than to changes in poverty alleviation.

## Population and wage labor

The 'mortality revolution,' as the economic historian Richard Easterlin calls it, involves radical changes in mortality rates, birth rates and population growth rates. As this process is theorized, it begins with an increase in productivity, due to the division of labor, which then leads to an increase in labor demand in urban areas, *where specialization in production and distribution goes furthest*. There is a turning point in mortality as paid employment spreads. 'A decrease in the demand for children is caused primarily by several processes linked to modern economic growth — education, urbanization, and the introduction of new goods' (Easterlin, 1998, p. 100). Universal schooling takes children away from work, so they are worth less as breadwinners, driving down birth rates. Paid women workers, with more education, prefer fewer children than foregone earnings, driving birth rates down further. Material aspirations rise and culture changes in favor of a pattern of consumption that is less family-centric and more oriented towards 'buying' rather than 'making' goods and services (Easterlin, 1998).

This epochal demographic shift tends to be slower under a regime of poverty alleviation. Because people tend to remain where poverty alleviation is administered, in the rural regions, culture changes relatively slowly. As it remains in tact, especially in the absence of land reforms or technological change in agriculture, population growth rates do not fall fast. Unemployment worsens and out-migration overburdens cities, reinventing the poverty cycle. Thus, the impact of poverty alleviation on radical institutional change is less positive than the impact of job formation.

Dementia over jobs and population growth rates have gone hand in hand; little external finance has flowed to either recently, and wages have sagged under population strains. In the 1970s, 'the World Bank's population advocacy had done much to legitimize the developmental significance of family planning' (Kapur *et al.*, 1997, pp. 344–345), but this stopped after negative fall-out from Indira Gandhi's forced sterilization program (and

China's one-child family). Both programs are now associated with gender bias in births, but they should also be associated with fast economic growth and large falls in birth and death rates, especially in China (China's poverty fell much faster than India's, as shown in Figures 1 and 2). Yet uncourageously, the World Bank took a more 'roundabout' approach to population, one in which 'family planning was integrated with *and partly disguised by* health and nutrition projects' (Kapur *et al.*, 1997, pp. 344-345; emphasis added).

Thus, as poverty alleviation spread, the two headlights guiding the way towards economic development were dimmed: job formation and the mortality revolution.

## Investing in the 'heart of darkness'

While the bottom up approach to poverty alleviation takes Say's Law for granted (employment — including self-employment at a living wage — is seen as the automatic reward of greater grass-roots effort), the top-down approach also requires an assumption: that there are, in fact, profitable investment opportunities in poor regions (rural or urban) that a private entrepreneur would consider investing in if government incentives were right (such as free land, good roads, cheap credit and hard-driving, docile workers). Together, these incentives might make an otherwise unprofitable investment in the short run profitable in the long run, as investments in learning bore fruit. The evidence from investment feasibility studies, or what the World Bank calls 'investment climate reports,' is almost always positive.[8] There *are* opportunities in impoverished lands for small factories, or agri-businesses, or service outlets, including some of Africa's poorest countries. A Chief Executive Officer from one of Korea's conglomerates (now defunct), which exported textiles in the 1970s to Indonesia and Africa, said:

> I can see money everywhere ... It is in America and in Africa, but you have to work hard to see it and to get it. If you try hard enough, you will see more money than you could possibly collect in your lifetime. (Harvard Business School, 1985, p. 9)

## Beyond micro-enterprises

Paid factory employment will only prosper in low-income regions if it can overcome the primary problem that has vexed entrepreneurs stuck in tiny, family firms: forming sustainable business enterprises that have some modicum of professional management. This is the primary challenge today to entrepreneurship in poor countries. Clifford Geertz, in his classic interpretive study of Javanese traders in 1963, *Peddlers and Princes*, emphasized this organizational weakness of Third World businesses: 'What the entrepreneurial group of Islamic small businessmen most lacks is not capital ... or drive ... or a sufficient market ... It lacks the capacity to form efficient economic institutions; it is a group of entrepreneurs without enterprises' (Geertz, 1963, p. 28). What can activists do to help?

Scientists and engineers can raise living standards by inventing something the developing world can 'make,' not only 'use.' They can put less (relative) weight on transferring technological innovations to poor countries that are designed to be consumed by the poor, like air-friendly charcoal briquettes for indoor cooking, and provide more products around which a business can start, like finding new markets for briquettes. The $100 laptop raises literacy, but just because millions of youth gain computer skills does not mean they can find gainful jobs. Paid work can be found in manufacturing computer parts.

## Conclusion

To slay the dragon of poverty, deliberate and determined investments in jobs above starvation wages must play a central role, whether for self-employment or paid employment. The grass-roots approach to solving poverty does not go far enough, because it aims only at improving the supply side of the labor market, making job-seekers more capable, and not the demand side, making new jobs available for them.[9] It acts as though new ways of earning a living emerge (at a positive wage) simply because the supply of job-seekers is better clothed, housed, and fed, or enjoys more human rights — which is the same fallacious reasoning behind Say's Law, to the effect that the supply of whatever an economy produces creates the demand to buy it (at a positive price). One ignores unemployment; the other ignores under-consumption. By not strengthening the demand side, 25 years of supply-side poverty alleviation has left poverty rates for the poorest people unchanged (assuming World Bank data are correct), including Africa's poor, the target of the attack on poverty (see Figures 1 and 2).

Employment generation is different from poverty alleviation because it has a concept behind it, 'capital.' This means that the labor market is influenced by, and influences, all flows through the savings–investment nexus, including accumulation, distribution and innovation. It is at the heart of political conflict. Multi-faceted policies, therefore, are required to promote employment growth, from fiscal and monetary to industrial and trade. Poverty alleviation has its policy rages, too, but they are more confined, outside the capital accumulation process. Still, the coordination of policies to create employment in the Third World's most impoverished regions is not impossible even if it is multifaceted. Excellent work in the 1970s was produced on the subject, only to be shelved in the 1980s for political reasons.[10]

Besides Keynesian and industrial policies to raise investment and employment, and to reverse brain-drain (which can alter a country's comparative advantage overnight), three changes in embedded practice might go a long way towards 'bringing employment back in'.

The first is to cease a heavy reliance at the grass-roots on volunteer, unpaid labor — it is necessary to form non-voluntary organizations along with non-governmental organizations. The greater the number of unpaid volunteers, as in healthcare workers, the greater the difficulty of creating paid professionals, as in nurses.

The second change is to strengthen the alliance between grassroots activists who are not hostile to government intervention and government bureaucrats who are involved in poverty reduction. Not just working together, but also working on a model for future collaboration, would lay the groundwork for a new generation to follow.

The third is to revolutionize foreign aid by tying it to jobs. For every dollar spent on poverty alleviation, a dollar should be spent in the poorest regions on employment creation, following the lead in rural employment generation established by China and Taiwan. Some aid donors could concentrate on the investment part of the project and other donors, with hands-on experience in business, could provide technical assistance on what is likely to work. Instead of buying a $100 laptop computer, developing countries could start competing with a $99 one!

## Notes

1 More than five years after the Millennium Developments Goals had been adopted, World Leaders at the World Summit, at the United Nations in September 2005, undertook the commitment to make the goals of 'full and productive employment and decent work for all' a central objective of (their) relevant national and international policies. This was followed by a ministerial declaration at the United Nations Economic and Social Council (ECOSOC) High-level segment in July 2006 expressing the same and the inclusion of a new target, echoing the commitment of the 2005 World Summit, under Millennium Development Goal Number 1 (Eradicate Extreme Poverty and Hunger). See United Nations (2007).

2 Studies that obtain other results typically compare micro-enterprises in both sectors, which miss the point — the formal sector has succeeded in building larger, professionally managed enterprises whose productivity may be higher than a micro-enterprise located in either sector (Gelb *et al.*, 2009).

3 For an excellent overview of the relationship between jobs and poverty, see Khan (2007).

4 ILO LABORSTA [www.laborsta.ilo.org].

5 For the underground industrial policies that have emerged as a result of restrictions on industrial policies by the World Trade Organization, see Amsden and Hikino (2000).

6 Rural electrification, despite its centrality to fighting poverty, has made notable gains in China, although little is written about this possibly because China's approach was not bottom up (Stanford University Program on Energy and Sustainable Development, 2006).

7 For the machine tool industry, see Amsden (1977).

8 A number of World Bank investment reports are mentioned in *The Bottom Billion*, which argues that the poorest countries are poor due to war but can be saved from free trade. Unfortunately, most world trade is now conducted within the confines of regional trade agreements, and many poor countries are not a part of any viable agreement. See Collier (2007).

9 Some grass-roots groups, of course, like OXFAM, do worry about the demand side.

10 One of the best studies, which combined poverty alleviation and job promotion, was done in Kenya by the International Labour Office (1974). It was experimental and tried to open

the doors to new ideas. One was that if income is re-distributed to the poor, employment will increase faster because the poor consume a bundle of goods made with more labor-intensive technologies than the rich.

## References


Acheson, D. (1969) *Present at the Creation: My Years in the State Department,* Norton, New York.

Amsden, A.H. (1977) 'The division of labor is limited by the 'type' of market: the taiwanese machine tool industry', *World Development,* 5, pp. 217–234.

Amsden, A.H. (1989) *Asia's Next Giant: South Korea and Late Industrialization,* Oxford University Press, Oxford and New York.

Amsden, A.H. (2001) *The Rise of 'the Rest': Challenges to the West from Late-Industrializing Economies,* Oxford University Press, New York.

Amsden, A.H. and Hikino, T. (2000) 'The bark is worse than the bite: new WTO law and late industrialization', *Annals,* 570 (July), pp. 104–114.

Banerjee, D. (2005) *Globaliisation, Industrial Restructuring and Labour Standards Where India Meets the Global,* Sage, Delhi.

Chen, Shaohua and Ravallion, Martin (2008) 'The developing world is poorer than we thought, but no less successful in the fight against poverty', *Policy Research Working Paper 4703,* The World Bank Development Research Group, [http://econ.worldbank.org/external/default/main?pagePK=64165259&piPK=64165421&theSitePK=469372&menuPK=64166093&entityID=000158349_20080826113239].

Collier, P. (2007) *The Bottom Billion: Why the Poorest Countries are Failing and What Can be Done About It,* Oxford University Press, New York.

Easterlin, R.A. (1998) *Growth Triumphant. The Twenty-first Century in Historical Perspective,* University of Michigan Press, Ann Arbor, MI.

Geertz, C. (1963) *Peddlers and Princes: Social Development and Economic Change in Two Indonesian Towns,* University of Chicago Press, Chicago, IL.

Gelb, A., *et al.* (2009) *To Formalize or Not to Formalize? Comparisons of Microenterprise Data from Southern and East Asia.* Center for Growth and Economic Development, Washington, DC.

Ghose, A.K. (2005) 'Employment in China: recent trends and future challenges', in *Employment Strategy Papers. Employment Analysis Unit, Empployment Strategy Department,* International Labor Organization, Geneva.

Harvard Business School (1985) *Daewoo group,* Harvard Business School, Boston, MA.

International Labour Office (1974) *Employment, Incomes and Equality: A Strategy for Increasing Productive Employment in Kenya,* ILO, Geneva.

International Labour Organization (2005) *World Employment Report 2004–05: Employment, Productivity and Poverty Reduction,* International Labour Organization, Geneva.

Kapur, D., Lewis, J.P. and Webb, R. (Eds) (1997) *The World Bank: Its First Half-Century,* Brookings, Washington, DC.

Khan, A.R. (2007) 'Growth, employment and poverty', in J.A. Ocampo and J.K. Sunderam (Eds), *Towards Full and Decent Employment,* Orient Longman for the United Nations, New York.

Sen, A. (2000) *Development as Freedom,* Anchor Books, New York.

Stanford University Program on Energy and Sustainable Development (2006) *Rural Electrification in China 1950–2004,* Stanford University, Stanford, CA.

United Nations (2007) *The Employment Imperative, Report of the World Situation 2007,* United Nations, New York.

# *Income Inequality and Employment Revisited: Can One Make Sense of Economic Policy?*

ROLPH VAN DER HOEVEN

*Rolph van der Hoeven is Professor of Employment and Development Economics at the Institute of Social Studies in The Hague, The Netherlands*

**Abstract** This article discusses growing inequalities in the context of employment and labour market policies and how the latter can contribute to lowering inequalities. It discusses what is meant by income inequality, why it is remains important to focus on income inequality, which measures of income inequality are relevant and how we have arrived at growing income inequality. A last section reviews what can be done about growing inequality. The current situation is dominated by globalization, which has influenced the functioning and outcome of various aspects of the labour market. Greater attention to labour market institutions and greater coherence between economic and labour market policies is therefore necessary to stem growing inequality. Past examples of combining growth with equitable income distribution are often examples of restrained capitalism. Either social pacts or government bureaucrats and political elites provided the restraint. The current crisis and the public concern for improved income equality might engender renewed political will to make employment creation and income distribution important objectives for economic policy-making.

## Introduction

Might income inequality at least be coming in from the cold? Chairman of the American Federal Reserve Board, Ben Bernanke (2007) lectures on the danger of growing inequality; there are debates in the *Financial Times*; the two 2007 issues of the World Economic Outlook of the International Monetary Fund (IMF) deal with growing inequality; and many governments, at least in their public statements at the United Nations, seem to be concerned with growing income inequality. Earlier, major UN organizations devoted their flagship reports to income inequality (for example, UNDESA,

2005). These were preceded by several research projects on inequality, notably those at the UN World Institute for Development Economic Research, at the beginning of this decade. Also, at the onset of the global financial crisis in the second half of 2008, voices have been raised to give greater attention to inequality and employment policies (see, for example, Alesina and Giuliano, 2009; International Labour Organization [ILO], 2008).

This article contributes to a reflection on concerns for growing inequality, and discusses this especially in the context of employment and labour market policies and how these can contribute to lowering inequalities. The first section discusses *what* we mean by income inequality. The second section argues why, despite various critiques, it is remains important to focus on *income* inequality and *which* measures of income inequality are relevant. Thereafter the paper reviews briefly *how* we have arrived at this growing income inequality.

A last section discusses *what* we could possibly do about growing inequality. The current situation is very much dominated by greater integration of various markets and splashes of technological development often called globalization. Globalization has influenced the functioning and outcome of various aspects of the labour market and a greater attention to labour market institutions and greater coherence between economic and labour market policies is a necessary condition to stem growing inequality.

## *What* do we mean with income inequality?

This article reviews growing income inequality at a national level: that is, income inequality between people and households within countries. In the current climate of cosmopolitan thinking one could argue that one rather needs to be concerned with inequality on a world scale, and do away with the notion of national identity and inequality. And indeed many studies have shown that inequality between nations has increased; for example, the ratio between the average income of the 20 richest nations and the 20 poorest countries has risen from 53 in 1960 to 121 in 2000 (World Commission on the Social Dimension of Globalization, 2004). But this process has been accompanied by a growing inequality within most countries (Cornia, 2004) and policy-making is mainly national: the World Commission on the Social Dimension of Globalization states that 'globalization starts at home' and argues that national policies can make a great difference. Paying attention to inequality at the national level therefore remains important.[1] This does not mean that no attention should be given to international inequality, as argued elsewhere.

The classical economists paid attention mainly to the distribution of income *between labour and capital* (factor income distribution). This distinction drove the great classical debates for many years. Less attention was given to this in the post-war period as neoclassical production functions often assumed a constant capital share. However, for good reasons, attention to factor income distribution is coming back — as will be discussed further on. After the Second World War, attention shifted to personal income or household income distribution. One can interpret personal income in three ways:

- The first is income earned from whatever activities are undertaken (by some analysts termed primary income): *primary* income is determined by markets and market institutions.
- The second interpretation of personal income is income after deduction of taxes and inclusion of transfer payments (sometimes called *secondary* income).
- Thirdly one can add to the secondary income the imputed benefits from public expenditure (sometimes labelled *tertiary* income).

Most policy discussions on inequality focus on secondary income inequality, and implicitly assume that redistributive policies are equivalent to tax policies (and then argue that globalization is restricting national tax policies so that politicians nowadays have a reduced set of tools). This article argues that policies are also required to stem primary and tertiary inequality, and that labour market and employment policies can be an important part of such policies.

## Why does it remain important to focus on *income* inequality?

Some argue that attention to income inequality is exaggerated as other aspects of life are equally or even more important: issues such as health, democratic participation, freedom, and so forth. Often statistics are used to show that inequality of life expectancy has declined or that increases in political rights have increased.

Recently, the Commission on Social Determinants of Health, which looked into the challenges of the global health system, published its report. An important finding of the report is that higher levels of inequality produce higher levels of ill-health *for all income groups*, rich as well as poor.[2] The report had three over-arching messages, the second of which was: 'Tackle the inequitable distribution of power, money and resources — the structural drivers of those conditions of daily life — globally, nationally and locally' (Commission on Social Determinants of Health, 2008, p. 2). So those who belittle the fact of growing income inequality will find little comfort in continuing to argue that we should look more at health inequalities, as the commission's report argues that a major determinant of health inequality is income inequality! Mkandawire (2004) has also argued that not all democracies necessarily pursue egalitarian polices.

Others argue that attention to income inequality is not necessary as long as the economy is growing and poverty declining.[3] This was actually one of the main tenants of the Millennium Development Goals, which concentrated on poverty reduction. Jolly (2007) and Vandemoortele (2003) are among those who have criticized the Millennium Development Goals for focusing insufficiently on inequality.

However, there are moral and economic reasons to be concerned with inequality *per se*. Cullity (2004) mentions four moral reasons:

1. Inequality as domination: imposing hardships on other groups.
2. Inequality of political and legal status as a consequence of income inequality.
3. Inequality as callousness: when others cannot meet their basic needs.
4. Brute inequality: inability of a society to include all groups in welfare enhancement.

An economic reason to be concerned with income inequality is that research over the past one and half decades has shown that there need not to be a trade-off between equality and growth, or between inequality and efficiency.

From the 1950s and into the 1970s, analytical emphasis was on probable trade-offs between growth and income distribution. This derived in part from Kuznetz's famous 'inverted-U hypothesis', which postulated that inequality would rise in the initial phases of development, and then decline after some crucial level was reached: hence policy action on reducing inequality would be unwarranted.[4] Growth theories could be cited in support of the hypothesis, such as the Lewis model of 'economic development with unlimited supplies of labour'. Also Kaldor's growth model, in which capitalists have higher marginal propensity to save than workers, implies that redistribution of profits raises the growth rate. This, however, is of less relevance to developing countries (Aghion *et al.*, 1999).

Focusing on the effects of inequality and growth, Cornia (2004) finds that there is a distinct non-linear relationship between initial income inequality and economic growth, and argues that too low a level of inequality is bad for growth (free-riding, high supervision costs), but also that too high levels of inequality can have serious negative consequences. Income inequality in most developing countries is currently in the high range. More recently, economists at the World Bank have taken up this point and make a distinction between deserved and undeserved income inequality or between good and bad income inequality (Ferreirra, 2007). This distinction brings in too much unnecessary value judgement, and the analytical approach of the non-linear approach is much preferred.

Birdsall (2005, p. 5) argues that income inequality in developing countries matters for at least three instrumental reasons:

- Where markets are underdeveloped, inequality inhibits growth through economic mechanisms.
- Where institutions of government are weak, inequality exacerbates the problem of creating and maintaining accountable government, increasing the probability of economic and social policies that inhibit growth and poverty reduction.
- Where social institutions are fragile, inequality further discourages the civic and social life that underpins effective collective decision-making that is necessary to the functioning of healthy societies.

*There is thus a growing consensus that countries with an 'initial condition' of a relatively egalitarian distribution of assets and income tend to grow faster than countries with high initial inequality. This is an extremely important conclusion, because it means that reducing inequality strikes a double blow against poverty.* On the one hand, a growth path characterized by greater equality at the margin directly benefits the poor in the short run. On the other hand, the resulting decrease in inequality creates in each period an 'initial condition' for the future that is growth enhancing. Thus, any growth path that reduces inequality reduces poverty through redistribution and *via* 'trickle down'.

*Thus, both on moral grounds as well as on analytical grounds, the concern for income inequality — and especially concern for growing income inequality — is a proper concern.*

Having established that concern for income inequality is justified, we have to face the question of how to measure income inequality. A subject widely researched and discussed. This article therefore does not dwell on this, with the exception of one point that has become relevant and can have a direct consequence on policy-making: a common measure used by many analysts is the so-called Gini ratio, which on a scale of zero to one indicates the level of inequality. The index is constructed in such a way that it gives importance to how income is redistributed around the middle incomes. But recently we have witnessed the phenomenon of growing inequality caused by top incomes (Atkinson, 2007), which some argue may not be always covered sufficiently by the changes in the Gini ratio. Leigh (2007), however, making use of detailed data for 13 developed countries, has found a strong and significant relationship between top income share and broader inequality measures such as the Gini ratio. Although it is not always correct to transpose research findings from developed countries to developing countries, there is some indication that more than average increases in top incomes can be indicative of an overall widening inequality and that therefore a general index, as the Gini index, capture such rises in top incomes.

*However, one phenomenon that is not picked up by general inequality statistics is gender inequality*. Elson (2007) and Heintz (2006) find that many factors are put forward to explain the gender gap in earnings — differences in education, shorter tenure in the labour market and interruptions in women's employment histories associated with raising children. Nevertheless, as Heintz reviews: a large quantity of research has shown that, even after controlling for education, age and job tenure, gender gaps in remuneration remain. In part, this is due to the persistence of earnings gaps within occupational categories (Horton, 1999), suggesting that wage discrimination remains influential. Research also suggests that earnings differentials between men and women are also apparent across the various forms of informal work (Chen *et al.*, 2005). However, Heintz argues that labour force segmentation is as important, if not more important, in determining the gap between women's and men's earnings. Women are disproportionately represented in lower paying forms of employment, often with fewer social protections and less stable incomes. Much less is known about the gender earnings gap in low income countries, where informal forms of employment, including wide spread non-wage employment, dominate. Also, the structure of production and responses to global integration can impact on changes in the gender income gap. For example, Seguino (2000) finds that capital mobility is one contributing factor to higher wage inequality in Taiwan. Since women are more concentrated in industries in which capital mobility is high, their bargaining power, and hence their wages, would fall relative to men as global integration progresses.

## *How* did income inequality develop over the past two decades?

Regarding *income and earnings inequality in industrialized countries*, Gottschalk and Smeeding (1997) observe that at any given time there are wide differences across modern countries in the level of earnings, and that nations with centralized bargaining (e.g. Sweden and Germany) have greater equality than nations with less centralized bargaining (e.g. the USA and Canada). They also observe in almost all industrialized countries some increase in wage inequality among prime-aged males during the 1980s. Wage inequality increased the most in the USA and the UK, and the least in the Nordic countries. The increased demand for skilled workers, coupled with differences among countries in the growth in the supply of skilled workers, explains a large part of the differences. Furthermore (and important for policy-making), they observe that institutional constraints on wage determination also seem to matter. The rise in relative unemployment rates among the least skilled in some, but not all, countries with centralized wage-setting institutions suggests that such institutional constraints were at least partially responsible for limiting the rise in inequality. For the USA they explain the rapid rise in earnings inequality by reference to a variety of structural changes in the economy such as changes in industrial structure; more foreign trade; more immigration; skill-based technical change; and the weakening of labour market institutions such as minimum wage setting and unionization that limit the effects of the free market. They cite studies that confirm the weakening of these two labour market institutions explains a large part, possibly even 50% cent, of the increase in the dispersion in wage earnings in the USA. Looking for common features and differences between the USA and European countries, Gottschalk and Smeeding argue that differences in wage-setting institutions may well account for some of the differences in the growth in inequality: 'There is certainly a *prima facie* case that countries with high union coverage on centralized wage setting were able to limit the growth in inequality' (1997, p. 653).

Regarding developing countries, Cornia (2004) argues that the past two decades have witnessed a *widespread and symmetric rise in within-country inequality in developing countries.* There are three possible explanations for this. First, limited migration to advanced nations did not help in equalizing the distribution of income in the countries of origin. Second, international financial flows have become less stable and more un-equalizing. And third, inequality was also influenced in a non-negligible way by domestic policy and institutional reforms — such as those of the labour market, financial sector, tax reform — which may have been introduced to facilitate the international integration of poor countries but which had unfavourable effects on labour income compared with profit income and wage differentials. Finally, Cornia argues, there are the inequality impacts of globalization. These contradict the predictions of standard theory, which is unable to capture the effect of other factors such as domestic institutional weaknesses, the complexity of trade and finance in a multi-country multi-goods environment, persistent and rising protectionism in the north and the equity impact of other domestic reforms that are often introduced to facilitate the drive towards globalization.

As argued above, neoclassical conventional wisdom sees the labour share in Gross Domestic product (GDP) as relatively constant. Research by Diwan (1999) and Harrison (2002), however, shows that the proportion of GDP that goes into wages and other labour income is variable over time. Harrison shows that, in the group of poorer countries, labour's share in national income fell on average by 0.1 percentage points per year from 1960 to 1993. The decline in the labour share accelerated after 1993, to an average decline of 0.3 percentage points per year. In the richer sub-group, the labour share grew by 0.2 percentage points before 1993, but then fell rapidly by 0.4 percentage points per year.

Harrison tested for factors that could explain changes in labour shares. Changes in factor shares are primarily linked to changes in capital/labour ratios. However, measures of globalization (such as capital controls or direct investment flows) also play a role. Exchange rate crises lead to declining labour shares, suggesting that labour pays a disproportionately high price when there are large swings in exchange rates (i.e. wages are more severely affected than GDP). Capital controls are associated with an increase in the labour share, an effect that Harrison attributes to the weaker bargaining position of capital *vis-à-vis* labour if the cost of relocating production increases with capital controls. The weak bargaining position of labour under open capital accounts is also a causal mechanism explored by Lee and Jayadev (2005). They found that financial openness exerted a downward pressure on the labour share both in developed and developing countries for the period from 1973 to 1995.

Harrison also finds that increasing trade is associated with a fall in the labour share. This result is robust across various specifications of the regression analysis. These results point to a systematic negative relationship between various measures of globalization and the labour share. Similarly, Vos (2007) argues that it is also clear that trade liberalization is no panacea for poverty reduction. Average welfare gains are mostly small, and in many instances have been inequality enhancing.

The overall decline in the labour share is partly explained by what some call the ratchet effect: after an economic shock or a financial crisis, the labour share in gross national income decreases but then in the phase of recovery increases less quickly as GDP increases (van der Hoeven and Saget, 2004). Some authors argue that the decline in labour share after economic shocks was, in effect, the consequence of a too high labour share before the crisis, thus partly blaming labour for the build-up of the crisis. However, only in a minority of cases have financial crises been caused by bidding up wages and labour shares. In most cases the crisis was caused by external events or rent-seeking behaviour of capital owners. In a study of the manufacturing sector in a large sample of developing countries, Amsden and van der Hoeven (1996) argue that a decline in real wages and a fall in the wage share of value added in most non-Asian developing countries in the 1980s and the 1990s reflect a redistribution of income from labour to capital, as low wages were made to bear the burden of uncompetitive manufacturers.

As the former chief economist of the IMF, Kenneth Rogoff, observed when he returned to academia:

> The simple truth is that corporations represent capital, and capital — in the form of factories, equipment, machines, money, and even houses — has been the single biggest winner in the modern era of globalization. Corporate profits are bursting at the seams of investors' expectations in virtually every corner of the world. … Many policymakers seem to be under the impression that surging profits are a purely cyclical phenomenon, Wait a bit, they predict, and wages will fully catch up later in the cycle. Not likely. Capital's piece of the pie has been getting bigger for more than 20 years, and the trend looks set to continue. (Rogoff, 2005)

Recent research by Daudey and Garcia Penalosa (2007) finds that factor distribution of incomes is an essential and statistically significant determinant of the personal distribution of income and that a larger labour share is associated with a lower Gini coefficient of personal incomes.

## *How* to react to the problem of growing income inequality?

We can distinguish four sets of reactions to growing income inequality:

- The question is wrong, because we are misreading the statistics (as discussed earlier, income is not important or we do not pick up lower prices of electronics that lower income groups consume, etc.).
- Income inequality is indeed increasing, but it is not a problem. It is either a temporary phenomenon in the course of development or an indication of the rewards of the current economic system.
- Growing income inequality is indeed a problem, but especially with current globalization there is little one can do (there is no alternative). This argument is usually based on the assumption that national governments cannot increase taxes and transfers as this would affect international

competitiveness or that governments in developing countries are incapable of dealing with income inequality.

- Growing income inequality is a problem, but with political will something can be done about it. Redistribution is necessary.

This article is mainly concerned with the fourth reaction. The remainder of this paper will discuss possibilities for redistribution and provide examples of policies of redistribution

Dagdevieren *et al.* (2004) have argued that implementing an agenda of redistribution involves major problems, but that these problems should not be exaggerated. In many developing countries, such problems might prove no more intractable than the problems associated with implementation of other economic policies, such as structural adjustment policies. An effective orthodox monetary policy is difficult to implement if a country is too small or underdeveloped to have a bond market. Similarly, replacing tariffs by a value-added tax would be a daunting task in a country whose commerce was primarily through small traders. The international financial institutions have recognized these constraints to adjustment programmes, and they typically made the decision that constrained implementation of such adjustment programmes was preferable to non-implementation. But the same argument can be made for a redistributive strategy: *to achieve poverty reduction, it might be preferable to redistribute growth imperfectly than to implement the* status quo *imperfectly.*

## Employment and income inequality as objectives of economic policy

A recent study on explanations for growing inequality over the past decade (Angeles-Castro, 2006) concludes that high employment levels reduce inequality and, especially, high employment levels in the industrial sector reduce inequality. *Targeting for employment and for reduction of income inequality can thus be combined objectives in policy-making.*[5]

What is the role of labour market institutions in this? New insights have been recently provided by Freeman (2007), who concludes — on the basis of an analysis of labour market institutions in developing and developed countries — that these institutions reduce inequality but have modest, uncertain or time-varying impacts on aggregate outcomes such as employment and other variables likely to be affected by wages.

One reason, Freeman argues, why effects other than on inequality may be modest is that the political economy of institutional interventions rules out collective bargaining settlements and regulations that are truly expensive to an economy. For example, no country would impose a minimum wage that disemployed a large fraction of the workforce; and no union or employer would sign a collective bargaining agreement that forced the firm to close. Taking this line of thinking to its logical conclusion, Freeman argues that economies that rely on well-functioning labour market institutions may have reduced the transaction costs of bargaining and developed long-term relations among parties such that they more often than not produce efficient outcomes as per the Coase Theorem. He concludes that to help assess these interpretations and increase our knowledge of institutions, reducing inequality requires inputs from areas of research that have played little role in the debate over the link between labour institutions on aggregate outcomes and argues that one such area is experimental economics. Evidence from laboratory experiments suggesting that people care about fair processes and outcomes and cooperate more than rational optimizing models of human behaviour suggest, opens the door for studies on the conditions needed for institutions to improve the market.[6]

Freeman's finding is very important because, if labour market institutions have as major objectives or outcomes a reduction of inequality, and have varied effects on growth and employment, and if higher employment is contributing to lower inequality as argued above, then policies aimed at strengthening well-functioning labour market institutions and having an explicit goal of increasing employment will contribute to lower inequality.

## How can employment or redistributive objectives make a difference? A few examples

### *Macro-economic policy*

The first illustration is in the realm of macro-economic policy. The World Bank has over the past five years become more concerned with growing inequality and has devoted various research publications to this. One example is the chapter of *Analyzing the Distributional Impacts of Reform, A Practitioners Guide* on 'Monetary and Exchange Rate Reforms' (Conway, 2005). It opens with a reference to the so-called 'policy trilemma' of international economic policies (see Mundell, 1963; Cohen, 1993; Obstfeld *et al.*, 2004). This states that national economic policy space is circumscribed by the impossibility of pursuing the following three policies simultaneously: open capital account, fixed exchange rates, and independent monetary policy. The trilemma posits that only two out of these three policies can be combined. For example, under a system of an open capital account and fixed exchange rates, countries cannot pursue an independent monetary policy, for example to stimulate employment growth, since interest rates are determined by world interest levels. Conversely, if countries need to undertake an independent monetary policy, they have either to revert to flexible exchange rates or opt for a closed capital account. The restriction of these options can hamper policies for full employment. The entire policy guide in the World Bank's publication is based on this observation; that is, an acceptance of mainstream economic theory. Had there been an explicit objective to put employment creation and inequality reduction as a primary objective, however, this work could have probed much more into exploring new policy avenues: more recent research argues that the policy trilemma, which has guided policy-makers for several decades, can be relaxed by avoiding the ultimate solutions referred to above and by looking beyond the traditional alternatives of fixed versus flexible exchange rates, or open versus closed capital accounts, to adopt intermediate options in these three policy domains — like a capital account management through the selective application of capital controls, or a managed real exchange rate (see Bradford, 2004).[7]

Although capital controls have, much like any other policy instrument, not always been fully effective in reaching their stated objectives (see Ariyoshi *et al.*, 2000), they have contributed to regaining greater policy autonomy in several cases. In Chile, for example, controls imposed on inflows have helped to reduce their level and to change the composition of inflows towards longer maturities, hence increasing the autonomy of monetary policy (Gallego *et al.*, 1999; see also de Gregorio *et al.*, 2000). The more controversial issue is controls on outflows, but Edison and Reinhart (2001) argue that such controls enabled Malaysia to stabilize exchange rates and interest rates during the East Asian crisis and to gain more policy autonomy. Kaplan and Rodrik (2001) conclude that the Malaysian approach has led to a faster economic recovery and to a smaller decline in real wages and employment than IMF policies would have done.

How could a system of a managed real exchange rate, the second element mentioned earlier, stimulate employment? Rodrik (2003) and Frenkel (2004) provide three channels. Active management of the real exchange rate would allow for higher capacity utilization in times of unemployment, if applied in combination with the appropriate mix of macro-economic and fiscal policies. It would also stimulate output growth and hence employment, if combined with appropriate industrial policies, as the experience in various Asian countries has shown. It could shift the sectoral composition of exports towards more labour-intensive goods, and hence increase the employment elasticity of the economy as a whole.

Employing a policy mix with intermediate options such as a managed capital account and a managed real exchange rate requires more fine-tuning and coherence in policies rather than relying on rule-of-thumb policy interventions. This necessitates national institutions with explicit mandates for employment and capabilities to achieve this (see van der Hoeven and Luebker, 2007).

Another possible, supplementary, element to relax the policy trilemma would be to include one or two additional policy instruments to complement the fiscal and monetary tools (see also Tinbergen, 1970 [1952]). Bradford (2004) suggests, for example, social pacts or coordinated wage bargaining to hold down inflation and so to 'free up' other policies aimed at growth and employment creation. Also, a greater concern for inequity and a reduction of national inequalities could contribute to reducing inflationary pressure and could be added either as part of a social pact or as a stand-alone policy instrument (see van der Hoeven and Saget, 2004). It is thus very important to have employment creation and equitable distribution as explicit policy objectives for macro-economic policies.

### Considering central banks as agents of development

A second example is that of considering central banks as agents of development, as suggested by Epstein (2007). He argues that an employment-targeting approach to central bank policy may seem quite alien to those schooled in the orthodox tradition of inflation targeting and financial liberalization, but that in fact this has been quite common historically in both currently developed and developing countries. Over the years, central banks have been seen as agents of economic development, not just agents of economic stabilization. And while sometimes central banks have failed quite spectacularly in this mission, there have been other important success stories, including important periods in the USA, the UK, France, Germany, Japan, South Korea and India, to name just a few examples.

As for developing countries, Amsden (2001, 2007) describes the key role that investment banks played in the industrialization success stories of countries such as South Korea, Taiwan, Malaysia, Brazil, Argentina and others in mobilizing and directing savings to key industrial sectors, and in particular to those specializing in exports. Epstein (2007) recalls that, in many of these cases, central banks were a key part of the government apparatus that played a supporting role by maintaining low interest rates, maintaining capital controls to help stabilize exchange rates at competitive levels, and sometimes engaging in direct lending for preferred purposes. Engaging in these developmental roles, using a wide variety of instruments, was widely seen as a key part of the central bank's mission. After the Second World War, there was a major transformation of central banking in the developing world. In many respects, these changes paralleled those in the developed world. Epstein deplores the resilience of inflation targeting and argues that inflation targeting is far from benign as it creates in central banks a *culture* of inflation focus, or even inflation obsession.[8] An explicit employment target besides an inflation target could change the mindset of traditional economists.

### Setting minimum wages

A third example is that of setting minimum wages. Several ILO studies (Saget, 2001, 2008) have observed that, as a consequence of structural adjustment and liberalization policies and a breaking down of trade unions and labour market institutions, the minimum wage in a sizeable number of countries is so low that it is does not contribute to reducing inequalities or poverty reduction and has become meaningless. In a second set of countries, the minimum wage appears to fulfil its objective of reducing poverty without hampering employment creation.[9] But there is also a set of countries where the minimum wage is very high: too high in fact to be considered a genuine minimum wage. This is the so-called 'maxi minimum wage' (Saget, 2008). Here, often, minimum wage legislation amounts to average wage fixation. Poorly developed collective bargaining is often a driving factor behind the emergence of such 'maxi minimum wages': minimum wage consultations are the only forum where trade unions can make their demands known, with the danger that the resulting minimum wage is not a genuine threshold but rather the actual wage earned by most formal workers. In such a process, countries are actually trying to pursue multiple goals with a single policy instrument: the minimum wage is used as a reference to fix wages and incomes policies, to get a grip on inflation and to promote social dialogue. As is known from macro-economic policy, one needs to have as many policy instruments as policy goals: the minimum wage-setting machinery is expected to respond to too many policy goals (Saget, 2008).

The interesting and policy-relevant conclusion is that both too low and too high minimum wages are an indication of malfunctioning labour markets. Well-functioning labour market institutions would contribute to more relevant income inequality and poverty-reducing minimum wages, without jeopardizing employment and economic growth. If employment and fair distribution of income was set as an over-arching policy goal, the credibility of such labour market institutions would have been strengthened.

## Conclusion

The three examples mentioned above demonstrate clearly that it is possible for economic policies to target better towards goals of employment creation and reduction of income inequality. The question of course is whether there is political will to do so; that is, *Can one make sense of current economic policy in the light of growing inequalities?* The answer to that question is no; or not yet. Economic policy needs to be embedded, or more deeply embedded, in a larger social construct that accepts equitable income distribution and employment creation as ultimate policy goals.

All this is perhaps utopian, but not necessarily so.

There have been spells in history that this was possible. For example, half a century ago, Dutch economic policy was based on five objectives:

- Full employment.
- Equitable income distribution.
- Shared economic growth.
- Price stability.
- Sustainable balance of payments.

These objectives were agreed in a social compact between workers, employers and governments of various political natures and were formulated in 1956 at the Social Economic Council of The Netherlands. They have guided for at least a decade a wide set of different economic policies (fiscal, monetary, sector, trade, consumption, price and income policies) combining economic growth with reducing primary, secondary and tertiary income inequality in The Netherlands.

Not only in The Netherlands but also in various other West European countries, the periods of the 1950s and the 1960s were characterized by rising employment, fairly equitable inequality and growth. Some analysts have labelled that period as the Golden Age: the willingness to set economic and social goals and to adhere to these goals contributed much to this. What is also remarkable is that a goal of achieving an equitable distribution of income was accepted, at a time when research on inequality and growth had not yet advanced as far as it has today and major research conclusions still pointed towards a trade-off between economic growth and reducing inequality. Yet, despite this assumed trade-off, maintaining an equitable distribution of income was accepted as one of the five basic economic goals.

Another example of a period in which countries grew fast and maintained a fairly equal distribution of incomes is the period 1965–1980, when the so-called Asian tigers laid the basis for their extremely fast development trajectory. This was achieved through a combination of redistributive policies (land redistribution and high investments in education) and of rapid but managed industrial development (Adelman, 1979; Amsden, 2001).

Although these two examples of combining growth with equitable income distribution may at first instance look very different, they have, as Singh (forthcoming ) has observed, at least one element in common: both are examples of restrained capitalism. In Europe the restraints came from social pacts and the functioning of the labour markets, while government bureaucrats and political elites provided the restraint in the Asian tigers.

The current crisis and the increased public concern for improved income equality might provide the basis for a renewed political coalition to again make employment creation and fair income distribution major objectives for economic policy-making. But it is far from clear whether in most countries such a coalition would have sufficient influence to drastically charge economic policy.

## Acknowledgments

This article is a revised version of an inaugural address at the Institute of Social Studies, September 2008. I would like to thank the editors of the *Journal of Human Development and Capabilities* and an anonymous referee for useful comments.

## Notes

1 During the 1980s and 1990s income inequality before taxes and subsidies was more or less the same in Finland and the UK, rising in both countries; but while income inequality after taxes and subsidies rose in the UK, it declined in Finland! (Atkinson, 2004).

2 *The Spirit Level* by Richard Wilkinson and Kate Pickett (2009) shows that this finding applies to many areas of social problems beyond health — levels of trust, mental illness, life expectancy, children's educational performance, teenage births, obesity, homicides, imprisonment rates, social mobility.

3 This observation is actually based on an economic concept that was made famous by the Italian economist Pareto, who argued that any outcome of a policy is optimal if at least one member of society sees his position improved by that policy and no one is worse off. This so-called Pareto optimality has guided neoclassical policy making for a long time.

4 Kuznetz's curve was based on the very limited amount of data as was then available — mostly from developed countries. The much greater quantity of data now available has discredited the Kuznetz's curve.

5 Their results correspond well with the observations made above that part of growing inequality can be explained by the policies undertaken during the process of liberalization and adjustment, including policies to make the labour market more efficient in order for a country to grow faster. van der Hoeven and Taylor (2000) have argued that the notion of efficient labour markets in most adjustment programmes was mainly based on considering the allocative efficiency of these markets, but that dynamic and redistributive efficiency were neglected during the adjustment programmes, leading to greater inequality.

6 A recent experiment is the so-called ultimatum game between two players, where the first player proposes to divide a cake or a sum of money in two, while the second player, the receiver, can only take or leave the proposition by the first player. Economic theory would posit that the receiver accepts all offers of various divisions made by the first player since each offer is greater than zero. But experiments show that most people reject an offer that is below 20% of the initial cake and are thus arbiters of fairness. However, experiments with chimpanzees showed that chimpanzees acted more as a *homo economicus* than the *Homo sapiens* (*The Economist*, 6 October 2007).

7 For example, in the case of China, research from the IMF argues that making the quasi-fixed exchange rate more flexible would allow the country to pursue a more independent monetary policy. The same paper also argues for a cautious approach to capital account liberalization, given the institutional weaknesses of China's financial system (see Prasad *et al.*, 2005). The argument could be extended to many other developing countries. Rather than abandoning capital controls altogether, they should remain a policy tool that can be used selectively.

8 'Millions of dollars are spent studying every aspect of inflation, but few aspects of unemployment; thousands of hours of the time of highly scarce, skilled economists are spent pouring over complex models designed to show how to get inflation down from 8 to 4 per cent, but not on how to create more and better jobs; and if other government officials or those in civil society ask the central bank to do something about employment creation, the central banks can respond, "that's not our job". More than anything else, the cost of inflation-focused monetary regimes is to divert the attention of the some of the most highly trained and skilled economists and policy makers in developing countries away from the tasks that previous generations of central bankers took for granted as being their main job: to help their countries develop, to create jobs, and to foster socially productive economic growth' (Epstein, 2007, pp. 92–122).

9 It has been argued that the existence of minimum wages results in greater informal employment. ILO (1997 ) shows, however, that minimum wages up to two-thirds of the level of wages of unskilled workers will not produce substantial increases in informality.

## References

Adelman, I. (1979) 'Redistribution before growth — a strategy for developing countries in development of societies: the next twenty-five years', proceeding from the Institute of Social Studies (ISS) Conference, The Hague, Martinus Nijhoff, pp. 160–175.

Aghion, P., Caroli, E. and Garcia-Penalosa, C. (1999) 'Inequality and economic growth: the perspective of the new growth theories', *Journal of Economic Literature*, 37, pp. 1615–1660.

Alesina, A.F. and Giuliano, P. (2009) 'Preferences for redistribution', *Working Paper 14825*, National Bureau of Economic Research, Cambridge, MA.

Amsden, Alice H. (2001) *The Rise of the Rest: Challenges to the West from the Late-Industrializing Economies,* Oxford University Press, Oxford.

Amsden, A. (2007) *Escape from Empire: The Developing World's Journey through Heaven and Hell,* MIT, Cambridge, MA.

Amsden, Alice and van der Hoeven, Rolph (1996) 'Manufacturing output, employment and real wages in the 1980s: labour's loss until century's end', *Journal of Development Studies,* 32(4), pp. 506–530.

Angeles-Castro, G. (2006) 'The effects of economic liberalization on Income distribution: a panel data analysis', in E. Hein, A. Heise and A. Truger (Eds) *Wages, Employment, Distribution and Growth,* Palgrave Macmillan, Basingstoke, pp. 151–180.

Ariyoshi, Akira, Habermeier, Karl Friedrich, Laurens, Bernard, Ötker, Inci, Kriljenko, Jorge Iván Canales and Kirilenko, Andrei (2000) 'Capital controls: country experiences with their use and liberalization', *IMF Occasional Paper No. 190,* International Monetary Fund, Washington, DC.

Atkinson, A. (2004) 'Increased Income Inequality on OECD Countries and the redistributive impact of the government budget', in G.A. Cornia (Ed.) *Inequality, Growth and Poverty in an Era of Liberalization and Globalization,* Oxford University Press, Oxford, pp. 221–248.

Atkinson, A.B. (2007) 'The distribution of earnings in OECD countries', *International Labour Review,* 156(1-2), pp. 41–60.

Bernanke, Ben S. (2007) 'The level and distribution of economic well-being', remarks before the Greater Omaha Chamber of Commerce, Omaha, Nebraska, 6 February, Federal Reserve Board, Washington, DC.

Birdsall, N. (2005) 'The world is not flat: inequality and justice in our global economy', *WIDER Lecture 9,* WIDER, Helsinki.

Bradford, Colin I. Jr. (2004) 'Prioritizing economic growth: enhancing macroeconomic policy choice', paper presented at the *XIX G24 Technical Group Meeting,* 27–28 September, Intergovernmental Group of Twenty-Four, Washington, DC.

Chen, M., Vanek, J., Lund, F., Heintz, J., Jhabvala, R. and Bonner, C. (2005) *Progress of the World's Women 2005: Women, Work, and Poverty,* UNIFEM, New York.

Cohen, Benjamin J. (1993) 'The triad and the unholy trinity: lessons for the Pacific region', in Richard Higgott, Richard Leaver, and John Ravenhill (Eds), *Pacific Economic Relations in the 1990s,* Allen and Unwin, London, pp. 133–158.

Commission on Social Determinants of Health (2008) *Final Report, Closing the Gap in a Generation,* WHO, Geneva.

Conway, P. (2005) 'Monetary and exchange rate reforms', in A. Coudouel and S. Paternostro (Eds), *Analyzing the Distributional Impacts of reform: A Paractioners Guide,* World Bank, Washington, DC., pp. 39–71.

Cornia, G.A. (Ed.) (2004) *Inequality, Growth and Poverty in an Era of Liberalization and Globalization,* Oxford University Press, Oxford.

Cullity, G. (2004) 'Equality and globalization', in K. Horton and K. Patapan (Eds), *Globalization and Equality,* Routledge, London, pp. 6–22.

Dagdevieren, H., van der Hoeven, R. and Weeks, J. (2004) 'Redistribution does matter: growth and redistribution for poverty reduction', in A. Shorrocks, and R. van der Hoeven, (Eds) (2004) *Growth, Inequality, and Poverty: Prospects for Pro-Poor Economic Development,* Oxford University Press, Oxford, pp. 197–220.

Daudey, E. and Garcia-Penalosa, C. (2007) 'The personal and the facor distributions of income in a cross-section of countries', *Journal of Development Studies,* 43(5), pp. 812–829.

de Gregorio, José, Edwards, Sebastian and Valdés, Rodrigo O. (2000) 'Controls on capital inflows: do they work?', *Journal of Development Economics,* 63(1), pp. 59–83.

Diwan, Ishac (1999) *Labor Shares and Financial Crises,* mimeo, World Bank, Washington, DC.

Edison, Hali, and Reinhart, Carmen M. (2001) 'Stopping hot money', *Journal of Development Economics,* 66, pp. 533–553.

Elson, D. (2007) 'Macroeconomic policy, employment, unemployment and gender inequality', in J.A. Occampo and K.S. Jomo (Eds), *Towards full and Decent Employment,* Zed Books, London, pp. 70–91.

Epstein, G. (2007) 'Central banks as agents of employment creation', in J.A. Occampo and K.S. Jomo (Eds), *Towards full and Decent Employment,* Zed Books, London, pp. 92–122.

Ferreirra, F.H.G. (2007) 'Inequality as cholesterol', in International Poverty Centre, *Poverty in Focus The Challenge of Inequality,* June, UNDP, Brasilia.

Freeman, R.B. (2007) 'Labormarket institutions around the world', *Paper 13242,* National Bureau of Economic research, Cambridge, MA.

Frenkel, Roberto (2004) 'Real exchange rate and employment in Argentina, Brazil, Chile and Mexico', paper presented at the XIX G24 Technical Group Meeting, 27-28 September, Intergovernmental Group of Twenty-Four, Washington, DC.

Gallego, Francisco, Hernández, Leonardo and Schmidt-Hebbel, Klaus (1999) 'Capital controls in Chile: effective? Efficient?', *Central Bank of Chile Working Paper No. 59,* Central Bank of Chile, Santiago de Chile.

Gottschalk, P. and Smeeding, T. M. (1997) 'Cross national comparisons of earnings and income inequality', *Journal of Economic Literature,* 35, pp. 633-687.

Harrison, A. (2002) *Has Globalization Eroded Labor's Share? Some Cross Country Evidence,* mimeo, National Bureau of Economic Research, Cambridge, MA.

Heintz, J. (2006) 'Globalization, economic policy and employment: poverty and gender implications', *Employment Strategy Paper 2006.3,* International Labour Organization, Geneva.

Horton, Susan (1999) 'Marginalization revisited: women's market work and pay, and economic development', *World Development,* 27(3), pp. 571-582.

International Labour Organization (1997) *1996 Labour Overview: Latin America and the Caribbean,* ILO Regional Office for the Americas, Lima.

International Labour Organization (2008) *World of Work Report 2008: Income Inequalities in the Age of Financial Globalization,* Geneva, ILO.

Jolly, R. (2007) 'Inequality in a historical perspective', in G. Mavratos and A. Shorrocks (Eds), *Advancing Development: Core Themes in Global Economics,* Palgrave, Basingstoke, pp. 63-73.

Kaplan, Ethan, and Rodrik, Dani (2001) 'Did the Malaysian capital controls work?', *NBER Working Paper No. 8142,* National Bureau of Economic Research, Cambridge, MA.

Lee, Kang-kook, and Jayadev, Arjun (2005) 'Capital account liberalization, growth and the labor share of income: reviewing and extending the cross-country evidence', in Gerald Epstein (Ed.), *Capital Flight and Capital Controls in Developing Countries,* Edward Elgar, Cheltenham, pp. 15-57.

Leigh, A. (2007) 'How closely do top income share track other measures of inequality', *Economic Journal,* 117, pp. 619-633.

Mkandawire, T. (2004) 'Disempowering democracies and the persistence of poverty', M. Spoor (Ed.) *Globalisation, Poverty and Conflict, A Critical Development Reader,* Kluwer, Dordrecht, pp. 117-153.

Mundell, R.A. (1963) 'Capital mobility and stabilization policy under fixed and flexible exchange rates', *Canadian Journal of Economics and Political Science,* 29(4), pp. 475-485.

Obstfeld, Maurice, Shambaugh, Jay C. and Taylor, Alan M. (2004) 'The trilemma in history: tradeoffs among exchange rates, monetary policies, and capital mobility', *NBER Working Paper No. 10396,* National Bureau of Economic Research, Cambridge, MA.

Prasad, Eswar, Rumbaugh, Thomas and Qing, Wang (2005) 'Putting the cart before the horse? Capital account liberalization and exchange rate flexibility in China', *IMF Policy Discussion Paper No. 05/1,* International Monetary Fund, Washington, DC.

Rodrik, Dani (2003) 'Growth strategies', *NBER Working Paper No. 10050,* National Bureau of Economic Research, Cambridge, MA.

Rogoff, K. (2005) *Hollywood's Favourite Villains,* November, [www.project-syndicate.org], accessed 7 September 2008.

Saget, C. (2001) 'Poverty reduction and decent work in developing countries: do minimum wages help?', *International Labour Review,* 140(3), pp. 237-269.

Saget, C. (2008) 'Fixing minimum wage levels in developing countries: common failures and remedies', *International Labour Review,* 147(1), pp. 25-42.

Seguino, Stephanie (2000) 'The effects of structural change and economic liberalization on gender wage differentials in South Korea and Taiwan', *Cambridge Journal of Economics,* 24(4), pp. 437-459.

Singh, A. (forthcoming) *Demand and Supply Factors in Economic Growth,* manuscript, ILO, Geneva.

Tinbergen, J. (1970) *On the Theory of Economic Policy,* 1st edn 1952, North-Holland, Amsterdam.

UN Department of Economic and Social Affairs (UNDESA) (2005) *The Inequality Predicament,* United Nations, New York.

Vandermoortele, J. (2003) 'Are the MDG's feasible?', *Development Policy Journal,* 3, pp. 1–21.

van der Hoeven, R. and Luebker, M. (2007) 'Financial openness and employment: the need for coherent international and national policies', in J.A. Occampo and K.S. Jomo (Eds), *Towards full and Decent Employment,* Zed Books, London, pp. 22–53.

van der Hoeven, R. and Saget, C. (2004) 'Labour market institutions and income inequality: what are the new insights after the Washington Consensus', in G.A. Cornia (Ed.) *Inequality, Growth and Poverty in an Era of Liberalization and Globalization,* Oxford University Press, Oxford, pp. 197–200.

van der Hoeven, R. and Taylor, L. (2000) 'Introduction: structural adjustment, labour markets and employment: some considerations for sensible people', *Journal of Development Studies,* 36(4), pp. 57–65.

Vos, R. (2007) 'What we do and don't know about trade liberalization and poverty reduction', *DESA Working Paper No. 50,* United Nations, New York.

Wilkinson, Richard and Pickett, Kate (2009) *The Spirit Level,* Allen Lane, London.

World Commission on the Social Dimension of Globalization (2004) *A Fair Globalization, Creating Opportunities for All,* Geneva, ILO.

# *Income Distribution under Latin America's New Left Regimes*

GIOVANNI ANDREA CORNIA
*Giovanni Andrea Cornia teaches economics at the University of Florence, Italy, and is former Director of the United Nations University World Institute for Development Economics Research*

**Abstract** This paper reviews the decline in income inequality that has taken place over 2002-2007 in most Latin American countries against the background of its steady increase over 1980-2002. The paper then analyzes the factors that could explain this trend reversal. It focuses in particular on favorable external conditions, cyclical factors, improvements in the distribution of educational achievements and the subsequent drop in skill-premium, and changes in macro-economic and social policies introduced in several countries, particularly by a growing number of left-of-center governments that have come to power during the past decade. An econometric test for the years 1990-2007 using a sample of countries covering the majority of the population in the region indicates that, in addition to a favorable business cycle and external conditions, a decline in skill premium and the new policy model of fiscally prudent social-democracy that is emerging this decade in much of Latin America impacted favorably the distribution of income. If this approach will survive the current crisis, much of the recent inequality decline is likely to become permanent.

## 1. Introduction

The gloom and doom caused in Latin America by the current financial crisis has obscured the positive changes that have taken place in the region since 2002. The most evident of them is the six-year uninterrupted economic expansion of 2003-2008 during which the average growth rate of Gross Domestic Product (GDP) averaged 5.5% a year, lower only to that registered over 1967-1974 (Ocampo, 2008). Such steady expansion of output was to some extent a rebound from the stagnation recorded during the 'half lost decade' of 1998-2002, but featured also a rise in the investment rate that grew from 16–17% to 21–22% of GDP over the same period, a level lower only to that reached at the end of the 1970s. The boom was accompanied also by a nine percentage points decline in the poverty head-count ratio and, central to the topic of this paper, a significant drop in income inequality.

Other important changes that are less frequently emphasized in the literature were recorded starting from the mid-1990s. The first concerns the steady gains in educational achievements realized since the beginning of the 1990s by both center-right and left-of-center (LOC) regimes — both social-democratic and populist — and the parallel decline in many aspects of educational inequality (Gasparini *et al.*, 2009). The second change is the slowdown in the growth of the labor force that, according to CELADE (2006), dropped from 3.1% in the 1990s to 2.2% during the current decade. Together with a faster growth of labor demand for unskilled workers and in the supply of skilled workers (see later), the slower increase in unskilled labor supply possibly contributed to reducing unemployment and halting the long-term rise in the wage premium. The third, and possibly most important, change concerns the shift towards democratization and the election of LOC governments (Panizza, 2005a). Indeed, during the past decade the political center of gravity of the region's shifted with surprising regularity towards political regimes that place greater emphasis on distributive and social issues while, at the same time, avoiding the populist excesses of the 1980s. However, the recent coup in Honduras and the election of a center-right president in Panama in July 2009 may signal that such trend has reached its zenith.

To what extent do these and other changes explain the decline in income inequality recorded since 2002 in most of the region? To what an extent are these changes permanent or to what extent will they be overturned by the current crisis?[1] These are the main issues explored by the paper. Section 2 reviews the recent decline in income inequality. Section 3 discusses the factors that could explain such decline. Section 4 tests econometrically the relative importance of these factors, while Section 5 concludes and offers a few conjectures on the inequality changes that may be expected in the future.

## 2. The distribution of income in Latin America in historical perspective

The colonial origins of income inequality in Latin America have been well documented in the classical work of Engerman and Sokoloff (2005). These authors theorized that high historical levels of inequality in the distribution of land, other forms of wealth, human capital and political power that benefited a tiny agrarian, mining and commercial oligarchy led to the development of institutions that perpetuated these inequalities, furthering their deleterious impact on long-run economic growth. Such hypotheses have been fully verified in Latin America. Indeed, with the exception of Uruguay and Argentina, in the early-mid 1950s, the Gini coefficients of the distribution of income in the region ranged between 0.45 and 0.60 (Altimir, 1996); that is, among the highest in the world (Klasen and Nowak-Lehman, 2009). The rapid growth that followed the adoption of the import substitution strategy in the 1950s and 1960s had — on average — a further un-equalizing impact. In contrast, during the 1970s inequality fell moderately in most of the region with the exception of the Southern Cone (Gasparini *et al.*, 2009) where an extreme version of the neo-liberal reforms had been implemented by military *juntas*. The combination of a rise in inequality over the 1950s-1960s and of a modest fall over the 1970s meant that, by 1980, all main Latin American countries had a higher income concentration than in the early to mid-1950s.

During the 'lost decade' of the 1980s, inequality in Latin America was affected by the 1982–1984 world recession, the debt crisis, a large decline in commodity prices, and the recessionary adjustments introduced to respond to these shocks. Altogether, the 1980s were characterized by regressive distributive outcomes and, during this period, income inequality fell only in Colombia, Uruguay and Costa Rica out of 11 countries with reliable data (Altimir, 1996). Despite the return to a moderate growth and extensive internal and external liberalization, income polarization did not decline during the 1990s — and in one-half of the cases it worsened further, if at a slower pace than in the 1980s (Gasparini *et al.*, 2009). A review of inequality changes over the 1990s based on 76 standardized surveys for 17 countries covering 90% of the regional population shows that inequality rose in 10 countries and stagnated or declined in seven countries (Székely, 2003). The worsening was particularly acute during the 'half lost decade' of 1998–2002. The income polarization of the 1980s and 1990s resulted from fast inequality rises during recessionary spells and slow inequality declines during periods of recovery. A key feature of the trend towards growing inequality was a decline in the labor share in total income and a parallel rise in the capital share. For instance, between 1980 and the late 1980s, the labor share declined by five or six percentage points in Argentina, Chile and Venezuela and by 10 percentage points in Mexico. Such a trend was not reversed during the mild recovery of 1991–1998 (Tokman, 1986). In several countries — as in Chile during the military dictatorship — the fall in the labor share was due, *inter alia*, to the relaxation of norms on workers dismissals, a reduction of the power of trade unions, the suspension of wage indexation, a cutback in public employment and in the coverage of the minimum wage, as well as to the reduction or elimination of wealth, capital gains and profit taxes. From an analytical perspective, the impact of the above changes on the labor share can be decomposed into five effects (Tokman, 1986). First, sluggish growth brought about a slowdown in jobs creation. Second, informal employment became much more common. Third, formal sector wages grew more slowly than GDP per capita. Fourth, minimum wages mostly fell in relation to

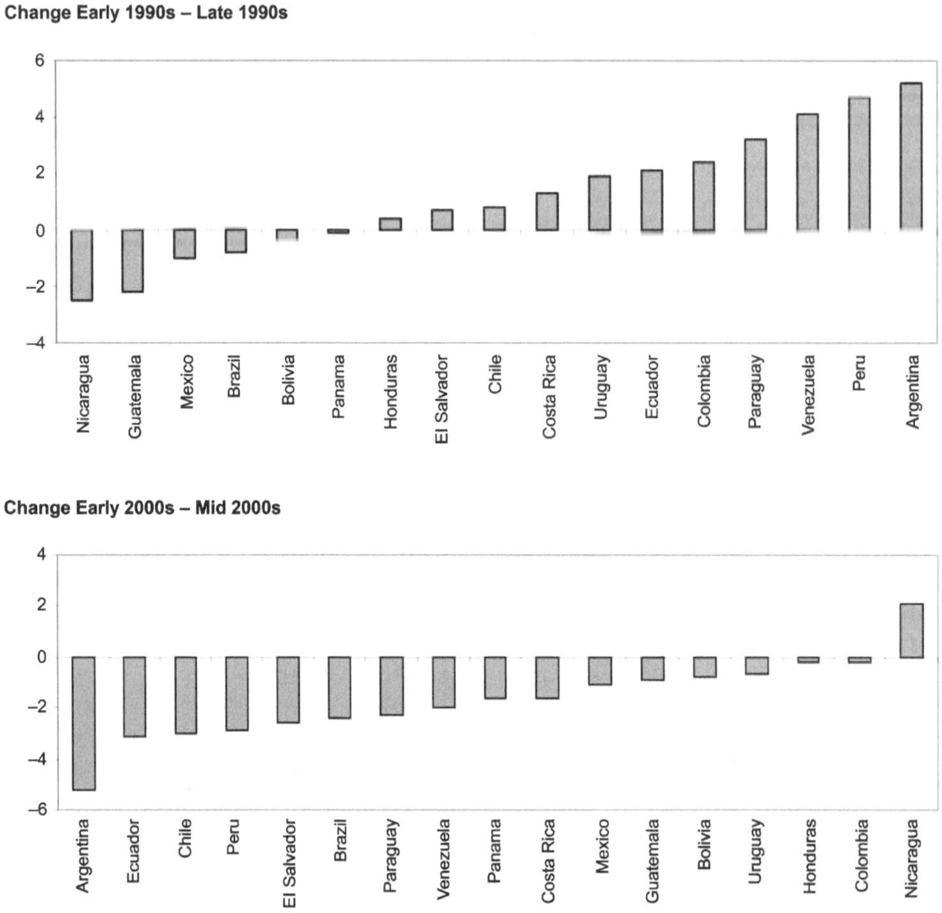


FIGURE 1. Changes in the Gini coefficients of the distribution of household income per capita, from the early to late 1990s and from the early to mid-2000s.
*Source*: Author's elaboration on CEDLAS database.

average wages. Fifth, the skill premium (i.e. the wage differentials by skill) widened particularly during the 1990s in parallel with widespread trade liberalization (Székely, 2003).

In contrast to the trends observed in the 1980s and 1990s, during the 2000s income inequality fell in most of the region, particularly since 2001-2002. Inequality declined between the early 2000s and the mid-2000s in all 17 countries analyzed, with the exception of Nicaragua (where inequality rose) and Honduras and Colombia (where it remained broadly constant). While the average decline in the Gini coefficient was of two or three points, in countries ruled for most of 2002-2007 by LOC governments, such as Argentina, Brazil and Venezuela, the drop was much more pronounced. Lustig (2009) arrives at similar conclusions, while noting further that the decline in income inequality observed in LOC countries was more pronounced among the populist than the social-democratic regimes. The recent decline in inequality was also characterized by greater convergence at a lower level of inequality, a trend opposite to that recorded during the prior two decades, when the countries' Gini coefficients converged at a higher level of inequality.[2]

## 3. Factors explaining the decline in income inequality over 2002–2007

Four groups of factors are discussed hereafter: the favorable external environment of 2002-2007, the rapid regional growth of GDP during this period, the longer term improvements in human capital formation and in its distribution, and the changes in economic and social policies part of the 'new LOC Latin American model' that is has been gradually taking shape during the past decade.

### *3.1 External conditions*

*3.1.1 Terms of trade gains.* Since the beginning of the new century, the rapid growth of China and other Asian countries exerted a favorable impact on the exports and economic performance of Latin America. The pull effect of Asian growth has entailed a large increase in Latin America's exports, which has become the most dynamic component of aggregate demand in the region. As a result, the regional export/GDP ratio rose from 13 to 22% of GDP between the average for the 1990s and 2006. The rapid increase in the value of exports was due to significant improvements in both export prices and volumes. In 2007 the index of the commodity prices exported by the region rose for the sixth year running, with the highest increases recorded by energy and agricultural products such as vegetable oils, flour and seeds (CEPAL, 2007a).

As a result, in 2007 the average regional terms of trade index exceeded by 33% its average level for the 1990s, generating in this way a positive yearly shock equal to 3.7% of the regional GDP between 2003 and 2007 (Ocampo, 2008). However, the terms of trade evolved in dissimilar ways within the region (CEPAL, 2007a). For instance, between the 1990s and 2007 the terms of trade index rose by 52% in South America, 21% in Mexico, and 13% for Mercosur, but fell by 13% in Central America, a region that depends on imported energy. Of the countries adversely affected by terms of trade changes, a first subset (Paraguay, Uruguay, Panamá and Nicaragua) further specialized in the export of traditional agricultural commodities. A second group (Costa Rica, El Salvador, Guatemala, and Honduras) switched to the export of textiles and recorded a rise in emigration (Perez Caldentey and Vernengo, 2008).

What was the probable impact of these changes in terms of trade and export volumes on income inequality? A partial equilibrium analysis suggests that, given the high concentration of the ownership of land and mines (particularly by foreign transnational corporations (TNCs))[3] prevailing in the region, the recent gains in terms of trade probably generated, *ceteris paribus*, a disequalizing effect on the functional and size distribution of income. Indeed, production in these sectors is very land, resource, and capital intensive, and their employment generation capacity is limited.[4] However, if these rents accrue to the state (as in Bolivia) or if private rents are taxed (as in Argentina) and the resources so obtained are redistributed in a progressive way, then the rise in land and mining rents can have a favorable distributive effect. Yet, the empirical evidence suggests a weak relation between terms of trade and tax/GDP and non-tax/GDP ratio in Latin America. The only relatively strong correlation ($r = 0.63$) between terms of trade and the non-tax revenue/GDP ratio was found for the eight main commodity exporters over 2003–2007 (Cornia and Martorano, 2009).

In the absence of a computable general equilibrium (CGE) model, the general equilibrium effects of the commodity boom on income inequality are even more difficult to map out. Improvements in the balance of payments due to terms of trade gains can, for instance, relax the foreign-exchange constraint to growth and stimulate production in labor-intensive industries with the effect of reducing income inequality. A second equalizing effect could occur via a reduction in interest rates (due to an expansion in money creation from abroad induced by growing export receipts) that would favor firms and households and penalize banks and rentiers. All in all, while it is plausible that the recent commodity bonanza had a favorable effect on growth, its impact on inequality remains uncertain.

*3.1.2 Rising migrant remittances.* During the past decade, Latin America enjoyed also a sharp rise in migrant remittances, which benefited in particular the Central American and Caribbean countries, Mexico and Ecuador. The surge in migration and remittances occurred mainly during the crisis years of 1998 and 2003, although it continued during the boom of 2003–2008. Official remittances to the region increased from US$2 to 59 billion dollars between 1980 and 2005 or from 0.23 to 2% of regional GDP (Table 1). In 2007, they accounted for 2.3% of the regional GDP (CEPAL, 2007a) but for over 11% in Central America, 2.8% in Mexico and about 20% in Grenada, Guyana and Jamaica. Interestingly, with the exception of Ecuador, remittances plaid a greater role in countries that did not experience terms of trade gains, meaning that Latin American countries support their current account balance by exporting either primary commodities or migrant labor, and only a modest amount of manufactured goods.

For the above group of countries, one may be tempted to establish a causal link between rising remittances and falling inequality. Yet the literature on the inequality impact of remittances suggests that their short-term and medium-term effect tends to be un-equalizing. Indeed, in developing countries mainly middle-class people are able to finance the high costs of illegal migration.[5] As a consequence, the remittances will accrue not to the poor

TABLE 1. Remittances/GDP in countries affected by positive and negative terms of trade

| | 1980–1990 | 1991–2001 | 2002–2006 |
|---|---|---|---|
| Countries that recently experienced *favorable* terms-of-trade effects | | | |
| Argentina | 0.07 | 0.22 | 0.38 |
| Bolivia | 1.98 | 2.17 | 2.51 |
| Colombia | 1.49 | 1.87 | 3.32 |
| Ecuador | 0.60 | 3.50 | 6.46 |
| Peru | 0.80 | 1.64 | 2.07 |
| Venezuela | −0.42 | −0.22 | −0.06 |
| Mexico | 0.96 | 1.19 | 2.36 |
| Average | 0.69 | 1.26 | 2.12 |
| Countries that recently experienced *unfavorable* terms-of-trade effects | | | |
| Dominican Republic | 4.40 | 8.67 | 11.37 |
| El Salvador | 8.85 | 14.01 | 15.86 |
| Guatemala | 1.51 | 1.95 | 10.47 |
| Honduras | 3.64 | 8.11 | 20.48 |
| Nicaragua | 5.48 | 10.05 | 14.84 |
| Paraguay | ... | 1.77 | 2.91 |
| Uruguay | 0.17 | 0.29 | 0.77 |
| Average | 3.59 | 4.91 | 8.85 |

*Source*: Adapted from Perez Caldentey and Vernengo (2008).

but mainly to middle-income groups. In addition, in the countries of origin the migration of skilled workers tends to raise their wage rate in relation to that of unskilled workers. Of course, the final distributive effect depends on if and how the families of migrants receiving remittances share them with the low-income groups. In addition, remittances may reduce inequality over the long term, if the creation of migrant networks in the countries of destination reduces migration costs, thus making migration accessible also to low unskilled workers. The long-term inequality impact of migration is mediated also by its effect on growth. In this regard, most of the available evidence (International Monetary Fund [IMF], 2005) shows that remittances raise current consumption, reduce volatility, and improve the creditworthiness in the countries of origin, but do not have a significant effect on the investment rate and the growth of GDP. In view of all this, one would not expect that migrant remittances plaid a central role in reducing income inequality, either directly or indirectly.

*3.1.3 Increasing availability of external finance.* Between 2004 and 2007, the region recorded a surge in capital inflows, the variation of which amounted to 2.4% of the region's GDP (Ocampo, 2008). Portfolio flows accounted for most of the rise in foreign financing while foreign direct investments (FDI) stagnated at 22% of the region's GDP. The portfolio flows mainly consisted in purchases of shares and securities in regional stock markets. As a result, the stock market capitalization of the seven largest regional economies quadrupled its value between middle 2004 and end

2007 (Ocampo, 2008). In addition, this large capital inflow facilitated the accumulation of international reserves that reduced country spreads on international loans, while the drop of international interest rates exerted a downward pressure on domestic rates. However, the increased availability of foreign finance benefited mainly large capital-intensive and skill-intensive companies and banks while it did not ease the financing problems of labor-intensive small and medium enterprises, possibly inducing in this way adverse distributional effects.

Also in this case, it is difficult to trace the indirect effects of financial exuberance on inequality. It is likely that — as in the case of terms of trade and remittances — the indirect effect on growth, employment and inequality was positive due to the relaxation of the balance of payments constraint. Yet financial exuberance caused also an appreciation of the real exchange rate that penalized the labor-intensive traded sector of the economy and, with it, the distribution of income (Taylor, 2004).

### *3.2 A positive business cycle*

As noted, from the end of 2002 the region recorded a strong recovery. The growth rate of GDP per capita doubled between the average of the 1990s and 2003–2007 in South America and improved by 50% in Central America. Only few countries (such as Chile, which recorded a Tiger-like growth already in the 1990s) did not improve their performance. While all countries improved their performance, in countries ruled by LOC governments the GDP growth was higher by about one point than in countries ruled by conservative regimes (Figure 2).

Economic theory suggests that in developing countries characterized by flexible labor markets an increase in GDP reduces inequality, as it tends to increase labor absorption and, under certain conditions, the wage rate, while a contraction of GDP raises inequality as wages drop and the workers made

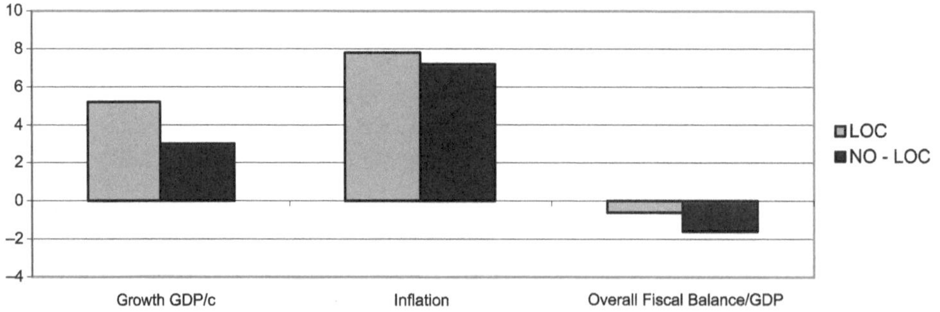


FIGURE 2. The 2007 macro-economic and 2003–2007 growth performance of LOC versus NO-LOC regimes.

*Note*: The inflation rate of LOC countries would be 6.6% (i.e. lower than the NO-LOC countries' average) if Venezuela (which recorded an average inflation of 21% during this period) is excluded.

*Source*: Author's elaboration on ECLAC's Badecon for the growth of GDP per capita and fiscal balance/GDP, and IMF's World Economic Outlook 2008 for inflation.

TABLE 2. Labor market trends for Latin America as a whole, 1990-2007

| | Participation rate (%) | Unemploy ment rate (%) | % wage earners or total workers | % formal sector workers | % workers paying social security | Average wages (constant 2000 US$)[a] | | |
|---|---|---|---|---|---|---|---|---|
| | | | | | | Average | Formal sector | Informal sector |
| 1990 | 63.8 | 6.2 | 62.6 | 55.0 | 63.3 | 384 | 372 | 278 |
| 2002 | 68.5 | 10.7 | 60.9[b] | 52.8 | 54.6* | 397 | 457 | 264 |
| 2005 | 70.1 | 9.7 | 61.4 | 53.7 | 59.4 | 405 | 449 | 267 |
| 2007 | 70.0 | 8.0 | 63.1 | 55.5 | 61.0 | 423 | 452 | ... |

*Note*: [a]The computation of the regional average is based on 13 countries, i.e., Argentina, Brazil, Costa Rica, Dominican Republic, Ecuador, Panama, Paraguay, Uruguay. For Chile, Colombia, Honduras, Mexico and Venezuela, the 2007 data are proxied by those of 2006. [b]Refers to 2000.
*Source*: compilation of different tables in CEPAL (2006 and 2008), IDLA database and OIT's 'Panorama Laboral' [http://www.oit.org.pe/WDMS/bib/publ/panorama/panorama08.pdf] for the percentage of wage earners and workers paying social security.

redundant are not covered by unemployment insurance. Past evidence from the region confirms this hypothesis (Altimir, 1993). A decline in inequality following a return to growth is, of course, far from automatic, as it depends on whether the growth pattern is pro-poor, neutral or immiserizing. Yet the evidence for the 2002-2007 period confirms that the vigorous recovery of those years, as well as the labor policies analyzed in Section 3.4, generated an equalizing effect on the distribution of wages. Urban unemployment dropped from 10.7 to 8% between 2002 and 2007 for the region as a whole (Table 2). Over 5.3 million new jobs were created — that is, at a much faster than during the previous decade. The new jobs were mainly taken by low-income groups, thus contributing significantly to the drop in wage inequality. Such improvements were more pronounced in the LOC than in the NO-LOC (Non-Left of Centre) countries. Indeed, between 2002 and 2007, the unemployment rate fell from 13.2 to 7.9% in the first group and from 10 to 8% in the second. Likewise, the average wage index rose from 98.6 to 103.7 in the LOC countries while it stagnated at 102 in the NO-LOC (Cornia and Martorano, 2009).

### *3.3 An improvement in the distribution of educational achievements*

Another important factor in the recent fall in income inequality is the rise in enrolment rates recorded at all educational levels since the early to mid-1990s (Gasparini *et al.*, 2009), and the subsequent reduction in enrolment inequality in primary and secondary education. For instance, the probability that a boy/girl from the bottom decile completes secondary school in relation to that of a child from the top decile rose from 36.7 to 50% between 1990 and

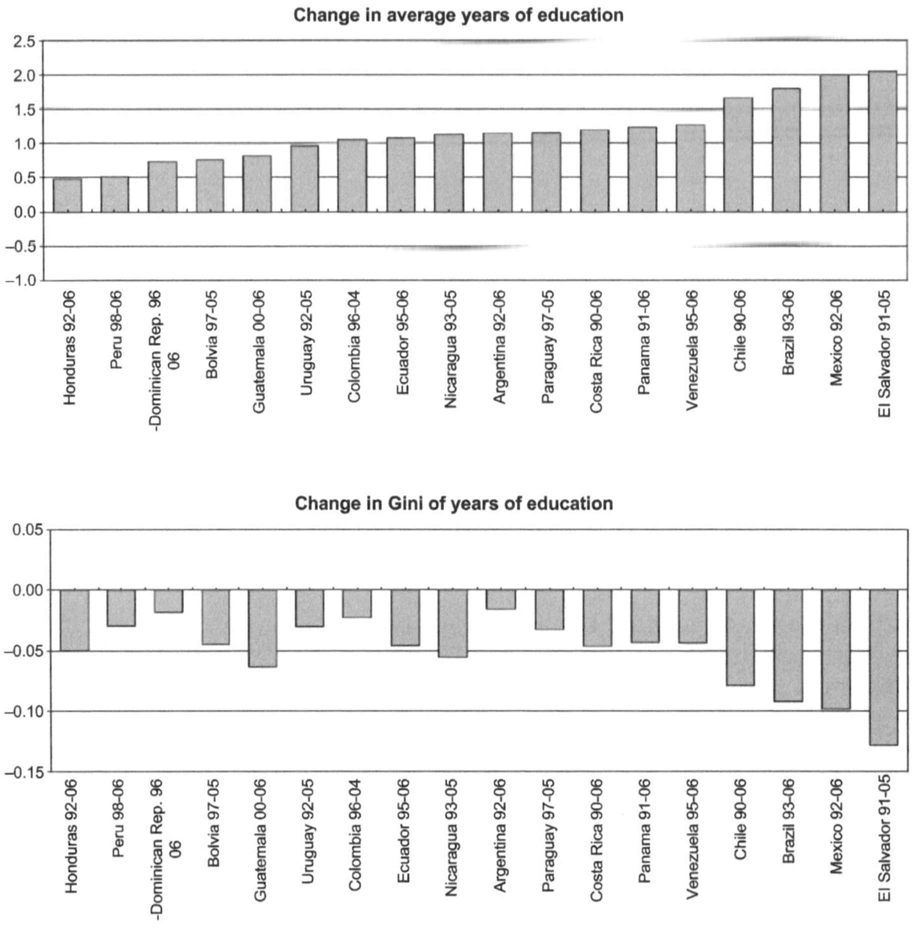


FIGURE 3. Percentage changes in average years of education of the adult population and the Gini of educational achievements between the mid-1990s and the mid-2000s in 18 Latin American countries
*Source*: Gasparini *et al.* (2009).

2005 (CEPAL, 2007b).[6] The surge in enrolments raised the average number of years of education of the working population, while reducing the inequality of its distribution in both LOC and NO-LOC countries (Figure 2). While the effect of these trends on the skill premium are not automatic, CEDLAS data confirm that the gains in human capital formation and educational inequality of the past 15 years were accompanied by a widespread drop in the skill-premium during the 2000s (Cornia and Martorano, 2009). In addition, a detailed study by Instituto de Pesquisa Economica Apliacada (IPEA) (cited in CEPAL, 2006 and 2008) that decomposed the fall in income inequality in Brazil over 2000–2006 confirmed that two-thirds of the decline was due to a fall in labor incomes inequality caused by a drop in educational inequality among workers and in wage premium by education level.

### *3.4 The spread of LOC regimes and the adoption of a new policy model*

Latin America has long been a symbol of authoritarian political systems, unequal distribution of assets, and limited redistribution by the state. However, during the past 20 years the political landscape has witnessed a steady drive towards democratization and, starting from the mid to late 1990s, a shift in political orientation towards LOC regimes. As documented by the results of different waves of the Latinobarometro,[7] such shift was to a large extent explained by growing frustration with the disappointing results of the Washington Consensus policies implemented in the 1980s and 1990s. Among other things, such policies caused a shrinkage of the industrial working class, a weakening of the unions, rising unemployment, and a substantial enlargement of informal sector and self-employment. The shift away from such approach began with the election in 1990 of Patricio Alwyn in Chile. It continued with the election of LOC leaders in the late 1990s and early 2000s, as in the case of Chavez in Venezuela in 1998, Lula in Brazil in 2002, Kirchener in Argentina in 2003, Tabarè Vasquez in Uruguay in 2004, Morales and Correa in Bolivia and Ecuador in 2006, Lugo in Paraguay in 2008, and Funes in El Salvador in March 2009. By mid-2009, of the 18 Latin American countries analyzed in this study, only Colombia and Mexico were run by center-right governments, while three are run by centrist regimes and 13 by LOC governments.

As noted by Panizza (2005a) and Lustig (2009), the LOC parties differ substantially among each other. Some of them can be defined as 'social-democratic', as in the case of Chile's Partido Socialista, Uruguay's Frente Amplio and Brazil's Partido dos Trabalhadores (Panizza, 2005a). These parties have their roots in organizations of the working class, but have evolved into broad coalitions comprising sectors of business and the middle classes, the urban and rural poor, the unemployed and the informal-sector workers. They have abandoned any notion of revolutionary break in favor of electoral politics and respect for the institutions of liberal democracy. In contrast, a second group of countries (such as Argentina and Ecuador) developed left-nationalist platforms, while Venezuela, Bolivia and Nicaragua (since 2007) are characterized by a radical-populist approach entailing a redistribution of assets nationally and internationally.

Matters of social justice and economic development are at the core of the new LOC parties' identity. However, in the pursuit of such objectives, the LOC parties (including the populist ones) avoided the ill-conceived approach to budget deficits and inflation typical of the populist policies of the 1980s (Dornbusch and Edwards, 1991). In fact, the LOC economic model incorporates into its paradigm liberal policies such as a sound fiscal policy and low inflation, an awareness of the inefficiencies associated with some forms of state intervention and protectionism, the primacy of the market in determining prices, regional trade integration and openness to foreign investment. At the same time, its concern for poverty and inequality, recognition of market failures and the increasing importance assigned to strengthening state institutions are in sharp contrast with the neo-liberal emphasis on shrinking the state and the self sustained role of the markets (Panizza, 2005a).

Despite this paradigmatic shift, measures to reduce the glaring wealth concentration existing in the region have seldom made their way on to the LOC governments' agenda, with the exception of Bolivia (which nationalized the mines and is planning a land reform), Venezuela (which renegotiated oil royalties and nationalized key industries, including steel, electricity and telecommunications) and, since 2007, Nicaragua. The moderate stance adopted by most LOC countries is probably explained by the fact that — in the absence of overwhelming political support, and in view of the heterogeneity of LOC coalitions — radical reforms would have generated tensions affecting business climate, capital flights, and electoral support. In addition, the advent to power of progressive regimes did not reduce the influence of dominant interest groups, which — although numerically small — are still powerful and can sway the public opinion on controversial issues. As a result, the LOC policy model resembles more the 'Redistribution With Growth' model (Chenery *et al.*, 1974) rather than the more radical 'Redistribution Before Growth' model, which sees the redistribution of assets and opportunities as a necessary step to exit the under consumption trap afflicting developing countries. In contrast, the measures in the field of labor market, social expenditure, and transfers have been more far-reaching.

LOC governments have thus developed a new economic paradigm and social contract that binds together their traditional and emergent constituencies through a combination of macro-economic stability, neocorporatist and participatory institutions, and redistribution via taxation and targeted social programs (Panizza, 2005b). The main components of the new model are reviewed hereafter.

*3.4.1 Macro-economic policies.* Overall, the measures introduced in this areas are broadly aligned to what can be defined a pro-poor macro-economic paradigm (Cornia, 2006). Its key elements are as follows.

- *A fiscal policy aiming at balancing the budget in the context of an expansionary expenditure policy.* Traditionally, Latin America adopted pro-cyclical expansionary fiscal policies that boost growth during periods of external buoyancy but build up vulnerabilities that explode when the favorable conditions disappear. This stance has been changed during the recent decade. A decline in the budget deficit was targeted in all countries, despite an increase in public expenditure (Figure 2). Overall fiscal deficits have typically been reduced below 1% of GDP (i.e. lower than the European Union and the USS) and in several cases were turned into surpluses. As a result, in 2006 and 2007 the average central government budget for the region as a whole was in equilibrium, suggesting a shift towards a countercyclical fiscal management (Ocampo, 2007). A strong version of such policy, which requires that the extra revenue collected during upturns is saved and is used to support public expenditure during bad years, was followed in Chile, Peru and Argentina. A 'weak version', consisting of balancing the budget or achieving a small surplus, then spending the extra revenue collected during the upturn, was followed by most countries due to the difficulties faced by democratic regimes in convincing the electorate about the need for fiscal austerity in periods of rising revenue (Ocampo, 2008).

- *Rising tax/GDP ratios*. Tax policy has undergone gradual but deep changes, both during the 1990s and even more so since 2002. As a result, the regional tax and non-tax revenue of the central government including social security contributions rose from 15% of GDP in 1990 to 17% in 2000, and 20.2% in 2007 (CEPAL, 2007a). Very large increases were recorded over 2002–2007 in Argentina and Brazil (9–10 points of GDP), Colombia (8.5 points), Bolivia (10 points), and Venezuela (6 points), and only Mexico experienced a small decline in the tax/GDP ratio (Cetrangolo and Sabaini, 2006). By the mid-2000s, Brazil, Argentina, Uruguay and Costa Rica had reached levels of taxation similar to those of the USA and Japan. In contrast, with tax/GDP ratios at around 10–12%, several Central American countries remained mired in a 'low revenue development trap' that makes them unable to fund pro-poor and pro-growth public goods. This revenue increase constitutes an important achievement, as inability or unwillingness to raise taxation was a main factor in the large accumulation of public debt during the 1970s, the debt crisis of the 1980s, and the macro-instability of the 1990s.

  The revenue increase resulted from a widespread reduction in excises and tariffs (following trade liberalization), a rise in indirect taxes (VAT *in primis*), an increase in personal and corporate income tax, and stagnation of wealth taxes and social security contributions (Table 3). LOC countries appear to have performed better, both in terms of additional revenue raised and of the progressivity of the tax instruments used (Cetrangolo and Sabaini, 2006). Countries benefiting from increases in the price of hydrocarbons, metals and agricultural exports recorded an important growth in public revenue.[8]

  While the improvement in terms of trade certainly contributed to raise the tax revenue/GDP ratio, it must be noted that its increase preceded the commodity boom and depended on broader efforts at widening the direct and indirect tax base and reducing evasion (Table 3). Several countries introduced a surrogate tax on financial transactions that, while potentially distortive (Cetrangolo and Sabaini, 2006), was a second best tool to tax assets the distribution of which is highly concentrated. In addition, Brazil and Argentina introduced selective export taxes that are very probably progressive, as they capture part of the land rent and windfall profits due to world price rises accruing to a sector characterized by high asset and income concentration. Overall, while tax systems in the region still have a long way to go to improve their progressivity, the recent revenue increase was in good part achieved by direct and other progressive taxes (Table 3).
- *Monetary policy and inflation targeting*. As suggested by the 'impossible trinity theorem', in economies with an open capital account, such as those

of Latin America, the monetary authorities can count only on few instruments (accumulation of reserves and sterilization) to control the fall in interest rates and credit expansion during booms generated by export bonanzas and large financial inflows. Argentina over 2002–2008 and Colombia in 2007, however, also reverted to capital controls (Ocampo, 2008). In most other countries, both LOC and conservative, monetary policy was either accommodating or neutral, tolerating therefore (with the major exception of Brazil) low or even negative real interest rates and higher inflation rates. Monetary policy aimed also at reducing the extensive dollarization of the financial system. Argentina conducted a radical de-dollarization during the crisis of 2002, and Peru adopted a policy of gradual de-dollarization, together with Bolivia and Uruguay. In particular, there was a tendency for foreign currency-denominated public-sector bonds issued on local capital markets to dwindle. Finally, there was a general strengthening of Central Bank independence.

- *Exchange rate regime.* With the exception of Brazil and Venezuela, most LOC and NO-LOC countries abandoned the free floats and fixed pegs regimes adopted during the prior decade, and opted instead for a competitive exchange rate regime or for managed floats aiming at preventing the appreciation of the real exchange rate. As noted by Ocampo (2007), consistently with this approach, Central Banks reduced the supply of foreign exchange through interventions in the currency market, adopted a coherent fiscal and policy, and in a few cases, introduced capital controls. The clearest example of this policy is given by Argentina, where the maintenance of a competitive exchange rate has been a cornerstone of macroeconomic policy (Frenkel and Rapetti, 2008).[9] In this country, the adoption of a competitive exchange rate shifted labor towards the unskilled labor-intensive traded sectors (mainly manufacturing) with a strong equalizing effect (Damill, 2004, cited in World Bank, 2005).

  In 2006 and 2007, this exchange rate policy came under pressure owing to large increases in export prices, capital inflows and remittances. As a result, the ensuing large current and capital account surpluses lead to a modest appreciation of 4.8% of the extra-regional real exchange rate for the region as a whole, with stronger effects felt in Colombia, Brazil and Venezuela (CEPAL, 2007a). Without a huge accumulation of reserves and parallel sterilization efforts by the central banks, several countries would have shown stronger symptoms of Dutch disease and accelerating inflation in the non-tradable sector, which — if uncontrolled — would have generated adverse growth and distributive impact (Taylor, 2004).
- *Trade and external indebtedness*. The free trade policies adopted in the past have not been overturned, in part because the newly adopted exchange rate policies offered some protection to the tradable sector. In contrast, the trend towards international trade integration was substantially reoriented. The Free Trade Area of the Americas seems to have stalled while, in contrast, regional trade integration developed rapidly, especially in the field of manufacturing exports. The free trade agreements

TABLE 3. Tax and non-tax revenue/GDP ratio of the central government in 1990, 2002 and 2007, and changes in tax structure in LOC and NO-LOC countries

| Tax revenue/GDP | | | Non-tax revenue/GDP | | | Country group | Changes over 2002-2007 (% points of GDP) | | | | |
|---|---|---|---|---|---|---|---|---|---|---|---|
| 1990 | 2002 | 2007 | 1990 | 2002 | 2007 | | Trade taxes | Excises + other ind. tax | VAT | Direct taxes | Social security |
| 17.5 | 19.2 | 23.7 | 5.4 | 5.3 | 5.9 | LOC | + 0.38 | − 0.23 | + 1.35 | + 2.56 | + 0.45 |
| 9.9 | 14.2 | 16.1 | 2.8 | 2.5 | 3.4 | NO-LOC | − 0.20 | − 0.72 | + 1.19 | + 1.49 | + 0.13 |

*Source*: Cornia and Martorano (2009).

with industrialized countries, in contrast, strengthened the exports of primary commodities — with the possible exception of Mexico, which increased its exports of manufactured goods — which in most cases have a high import content and limited backward and forward linkages. LOC governments have also attempted to reduce their dependence on foreign borrowing. Existing short-term stabilization agreements with the IMF were generally not renewed, while Brazil (in 2005) and Argentina (in 2006) prepaid their outstanding debt to the IMF. A few countries also restructured their foreign debt, as in the case of Argentina who successfully renegotiated its debt at a 70% discount. As a result, Latin America's gross foreign debt declined from 42% of the regional GDP in 2002 to 20% in 2007, while the debt net of foreign reserves fell from 33 to 8% of GDP.

### *3.4.2 Labor market, income, and social policies.*

- *Labor market policies.* The LOC's policy model differs from the liberal one in terms of the extent to which labor policies explicitly address the problems of unemployment, informalization and instability, falling unskilled wages, diminishing coverage of social security, and weakening of institutions for wage negotiations and dispute settlements. Argentina enacted income policies to strengthen the purchasing power of poor and middle-income families, including a rise in minimum wages, a large-scale public work program, a deliberate attempt to extend the coverage of formal employment, and the re-birth of trade unions. In Uruguay, the Frente Amplio administration reinstated the tripartite collective bargaining bodies comprising representatives of business, unions and government that negotiate wage settlements for the main industries. In Brazil, the government set up an Economic and Social Development Council composed of representatives of business, labor and a wide variety of civil society organizations to advise on economic and social issues. At the same time, most LOC governments decreed hikes in minimum wages that were sizeable but far from excessive. Such restraint reflected the greater concern of policy-makers for creating jobs than for improving earnings. It also reflects the recognition that, unless backed by increases in productivity, nominal wage raises may fuel inflation with scant effect on real wages.

The empirical evidence suggests that the increases of minimum wages adopted during the 2000s probably produced an equalizing effect. Indeed, a study on 19 Latin American countries over 1997–2001 (Kristensen and Cunningham, 2006) shows that minimum wages[10] raised the pay at the bottom of the distribution and were generally associated with lower dispersion of earnings, as minimum wages were found to lift wages in both the formal and informal sector. Indeed, although they are not binding in the informal sector, the study found that in 14 of the 19 countries analyzed the minimum wages enhanced the wage distribution also in this sector. This suggests they represent a sort of 'fair reservation wage' below which the supply of unskilled labor falls. Table 2 suggests also that in the 2000s wage employment rose faster than self-employment, signifying that the policy of 'formalizing employment' produced some results. A third factor was a decline in the wage premium of skilled workers, due to a growing supply of educated workers (Section 3.3), and a shift of production towards the more unskilled labor-intensive tradable sector.

- *Rising public social expenditure and redistribution.* Public social expenditure started rising already in the early to mid-1990s but accelerated its upward trend since the early 2000s in most of the region (Table 4), especially in LOC countries. Most of the expenditure increase concerned social security, social assistance and education (Kristensen and Cunningham, 2006). The rise was nearly universal, and of the 21 countries of the region only Ecuador had in 2005 a social expenditure/GDP ratio lower than in 1990–1991 (CEPAL, 2005). There still is a huge intra-regional variation in social expenditure[11] but it appears that the recent rise was proportionately greater in low-income countries. A first factor in the public expenditure rise was the increase in tax/GDP ratios. Changes in the structure of public expenditure also played a role. For instance, the debt cancellation enjoyed by highly indebted poor countries countries permitted reallocating to social activities monies used to service the foreign debt,[12] while recipients of official development assistance increased their social expenditure, possibly due to growing 'social conditionality' for the achievement of Millennium Development Goals.

The rise in public social expenditure probably generated positive redistributive effects. Analysis of public social expenditure by income quintile for 18 countries over 1997–2003 (CEPAL, 2007a; Gasparini, 2007) suggest that: all components of public social expenditure (including social security) are less concentrated than private incomes; expenditures on primary education and social assistance are strongly progressive, those on secondary education and healthcare are mildly progressive or broadly proportional (in the case of health, it depends on the approach to its financing), and those on tertiary education are as concentrated as the distribution of income. In turn, expenditure on social security (pensions, unemployment insurance) is slightly less concentrated than that of private income, as it focuses on formal sector workers and only seldom provides non-contributory benefits to informal sector workers and their families. These are average regional data and things vary between the three main country groups in the region (Table 5, panel b). Furthermore, there are indications (CEPAL, 2005) that the incidence of such public expenditure is becoming more progressive, although at different speeds across the region, as shown by the increase in enrolments in secondary education mentioned above, greater access to health services, social assistance (see below) and anti-poverty programs.

As shown in Table 5, social security expenditure is not progressive, as it mainly covers formal-sector workers with stable employment. This raises the question of how best can government expand social security coverage, whether by extending the formal sector or by setting up solidarity-based, non-contributory, universal funds providing basic benefits (such as minimum pensions) to informal sector workers and their families. Both approaches were adopted in recent years, although the latter was more common. For instance, several LOC countries (Argentina, Bolivia, Brazil, Chile and Costarica) introduced non-contributory social pension that started addressing this problem (Table 6).

Prior to the recent changes in tax and expenditure policies, the overall redistributive effect of tax-and-transfer operations in Latin America was much smaller than in the OECD, with the exception of Argentina and Costa Rica. An analysis of tax incidence in 11 Latin American countries for the late 1990s and 2001–2002 (Cetrangolo and Sabaini, 2006) concluded that the distribution of income after taxation (but before transfers) remained broadly unchanged and worsened in Mexico and Nicaragua, as the tax system mainly relied on regressive or proportional taxes. In contrast, in most countries public expenditure redistributed income in a perceptible way. Yet, as noted above, the increase in income and wealth taxes recorded between the mid to late 1990s and 2007 in several countries should have improved, if moderately, the progressivity of the tax system, although no new analyses are available in this regard.

- *Conditional transfer programs.* During the past 10–15 years most governments introduced targeted social assistance programs to complement the coverage of formal social security. Contrary to the small, donor-dependent, and poorly sequenced and targeted Social Emergency Fund and Social Investment Fund introduced in the late 1980s to soften the resistance to and impact of structural adjustment, conditional transfers are better funded by the state (second column of Table 7), cover an important share of the population at risk, and are directed to old and new political constituencies such as the urban and rural poor. Such programs include: conditional transfers aiming at reducing poverty and child labor and at ensuring that children remain in school, and have access to health services and proper nutrition (as in the case of Brazil's famous *Bolsa Familia*); temporary employment schemes for the construction of public infrastructure (as in Argentina's *Programma Jefas y Jefes de Hogares* and Uruguay's PANES); training of unemployed workers and youth with the aim of facilitating their access to formal sector jobs; subsidized formal sector employment for the youth; and the promotion of small and

TABLE 4. Average public social expenditure/GDP in LOC versus NO-LOC countries

| Year | Social public expenditure as percentage of the GDP | | | | |
|---|---|---|---|---|---|
| | Total | Education | Health | Social security | Housing |
| 1990 | 9.0 | 2.8 | 2.1 | 3.3 | 0.7 |
| 1996 | 10.9 | 3.4 | 2.4 | 4.0 | 1.0 |
| 2003 | 12.8 | 4.3 | 2.8 | 4.6 | 1.1 |
| Around 2006 | 13.3 | 4.3 | 2.9 | 4.6 | 1.4 |
| LOC Δ (2006–2003) | 1.33 | 0.20 | 0.38 | 0.46 | 0.29 |
| NO-LOC Δ (2006–2003) | 0.48 | −0.12 | 0.06 | 0.11 | 0.43 |

*Note*: Data refer to the 18 countries analyzed in this study, including Bolivia (on the basis of national data) omitted in similar CEPAL studies (CEPAL, 2007b).
*Source*: Author's elaboration on the basis of the ECLAC database Badenso.

TABLE 5. Incidence of government expenditure by quintile (18 countries, 1997–2004) and concentration coefficients of the public expenditure by three country groups

| Panel a: shares of total public expenditure by sector and income quintile | | | | | Expenditure sector | Panel b: concentration coefficients of public expenditure | | |
|---|---|---|---|---|---|---|---|---|
| I quintile | II quintile | III quintile | IV quintile | V quintile | | Group 1 | Group 2 | Group 3 |
| 7.4 | 6.5 | 6.3 | 5.9 | 5.6 | Education | −0.067 | 0.116 | −0.138 |
| 5.1 | 4.7 | 4.2 | 4.0 | 3.7 | Health | 0.074 | −0.073 | −0.192 |
| 2.0 | 2.8 | 4.3 | 6.3 | 16.5 | Social security | 0.504 | 0.568 | 0.349 |
| 3.3 | 2.1 | 1.6 | 1.3 | 1.1 | Social assistance | −0.089 | −0.154 | −0.484 |
| 0.8 | 0.9 | 1.1 | 1.4 | 0.9 | Housing | 0.206 | 0.067 | −0.026 |
| 19.6 | 17.0 | 17.5 | 18.9 | 27.8 | Total | 0.143 | 0.042 | 0.044 |

*Note*: Group 1 includes Bolivia, El Salvador, Guatemala, Honduras, Ecuador, Nicaragua, Paraguay, and Peru. Group 2 includes Colombia, Dominican Republic, Mexico, Panama, and Venezuela. Group 3 includes: Argentina, Brazil, Chile, Costarica and Uruguay.
*Source*: Elaboration on CEPAL (2007b).

medium enterprises. Several studies document the favorable distributional impact of such transfers. For instance, an IPEA study (cited in CEPAL, 2006) found that in Brazil government transfers (social pensions and *Bolsa Família*) explained one-third of the decline in income inequality observed between 2000 and 2006.

## 4. Regression analysis

### *4.1 Data-set and matrix of correlation coefficients*

The understanding the relative impact on inequality of the factors discussed in Section 3 required one to compile a data-set on Income Distribution in

TABLE 6. Coverage of non-contributory pensions in Latin America

| | Age of eligibility (years) | Universal or means tested | Amount paid/ month (US$) | % population over 60 years | % pop >60 years receiving a pension | Cost of pension as % of GDP |
|---|---|---|---|---|---|---|
| Argentina | 70+ | Means | 88 | 14 | 6 | 0.23 |
| Bolivia | 65+ | Universal | 18 | 7 | 69 | 1.30 |
| Brazil 1 | 67+ | Means | 140 | 9 | 5 | 0.20 |
| Brazil 2 | 60/55+ | Means | 140 | 9 | 27 | 0.70 |
| Chile | 65+ | Means | 75 | 12 | 51 | 0.38 |
| Costa Rica | 65+ | Means | 26 | 8 | 20 | 0.18 |
| Uruguay | 70+ | Means | 100 | 17 | 10 | 0.62 |
| Memo item | | | | | | |
| Lesotho | 70+ | Universal | 21 | 8 | 53 | 1.43 |
| Mauritius | 60+ | Universal | 60 | 10 | 100 | 2.00 |
| South Africa | 65/58+ | Means | 109 | 7 | 60 | 1.40 |

*Notes*: Brazil 1 and Brazil 2 = Beneficio de Prestacao Continuada; Previdencia Rural.
*Source*: HelpAgeInternational (2006).

TABLE 7. Summary of some main social programs introduced in recent times in the region

| Program (reference year) | Cost (% of GDP) | Number of beneficiaries | Monthly subsidy |
|---|---|---|---|
| Plan Jefas y Jefes (Argentina, 2002) | 0.80 | 1.85 million workers | US$45 (2002), US$ 150 (2007) |
| Plan Nacional Emergencia (Bolivia, 2002) | 0.86 | 1.6% of active population | US$63 wage manual workers |
| PANES (Uruguay, 2005) | 0.50 | 7.2% of active population | US$55 |
| Bolsa Familia (Brazil, 2005) | 0.36 | 11.1 million families | R$ 62 for poor families, R$15 for children, R$30 for youth |
| Chile Solidario (Chile 2005) | 0.08 | 256 000 families | US$8–21 depending on poverty intensity |
| Oportunidades (México, 2006) | 0.40 | Five million families (18% of population) | US$12–74 depends on education level, US$17 family health |
| Bono desarrollo umano (Ecuador 2005) | 0.60 | Five million people (40% of population) | US$15 |
| Familias en accion (Colombia 2007) | 0.20 | 1.7 million families | US$8–33 (educational subsidy/ child), 30 US$ (health subsidy/ family) |

*Source*: Author's compilation from Fiszbein and Schady (2009) and Bouillon and Tejerina (2007).

Latin America (IDLA). IDLA includes annual data for 18 Latin American countries, for the 18 years 1990–2007 and the variables presented in Table 8. The database thus includes 324 (18 × 18) cells for each variable, although missing data reduce the number of data strings with non-zero cells. The dependent variable is the Gini coefficient of the distribution of household disposable income.[13] The explanatory variables included in the regression are described in Table 8. They belong to five sets of factors:

TABLE 8. Definition, description and data sources of the variables used in regression analysis

| Variable name | Variable label | Source | Unit of measure |
|---|---|---|---|
| Gini | Gini coefficient of the current distribution of disposable household income per capita | See footnote 15 | Percentage points |
| GDP per capita | Per-capita average annual growth rates GDP at constant market prices | ECLAC | Percentage based on US$ figures at constant 2000 prices |
| Gini education — 1 | Education Gini index for working population 25–64 years old, lagged one year | SEDLAC | Percentage points |
| Tot-fob | Terms of trade, fob | ECLAC | Index, 2000 = 100 |
| Remittances | Workers' remittances/GDP | UNCTAD | Percentage of GDP |
| FDI | Net stock of foreign direct investment/GDP | UNCTAD | Percentage of GDP |
| Capital flows | Portfolio investment/GDP | ECLAC | Percentage of GDP |
| REER | Indices of Real Effective Exchange Rate | Economic Survey of Latin America and the Caribbean | Index, 2000 = 100 |
| Min-wage | Minimum wage | ECLAC | Index, 2000 = 100 |
| Direct tax | Taxes on income, profits, capital gains, property/GDP | ECLAC | As a percentage of GDP |
| Indirect tax | (General taxes on goods and services + taxes on specific goods and services)/GDP | ECLAC | As a percentage of GDP |
| Public expenditure on social security | Public expenditure on social security and social assistance/GDP | ECLAC | As a percentage of GDP |
| Q5/Q1 pensions | Ratio of pensions coverage by quintile | Rofman *et al.* (2008) | Ratio |
| Social-democratic | Dummy denoting a country/year with a social-democratic government | Author's compilation | One, social-democratic; zero, all other cases |
| Populist | Dummy denoting a country/year with a radical-populist government | Author's compilation | One, populist; zero, all other cases |

*Source*: Author's compilation.

- the *current business cycle* — measured by the growth rate of GDP per capita, and expected *ex ante* to have a negative sign;
- the *distribution of human capital* — that is, the Gini of the distribution of years of education among workers lagged one year, expected *ex ante* to reduce inequality;
- *external conditions* — that is, international terms of trade, migrant remittances (both of which have an uncertain *ex ante* effect on inequality, besides the effect mediated through other variables), as well as FDI and portfolio flows (expected *ex ante* to have a un-equalizing effect), besides the effects mediated through GDP growth and other channels;
- *public policies* — which include the Real Effective Exchange Rate (REER) that proxies *macroeconomic policy*, and which is expected to reduce inequality for the reasons given in Section 3 (the minimum wage interacted with the share of formal sector workers (expected *ex ante* to reduce inequality) as proxy *labor market policies*); and for *redistributive policies*, the following variables were used in regression analysis: the ratio of direct to indirect taxes, the share of public expenditure on social security as a share of GDP (both expected to reduce inequality) and the ratio of pension coverage in the top versus bottom quintile; and
- two political dummy variables — that is, the '*social democratic*' *dummy*, which is equal to one when a country is ruled by a social-democratic government and zero in all other cases; and the '*populist*' *dummy*, which takes the value of one in the years during which Venezuela, Bolivia and Nicaragua were ruled by a radical-populist regime and zero in all other cases. Both dummies are expected to reduce inequality (beyond the impact of the progressive policies introduced by these regimes).

Analysis of the matrix of bilateral correlation coefficients (omitted for reasons of space) among the 14 explanatory variables included in regression analysis shows that — of the 88 bilateral correlation coefficients contained in such a matrix — only that between the 'ratio of pensions coverage between the top and bottom quintile' and 'public expenditure on social security' is sizeable ($r = -0.64$) and can cause multicollinearity problems. Another four coefficients have values of around 0.5, while all others are very low values (0.002–0.3) suggesting that the explanatory variables are independent among each other, that problems of multicollinearity should be limited, and that — contrary to what could be suggested by economic theory — there is no need to develop a structural multi-equation model.

### *4.2 Estimation procedure and regression results*

The IDLA database is organized as a tri-dimensional matrix, with 18 countries on one axis, 18 years on the second and the dependent, and 14 explanatory variables on the third. Such a kind of data-set demands that the procedure chosen for the estimation of the determinants of income inequality takes into account that each country is observed over several periods. Such model takes therefore the following form.

$$GINI_{it} = a + \beta X_{it} + \eta_i + y_t + u_{it}$$

where $Gini_{it}$ is the coefficient of the distribution of household disposable income per capita, $X$ a vector of 14 explanatory variables (Table 8), the subscripts $i$ and $t$ represent, respectively, the countries and the years of the panel, $\eta_i$ the error term for each country, $y_t$ the error term for each year, and $u_{it}$ a joint error term for countries and time periods, while $\alpha$ and $\beta$ are parameters to be estimated. Given the nature of this data-set, the ordinary least squares procedure tends to yield inefficient and distorted estimates of the values of $\alpha$ and $\beta$ (Baltagi, 2005). The estimation procedure best suited to situations in which $u_i$ varies from country to country is the fixed effects model in which $u_i$ is not treated as a random variable. This means that this estimation procedure generates, for each of the 18 countries considered, an intercept that captures specific country effects reflecting differences in geography, institutions and unobservables. The Hausman test confirms that the fixed effects model is preferable to the random effect model.

The regression analysis has been carried out as follows: the ratio of pension coverage of the top to the bottom quintile has been dropped due to multicollinearity problems mentioned above, while the capital flows/GDP ratio was also dropped due to lack of sufficient data. To capture the progressivity of the tax system, the ratio of direct taxes/GDP was divided by that of indirect taxes/GDP (and further standardized by the overall tax/GDP ratio). The regressors have been introduced in a stepwise mode starting with the two political dummies ('social democratic' and 'populist'), followed, one by one, by the different sets of factors discussed in Section 3; that is, the growth rate of GDP, educational inequality of the labor force, external economic conditions (terms of trade, remittances, and FDI), macro-economic policies (proxied by the real exchange rate expressed in quadratic form), labor market policies (proxied by the minimum wage index interacted with the share of formal sector employment), and redistributive policies (i.e. the ratio of direct to indirect taxes, and social expenditure/GDP). The introduction of each new variable entails a reduction in the number of observations, which drops from 301 in Model 1 to 222 in Model 8.

The results show that, when introduced all alone, the two dummy variables are highly significant, with the 'populists' having a somewhat bigger redistributive (1.9 Gini points) effect than the 'social-democrats' (1.4 Gini points). As expected, with the introduction of other variables (particularly the policy variables) the parameters of the two dummies decline in value and lose significance, although they remain significant in most of the eight models in Table 9. The populist dummy is non-significant in three of the eight models, probably because the small number of years in which this variable takes values different from zero, while the 'social democratic' is non-significant only in one model. Most importantly both dummies are significant

TABLE 9. Fixed effects regression results (dependent variable: Gini coefficient of the distribution of disposable income/capita)

| Variable (sign expected *ex ante* on the basis of theory) | Model 1 | Model 2 | Model 3 | Model 4 | Model 5 | Model 6 | Model 7 | Model 8 |
|---|---|---|---|---|---|---|---|---|
| Dummy social democratic (–) | −1.3920 | −1.3593 | −1.1736 | −0.9949 | −1.0235 | −0.7252 | −0.5033 | −0.6978 |
| | [0.3962]*** | [0.3983]*** | [0.3872]*** | [0.3975]** | [0.4283]** | [0.4431]* | [0.4503] | [0.4152]* |
| Dummy populist (–) | −1.9185 | −1.9045 | −1.0883 | −0.012 | 0.0632 | −0.3148 | −1.3174 | −1.4073 |
| | [0.6777]*** | [0.6706]*** | [0.6343]* | [0.7211] | [0.7575] | [0.7697] | [0.7097]* | [0.7236]* |
| Growth rate of GDP/per capita (–) | | −0.0545 | −0.0769 | −0.0444 | −0.0402 | −0.0364 | −0.0471 | −0.0538 |
| | | [0.0375]∧ | [0.0313]** | [0.0316]∧ | [0.0330] | [0.0336] | [0.0333]∧ | [0.0316]* |
| Gini distribution of years of education (−1) (+) | | | 0.6892 | 0.701 | 0.666 | 0.637 | 0.6114 | 0.6212 |
| | | | [0.1008]*** | [0.1089]*** | [0.1106]*** | [0.1162]*** | [0.1144]*** | [0.1216]*** |
| International terms of trade, fob (+,– ) | | | | −0.0195 | −0.0202 | −0.019 | −0.0154 | −0.0128 |
| | | | | [0.0085]** | [0.0086]** | [0.0089]** | [0.0086]* | [0.0091]∧ |
| Migrant remittances/GDP (+, –) | | | | 0.0446 | 0.0356 | 0.0359 | 0.0459 | 0.1102 |
| | | | | [0.0612] | [0.0627] | [0.0628] | [0.0625] | [0.0684]∧ |
| Net FDI stock/GDP (+) | | | | 0.0381 | 0.0365 | 0.0348 | 0.0318 | 0.0610 |
| | | | | [0.0134]*** | [0.0130]*** | [0.0134]*** | [0.0137]** | [0.0123]*** |
| REER (–) | | | | | −0.0689 | −0.0786 | −0.0848 | −0.0725 |
| | | | | | [0.0293]** | [0.0293]*** | [0.0293]*** | [0.0303]** |
| $REER^2$ (+) | | | | | 0.0002 | 0.0003 | 0.0003 | 0.0003 |
| | | | | | [0.0001]** | [0.0001]*** | [0.0001]*** | [0.0001]*** |
| Minimum wage index * share of formal sector employment (–) | | | | | | −0.0256 | −0.0258 | −0.0198 |
| | | | | | | [0.0105]** | [0.0104]** | [0.0115]* |
| Share of direct tax/indirect tax on tax/GDP (–) | | | | | | | −0.105 | −0.0993 |
| | | | | | | | [0.0229]*** | [0.0244]*** |
| Public expenditure on social security/GDP (=,–) | | | | | | | | −0.3183 |
| | | | | | | | | [0.1495]** |
| Constant | 53.0059 | 53.1929 | 29.3445 | 29.6811 | 35.3471 | 38.5238 | 39.7936 | 39.5974 |
| | [0.3069]*** | [0.3235]*** | [3.4399]*** | [4.2750]*** | [4.9764]*** | [5.4184]*** | [5.3625]*** | [5.7001]*** |
| Year dummies | Yes | Yes | Yes | Yes | Yes | Yes | Yes | yes |
| Observations | 301 | 301 | 252 | 251 | 246 | 241 | 239 | 222 |
| *R*-squared | 0.17 | 0.17 | 0.30 | 0.34 | 0.35 | 0.36 | 0.38 | 0.45 |

*Note*: ***Significant at 1%; **significant at 5%; *significant at 10%; ∧significant at 18%.
*Source*: Author's calculations.

in the most complete model (i.e. Model 8). In turn, GDP growth has, as expected, a negative sign and is generally, if weakly, significant. But it appears to have a limited impact on income inequality; for instance, a 6% growth of GDP per capita reduces inequality by 0.2–0.4 Gini points, depending on which of the eight models of Table 9 is selected. The Gini of educational achievements is strongly and significantly related to the Gini income, and its parameters range between 0.6 and 0.7 in all models in which such variables are included. This means that the observed average drop of two or three points in the Gini of educational achievements over 2002 and 2007 (with higher values for Brazil and Guatemala) explains 1.5–2 points of the decline in the Gini of disposable during the same period. As for the impact of the international environment, the terms of trade turns out to reduce inequality moderately. For instance, given their 33% improvement in relation to the 1990s, and given values of the regression parameters ranging between –0.13 and –0.020, the average Gini decline during the 2000s due to this variable is estimated at about 0.4–0.6 points. In turn, migrant remittances are non-significant in all specifications, while FDI/GDP appears strongly and very significantly un-equalizing but rose only minimally during the past decade. Also the parameters of the linear and quadratic terms of the REER are strongly significant, confirming that, for instance, a 20% devaluation of REER reduces income inequality by about 1.2 points. As for the redistributive policies, the regression analysis corroborates the predictions of Section 3 about of their equalizing impact. For instance, doubling of the minimum wage index and considering the three percentage points expansion of the formal employment on the total (Table 2) would induce a drop in income inequality by some 1.2 Gini points. Likewise, the 1.3 percentage points rise in public social expenditure observed in LOC countries over 2003–2006 (Table 4) induced a statistically significant drop in the Gini of income inequality of about 0.4 points. A bit less marked but highly significant and with the expected sign is the parameter of the ratio of direct to indirect taxes.

All in all, Table 9 — and in particular Model 8 — shows that all the signs of the estimated parameters coincide with those expected *ex ante* on the basis of the theories discussed in Section 3. The parameters are also stable across the different specifications, a sign that their values are correctly estimated and sufficiently reliable for computing the relative weight of each set factors used to explain the inequality decline observed between 2002 and 2007. Among all the variables considered, those with the biggest impact on income inequality are (in descending order): the drop in the Gini of educational achievements due to sustained investments in education that affected the skill premium; the choice of an appropriate REER; the labor market and social expenditure policies; and the 'social democratic' and 'populist' dummies that measure the effect on inequality of progressive policies and conditions other than those explicitly considered in the regression analysis. The terms of trade gains and the growth recovery also contributed to the decline in inequality over 2002–2007 but in a quantitatively less important way, while migrant remittances and portfolio flows were not significant, and the stock FDI/GDP (which changed little over 2002–2007) had a lesser impact on inequality, although its parameter is highly significant.

These satisfactory results have to be probed for the possibility of reverse causation and endogeneity. Reverse causation is normally tested by means of the Granger test. However, such a test is not suitable for the IDLA data-set in which each variable has at most 18, and often fewer, observations. It is therefore more appropriate to deal with this problem from a theoretical standpoint.[14] In turn, a solution of possible problems of endogeneity requires developing a simultaneous equations system, which is difficult in a panel with only 18 observations. This means that the results in Table 9 are to be interpreted as correlations rather than causal explanations, although the theoretical discussion in Section 3 lends support to a prudent causal interpretation of the results obtained.

On the whole, it appears that improvements in educational inequality, favorable terms of trade, and pro-poor policies contributed to reduce income inequality. These results contradict the conclusions of Perez Caldentey and Vernengo (2008), according to which the recent growth acceleration and fall in inequality have nothing to do with the policy changes introduced by governments in the economic and social sphere. These authors are right, however, in noting that the recent developments have only minimally reduced the dependence of the region on the export of primary commodities

## 5. Tentative conclusions: is 'prudent redistribution with growth' reducing income inequality in Latin America? Will the current crisis undo it?

The spread of democracy and dissatisfaction with Washington Consensus policies have lead to the elections of LOC governments that introduced — thanks also to favorable external conditions — economic reforms broadly inspired by a 'prudent redistribution with growth' paradigm committed to reducing the inequality inherited from the colonial past and exacerbated by the liberal policies of the 1980s and 1990s. With the exception of Venezuela and Bolivia, the new policy model did not introduce radical measures altering the distribution of assets. Rather, it emphasized orthodox objectives such as macro-economic stability, fiscal prudence, and the preservation of free trade and capital flows. Yet, in a clear departure from the 1990s, the new model relies on managed exchange rates, a neutral or counter-cyclical fiscal policy, reduced dependence on foreign capital, rapid accumulation of reserves, and an active role of the state in the field of labor and social policies.

In addition, as in the European social democracies, LOC and moderate center-right governments raised the tax/GDP ratio (a trend facilitated but not fully explained, neither in its timing nor in its extent, by the recent gains in terms of trade gains) as well as public spending on education, conditional cash transfers, and other forms of social assistance. There is micro-evidence that higher public and private spending reduced inequality in education, improved the distribution of human capital among the workforce, and reduced the skill premium. Redistribution was also pursued via macro-policies favoring the labor-intensive traded sector as well as changes in labor market policies and institutions. Also in this case, the changes introduced were far from radical and yet helped increasing labor participation and the share of workers covered by formal contracts, and reducing unemployment.

Beyond the problems posed by the current financial crisis, the Latin American governments still face formidable hurdles in deepening these reforms. First, the trend towards rising taxation and social expenditure needs to continue in part of the region with the objective of building a lean welfare state that avoids the high costs of the European model but offers universal coverage. Second, the fiscal revenue needed to sustain future social expenditure will have to come from a diversification of the economy into new labor-intensive and skilled-intensive sectors. Third, an intensification of the new policy model by LOC governments in the region faces considerable political opposition, as shown by the case of Bolivia and Argentina, where interest groups have nearly stalled attempts at redistribution. Meanwhile, the financial crisis may dig a gap between the responses expected from LOC governments and what they can actually do under the recessionary conditions of 2009 and part of 2010. An unchecked deterioration of living conditions might lead to a collective perception that the crisis is due to inadequate policy responses. Failure to stay — if in part — the new policy course may cause a credibility gap, undermine electoral support, and push the region towards its traditional path of unequal development or towards more radical solutions, possibly overturning in this way the inequality gains of the recent past.

A simulation of Model 8 in Table 9 suggests that income inequality is likely to have stagnated in 2008 and to have risen by two or three points in 2009 due to deterioration in some of the model's explanatory variables, such as terms of trade, migrant remittances, growth of GDP per capita, and so on. Adverse changes in other variable not included in the model — such as drop in capital inflows, rising interest spreads on international loans, and rises in capital flights — may affect further income inequality. These recessionary pressures are very likely to cause a decline in tax revenue, a phenomenon that may be aggravated by the tax cuts introduced as relief measures as part of the policy response to the crisis. The ability to redistribute via the budget would thus be eroded, unless a counter-cyclical fiscal policy is adopted.

On the positive side, it must be noted that the current crisis hits a region in better conditions than those prevailing on occasion of the crises of 1982–1984 and 1998–2002. To start with, the crisis is mainly a real economy crisis, and not a financial crisis, as in the USA or as experienced in the region during the 1980s and 1990s. This means that fewer funds are needed than in the past to recapitalize ailing banks. Second, many countries of the region are in a position to adopt counter-cyclical fiscal policies and to incur substantial deficits for a couple of years, thanks to declines in the public debt/GDP ratio, large accumulation of currency reserves, and decline in inflation achieved in the first part of the decade (see Section 3). Central Banks can also carry out a more flexible monetary policy without endangering their inflation targets. In turn, the devaluation of the exchange rate is likely to raise the REER (correcting in this way its recent appreciation in some countries, Brazil ahead of all) with a possible favorable impact on inequality. Third, the impact of the recession via the international trade will not affect all countries equally hard. Mexico, Central America and other nations strongly integrated with North America and Europe are likely to suffer an important trade shock, but the Andean and Southern Cone nations that have been increasingly trading with East Asia are likely to be less affected due to the milder recession experienced by this region. Fourth, most countries have introduced in the recent years important public works and cash transfer programs (Table 7). At the moment, 85 million Latin-Americans receive a subsidy under some kind of conditional cash transfer scheme (United Nations Development Programme, 2009). This prior institutional development ought to facilitate the expansion of safety nets during the crisis and preserve in this way some of the recent inequality decline, although not all countries may have the capacity to do so in a timely manner. Finally, current and future inequality trends will depend on the ability of governments to sustain the measures introduced during the recent past in the field of direct taxation, social expenditure, labor market policies and a gradual drive towards an integrated, universal social protection system. As noted, the counter-cyclical fiscal policy followed in the first part of this decade should permit one to sustain some of these programs in the years ahead and to preserve part of the inequality gains achieved during the recent past.

## Acknowledgements

I would like to acknowledge the comments on prior versions of this paper received from an anonymous referee, as well as from Francois Bourguignon, Guillermo Cruces, Michael Grimm, Rafael de los Hoyos, Saul Keifman, Stefan Klasen, Juan Carlos Moreno-Brid, Abijit Sen, Rolph van der Hoeven and participants to conferences or seminars held at ISS-Den Haag (18 September 2008), University of Montevideo (30 September 2008), UN House in Asuncion (2 October 2008), CERDI-University of Auvergne (5 December 2008), TISS-Bombay (13–15 March 2009), EcIneq conference in Buenos Aires (18–19 July 2009), and PegNet conference of Den Haag (3–4 September 2009). I would also like to thank Bruno Martorano for outstanding research assistance. Of course, all remaining errors are only mine.

## Notes

1 CEPAL's Economic and Social Survey 2008–2009 predicts a 1.9% fall in GDP in 2009 and a recovery of 3.1% in 2010, with a cumulative loss of 10 points of GDP growth in relation to the 2003–2008 trend.

2 The coefficient of variation of the national Gini indexes fell from 0.10 to 0.07 over 1992–2006 (Gasparini *et al.*, 2009).

3 An important part of the gains in terms of trade left the region in the form of profit remittances, as the exploitation of natural resources in Latin America is often in the hands of TNCs. Chile and Peru account for over one-half of the regional outflow of profit remittances, although they account for only 8% of the region's GDP.

4 For instance, in Argentina, agriculture accounts for a modest 8% of the total labor force.

5 However, in Mexico most of the migrants come from low-income groups (communication from Rafael de los Hoyos).

6 However, during the same period, the gap between rich and poor in accessing tertiary education widened.

7 Corporación Latinobarómetro is a non-profit non-governmental organization based in Santiago, Chile. Since 1995 it has carried out polls on various political topics by surveying 19 000 households from 18 countries of the region [http://www.latinobarometro.org].

8 Governments developed a variety of fiscal mechanisms for appropriating part of the increase in commodity prices (CEPAL, 2007a, p. 31). Argentina financed part of its spending from resources generated by export duties. In turn, Venezuela, Bolivia and Chile created new taxes to increase the revenue generated from their non-renewable resources. As a result, the share of fiscal resources represented by such revenue in Bolivia, Chile, Colombia and Mexico rose from of 27.8%, 7.6%, 9.9% and 29.4% in the 1990s to 34.8%, 20%, 14.2% and 37.5% in 2006–2007.

9 Such policy requires that the build-up of international reserves during upturns be matched by measures to sterilize their monetary impact. Sterilization of this type is easier when there is a fiscal surplus. Otherwise it is necessary to sterilize via a mix of traditional open market operations, sales of central bank bonds in the market, or higher reserve requirements. For this reason, a fiscal surplus is an essential complement to the policy aiming at maintaining a stable and competitive real exchange rate.

10 Minimum wages varied between 20 and 143% of low-skilled wages, with the number of beneficiaries varying between 1 and 20% of the labor force.

11 In 2005, Cuba, Uruguay, Brazil, Argentina, Bolivia, Costarica and Panama had social expenditure/GDP ratios of 15–20% (near the OECD level), but most Central American and Andean countries had ratios below 10%.

12 Since 1996–1997, Bolivia, Honduras and Nicaragua enjoyed debt cancellations equal to 5%, 6% and 2% of their GDP.

13 Of the (18 x 18) 324 observations of the Gini coefficient of income inequality, 175 derive from the SEDLAC database [www.depeco.econo.unlp.edu.ar/sedlac/eng/statistics.php] and are obtained through a standard procedure using household surveys data, 11 are taken from WIDER's WIID2c [www.wider.unu.edu/wiid/wiid.htm], three from Badeinso-Eclac 2008 [www.eclac.cl/estadisticas/bases/], 13 from WDI 2007, and one (Argentina in 2007) from national sources. Ninety-eight data-points were interpolated by filling gaps of one or two years in time series with stable trends. In three cases, interpolation was used to fill gaps of three years, and in three cases of four years; that is, for a total of 21 data-points referring mostly to the early 1990s. Finally, 23 cells (for Ecuador, Guatemala, Nicaragua, and Paraguay in the early 1990s) remain blank. A successful check was carried out to ensure that the data filled in by interpolation replicated the trend of other income concepts with available data. In most cases, the data refer to disposable household income per capita. In a few cases, it was not possible to find out the income concept used for computing the Gini coefficients, as this information was not included in the survey questionnaires. This might introduce some error in the measurement of the dependent variable. However, as it was possible to verify a strong co-variance between trends of Gini coefficients based on different income concepts, this bias may affect the value of the country intercepts in the fixed effect estimation, without affecting the parameters of the explanatory variables. All data cover the nation as a whole, except for Argentina (where surveys initially covered the Greater Buenos Aires, then the 15 main cities, and later the 28 main cities), Bolivia

(where between 1990 and 1995 the coverage was only urban), and Uruguay (urban coverage only).

14 In this regard, it must be noted that reverse causality makes no sense in the majority of the relations in Table 9. For instance, it is not plausible that changes in domestic inequality affect the real exchange rate, or can affect lagged, exogenous or policy variables (such as Gini income 1990, migrant remittances, terms of trade, ratio of direct/indirect taxes, ratio of pension coverage Q1/Q5, and minimum wage). Also, a fall/increase in Gini income may affect the Gini of years of education only after a considerable lag. It is also implausible that a decrease in inequality will affect the expenditure on social insurance/GDP, which depends on the coverage of formal employment as far as pensions are concerned, and on tax revenue and public expenditure allocation for conditional cash transfers. The only relation in which reverse causation may be plausible is that between the Gini inequality and the growth rate of GDP per capita. In this case, however, this relation would be characterized by time lags, thus excluding the possibility of reverse causation on synchronous data. Furthermore, the literature on the impact of higher inequality on GDP per capita growth is not unanimous. Neokeynesian and neoclassical models postulate a positive relation between these two variables, while 'political economy' and 'incentives' models assume a negative one. On the whole, reverse causality does not seem plausible.

## References

Altimir, Oscar (1993) 'Income distribution and poverty through crises and adjustment', paper presented at the *ECLAC/UNICEF Workshop on Public Policy Reforms and Social Expenditure,* Santiago, Chile, 14-15 June.

Altimir, Oscar (1996) 'Economic development and social equity', *Journal of Interamerican Studies and World Affairs,* 38(2/3), pp. 47-71.

Baltagi, Badi H. (2005) *Econometric Analysis of Panel Data,* John Wiley and Sons, Chichester.

Bouillon, Cesar Patricio and Tajerina, Luis (2007) *Do We Know What Works?: A Systematic Review of Impact Evaluations of Social Programs in Latin America and the Caribbean,* Inter-American Development Bank, Washington, DC.

CELADE (2006) *América Latina y el Caribe: Observatorio Demográfico N° 2,* October, CEPAL, Santiago.

CEPAL (2005) *Panorama Social de America Latina,* CEPAL, Santiago de Chile.

CEPAL (2006 and 2008) *Panorama Social de America Latina,* CEPAL, Santiago de Chile.

CEPAL (2007a) *Preliminary Overview of the Economies of Latin America and the Carribean, 2007,* CEPAL, Santiago de Chile.

CEPAL (2007b) *Panorama Social de America Latina,* CEPAL, Santiago de Chile.

Cetrangolo, Oscar and Sabaini, Gomez (2006) 'Tributacion en America Latina: En busca de nuevas agenda de reformas', *Libros de la CEPAL No. 93,* December, CEPAL, Santiago de Chile.

Chenery Hollis, Ahluwalia, Montek, Bell, Clive, Duloy, John and Jolly, Richard (1974) *Redistribution with Growth,* Oxford, Oxford University Press.

Cornia, Giovanni Andrea (2006) *Pro-poor Macroeconomics: potential and limitations,* Palgrave McMillan, London

Cornia, Giovanni Andrea and Martorano, Bruno (2009), 'What explains the decline of income inequality during the last decade?', paper presented at the *Overcoming Persistent Inequality and Poverty Conference in honor of Frances Stewart,* Oxford Department of International Development, 17-18 September.

Dornbush, Rudiger and Edwards, Sebastian (1991) *The Macroeconomics of Populism in Latin America,* University of Chicago Press, Chicago and London.

Engerman, Stanley L. and Sokoloff, Kenneth L. (2005) 'Colonialism, inequality and long run paths of development', *Working Paper 11057,* NBER, Cambridge, Mass.

Fizsbein, Ariel and Schady, Norbert (2009, *Conditional Cash Transfers: Reducing Present and Future Poverty,* World Bank, Washington, DC.

Frenkel, Roberto and Rapetti, Martín (2008) 'Five years of competitive and stable real exchange rate in Argentina, 2002–2007', *International Review of Applied Economics*, 22(2), pp. 215–216.

Gasparini, Leonardo (2007) *Monitoring the Socio-Economic Conditions in Argentina 1992–2006*, mimeo, June, CEDLAS, Universidad Nacional de La Plata, La Plata.

Gasparini Leonardo, Cruces, Guillermo, Tornarolli, Leopoldo and Marchionni, Mariana (2009) 'A turning point? Recent developments on inequality in Latin America and the Caribbean', *Documento de Trabajo Nro. 81*, February, CEDLAS, Universidad Nacional de La Plata, La Plata.

HelpAgeInternational (2006) [www.helpage.org/Home].

Klasen, Stephan and Nowak-Lehman, Felicitas (2009) *Poverty, Inequality and Policy in Latin America*, Cesifo Seminar Series, The MIT Press, Cambridge, MA.

Kristensen, Nicolai and Cunningham, Wendy (2006) 'Do minimum wages in Latin America and the Carribean matter? Evidence from 19 countries', *World Bank Policy Research Working Paper No. 3870*, March, World Bank, Washington DC.

International Monetary Fund (2005) *World Economic Outlook: Globalization and External Imbalances*, April, IMF, Washington, DC.

Lustig, Nora (2009) 'La pobreza y la disegualdad en America Latina, y los gobiernos de la Izquirda', *Cuadernos del Consejo Mexicano de Asuntos Internacionales, No. 7.*

Ocampo, José Antonio (2007) 'The macroeconomics of the Latin American economic boom', *CEPAL Review*, 93. pp. 7–28.

Ocampo, José Antonio (2008) 'The Latin American economic boom', *Revista de Ciencia Política*, 28(1), pp. 7–33.

Panizza, Francisco E. (2005a) 'Unarmed utopia revisited: the resurgence of left-of-centre politics in Latin America', *Political studies*, 53(4), pp. 716–734.

Panizza, Francisco E. (2005b) 'The social democratisation of the Latin American left', *Revista Europea de Estudios Latinoamericanos y del Caribe*, 79, pp. 95–104.

Perez Caldentey, Esteban and Vernengo, Matías (2008) *Back to the Future: Latin America's Current Development Strategy* [www.networkideas.org/featart/aug2008/fa02_Back2 Future.htm].

Székely, Miguel (2003) 'The 1990s in Latin America: another decade of persistent inequality but with somewhat lower poverty', *Journal of Applied Economics*, VI(2), 317–339.

Taylor, Lance (2004) 'External liberalization, economic performance and distribution in Latin America and elsewhere', in Giovanni Andrea Cornia (Ed.), *Inequality, growth and Poverty in an Era of Liberalization and Globalization*, Oxford University Press, Oxford, pp. 166–196.

Tokman, Victor (1986) 'Ajuste y Empleo: Los Desafios del Presente', PREALC, Regional Employment Programme for Latin America and the Caribbean, mimeo. Santiago, Chile.

United Nations Development Programme (2009) 'The global financial crisis: social implications for Latin America and the Caribbean', *Crisis Update No. 2*, 10 February, Regional Bureau for Latin America and the Carribean, New York.

World Bank (2005) *Argentina: Seeking Sustained Growth and Social Equity: Observations on Growth, Inequality and Poverty*, 21 October, World Bank, Washington, DC.

# *Does Fast Growth in India and China Help or Harm US Workers?*

ALEX IZURIETA and AJIT SINGH
*Alex Izurieta is Senior Economic Affairs Officer in the Development Policy and Analysis Division of the United Nations Department of Economic and Social Affairs and Research Associate at the University of Cambridge, UK*
*Ajit Singh is Emeritus Professor of Economics at Cambridge University and Senior Research Fellow at the Judge Business School Cambridge, UK*

**Abstract** A major issue today is whether globalization of the world's labour, capital and product markets, together with rapid economic growth in India and China, will have an adverse effect on workers in the US and other advanced countries. Simulations of different scenarios using the Cambridge-Alphametrics Model of the World Economy indicate that, at a bloc-disaggregated level, there are severe supply-side constraints relating particularly to natural resources (energy and raw materials) that thwart the expansionary demand effects of fast growth in India and China. This analysis is based on long-term trends in the world economy prior to the current global financial crisis. However, for the sake of completeness, it also comments on the likely implications of this crisis for the USA and other advanced country workers.

## Introduction

Based on long-term trends in the world economy over the past two decades (up to 2007) — that is, not taking into account the current global financial turmoil — the simulation analysis presented in this paper suggests that there is an ultimate conflict between the interests of workers in the North (advanced countries [ACs]) and the South (developing countries [DCs]). This conflict would arise *if* China and India were to grow at their desired fast rates of growth in order to reduce their backlog of unemployment and under-employment of their large agrarian workforces. The fast growth rates of these two economies would lead to continuing high growth of demand for the world's natural resources (energy, minerals and other raw materials and food). Given short time constraints on expansion of these resources and consequent high prices, this would only be compatible with less than full employment growth rates in the G7 countries

This paper firstly discusses the impact on labour markets in ACs of the integration of the two giant fast-growing countries, China and India. Secondly, it raises the question of a binding supply constraint on natural resources and shows, using model simulations, that if such constraints are alleviated then full employment growth for both North and South can be achieved. The main policy conclusion is that full employment of workers worldwide requires close cooperation between governments to resolve this potential conflict by taking measures such as international pay coordination policies, cooperation over technological developments, and fiscal policy to help manage global demand among other things.

On empirically less rigorous and essentially *a priori* grounds, some leading economists have argued that, even though over the past two decades the gradual integration of developing countries such as those in Latin America with the liberalized global economy may not have had a serious negative impact on wages and employment in advanced countries, the integration of China and India is most likely to do so both now and in the future. This is because the latter integration means a sudden doubling of the globalized labour force without a concomitant increase in capital per worker.[1]

The intellectually most cogent and vigorous expression of this view is presented in Freeman (2005), an eminent US labour economist with evident sympathies for trade unions. Freeman could fairly be regarded as representing the pro-labour US intellectual opinion. In the present context, his research also draws its significance from a seminal article (Freeman, 1995) that he wrote 12 years ago with the mischievous title 'Are Your Wages Set in Beijing?' At that time, Freeman argued that this was not the case because there was insufficient integration between the US and Chinese labour markets to warrant such a conclusion. Today Freeman is more likely to reach the opposite conclusion. In his recent work (Freeman, 2005) he suggests that, even if trade with the South may not previously have seriously disadvantaged workers in rich countries, the fast integration of the giant economies of India and China with the international economy is likely to have in the future profoundly unfavourable repercussions for AC workers.

The present paper argues against this pessimistic thesis. This is basically on two grounds: it does not take into account the demand-side effects of fast growth in India and China; and it ignores the dynamism of the US real economy and its innovative large corporations, capable of contributing to the technological developments that are necessary to overcome the impending natural resource constraints that are likely to be otherwise binding.

The paper first carries out an intellectual evaluative exercise of these opposing arguments about the effects of fast growth in India and China on the US economy and the world economy. It next uses an econometric model of the world economy to simulate the results of alternative policy choices in facing binding resource constraints.

Although most of this paper is based upon the analysis of economic forces in the period preceding the current financial crisis (i.e. before 2008), for the sake of completeness we nevertheless offer some brief comments on the crisis in the light of the preceding analysis.

## Fast economic growth in China and India

One heartening feature of the evolution of the world economy during the past two to three decades has been the outstanding economic success of China and India — two of the world's most populous and hitherto extremely poor countries. Starting with the world's largest absolute numbers of people living in poverty, in narrow economic terms the two countries have achieved impressive growth. Figure 1 provides a broad-brush statistical profile of Gross Domestic Product (GDP) growth over the past four decades for China, India, and all medium-income and low-income countries (namely, DCs) and for the world economy as a whole. China has undoubtedly been the fastest growing country in the world over the past quarter of a century, achieving historically unprecedented, almost double-digit, growth rates since 1980. Similarly, although not as fast as China,

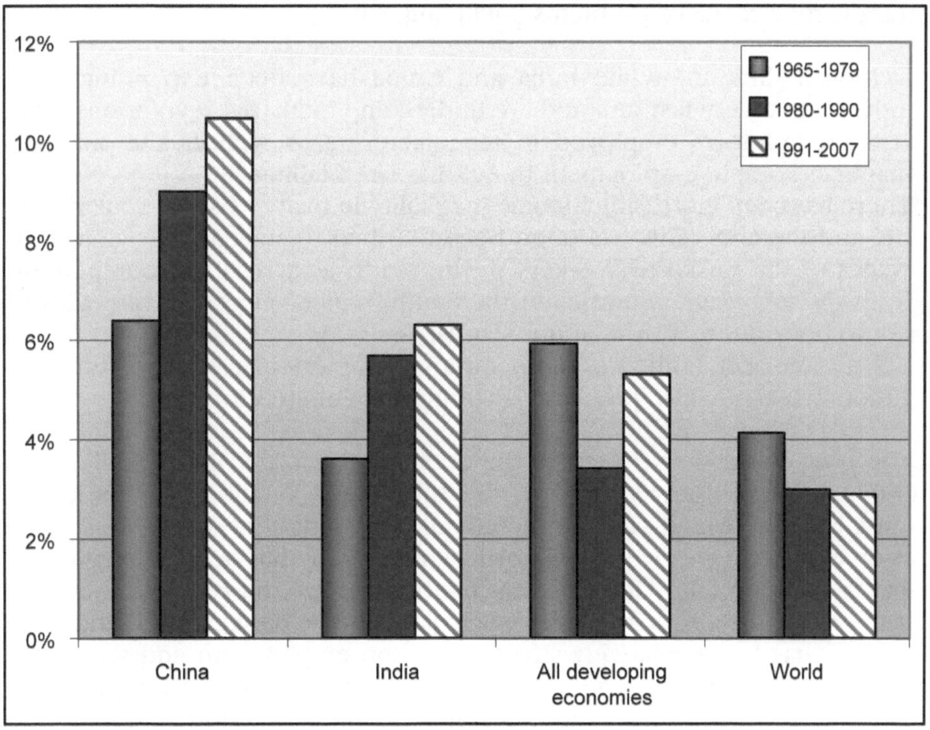


FIGURE 1. Trends in real GDP growth: China, India, developing economies and the world, 1965–2003 (average annual percentage growth).
*Source*: Adapted from Dasgupta and Singh (2005).

India's economic growth has also been one of the highest in the world since 1980, its per capita growth rate tripling between 1950–1980 and 1980–2005 (Kelkar, 2004). India was among the 10 fastest growing countries in the world over each of the two decades 1980–1990 and 1990–2000. This record is unmatched by any country other than China. Indeed, the acceleration of growth in India and China in the past quarter-century is particularly remarkable, as it has taken place during a period of deceleration in world economic growth (as compared with the Golden Age of the 1950s and 1960s). Fast economic growth has led to large-scale income poverty reductions in both countries, although the extent in the Indian case since 1990 is still debated. There have also been huge improvements in human development indicators. For recent contributions to this debate see, for example, Sen and Himanshu (2004), Srinivasan (2003) and United Nations Development Programme (2005, Box 1.3).

The rapid economic expansion of these two giants has given rise to serious concerns in advanced nations regarding both the short-term and long-term implications for their peoples. Since the end of the 'golden age' of fast economic growth in the North in the mid-1970s, most of these economies have suffered from serious labour market difficulties. Specifically, workers and trade unions blame competition from low-wage economies such as China and India for a range of problems, including:

- Deindustrialization: while India and China have been expanding their industry at a very fast rate and are undergoing industrial revolutions,[2] the absolute numbers employed in manufacturing as well as the share of manufacturing in employment in ACs has been falling.
- There has been increasing income inequality in many ACs, particularly the UK and the USA. This has often been ascribed to stagnant or falling real wages of the unskilled workers in the North as a result of competition from the low-wage countries of the South, which, moreover, are alleged not to obey international labour standards.
- There have been high rates of unemployment particularly in the European Union, which are also popularly attributed to competition from the South.

In the post-World War II period, the economics profession, as well as the traditional liberal establishment in the USA, have favoured free trade and taken a broadly benign view of the effects of competition from poor countries on economic welfare in the North. This position has been backed up by research. Despite following different methodologies, the research indicates that the effects of globalization, in particular of trade between rich and poor countries, has had a relatively small impact on employment and wages for workers in advanced countries such as the USA. The labour market problems of advanced country workers are attributed in this analysis much more to the nature of the new technology rather than to globalization.[3] However, it is precisely this favourable perspective on globalization that has seriously been challenged by Freeman.

## The threat for advanced countries from new globalizers: the Freeman thesis

Freeman's new post-1995 line of thought, which regards globalization as a potentially major threat for the North's workers, chimes in very well with popular sentiment in ACs. Opinion polls indicate 6 out of 10 citizens in the USA are not persuaded by the supposed benefits of globalization. This is quite remarkable in view of the fact that the US economy has recorded the strongest growth rate of all major economies in the past 10 years (Martin and Rowthorn, 2005). However, US wages and salaries have been more volatile than before, and on a declining trend in real terms in some categories, which suggests that the general scepticism about globalization is perhaps not so remarkable after all. Freeman's (2005) contribution provides a formidable and sophisticated articulation of this sentiment. Further, in addition to the short term, Freeman is very much concerned with the potential adverse long-term effects of global economic integration. The latter aspect adds to the weight of Freeman's analysis.

The essential basis for Freeman's argument is his observation that the global labour force has all of a sudden doubled with the entry of India, China and former Soviet bloc countries into the liberalized global market in the recent period. He suggests that in 1985 there were about a billion workers who competed with each other under 'globalization'; that is, these countries by then had achieved more or less free trade and more or less free capital movements amongst themselves. This globalized countries group at the time consisted of the OECD economies and Latin America. According to Freeman's estimate, approximately 960 million people worked in these countries in 1980. By the year 2000, the size of this labour force had increased to 1460 million workers, mainly through population growth in the developing countries part of this group. However, with the entry of India and China and the former Soviet bloc countries into the globalized economy around 2000, the global labour force suddenly doubled to three billion, of which nearly half (i.e. 1.47 billion) were the Chinese, Indian and other new entrants to the labour force (see Figure 2). This doubling of the labour force of the world's integrating liberal capitalist economy, Freeman suggests, has, on the whole, pleasant consequences for low-income countries such as India and China, but potentially rather unpleasant outcomes for high-wage workers in rich countries.

Freeman notes that these additional 1.5 billion workers from the newly globalizing countries had brought very little capital with them. As a result, the global capital labour ratio was cut to 55% of its pre-2000 level. This decline in the world capital labour ratio not only reduces average productivity and real wages but also makes capital scarce, shifting the balance of power towards it.

The conventional analysis of North–South trade involves the notion that countries should produce according to their comparative advantage, with rich countries specializing in skill-intensive or capital-intensive products and

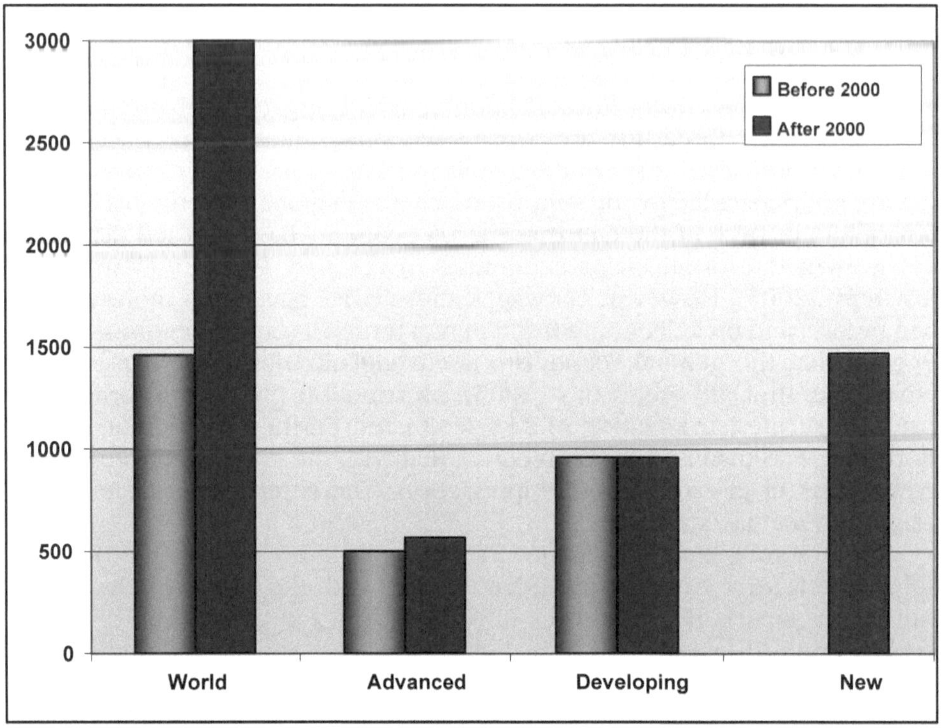


FIGURE 2. The evolution of economic activity per region.
*Source*: Freeman (2005).

poor countries in labour-intensive and less skilled products. Freeman regards this theory as obsolete in view of the outsourcing of many skill-intensive jobs to the South and the ability of countries like India and China to produce more absolute numbers of engineers and science graduates than the USA. In 2003 China graduated 325 000 engineers and the USA only 65 000. Even taking into account the technical superiority of the American engineers over the Chinese, this difference is too large for US comfort. Freeman argues that the probability of achieving technological innovations depends on the *absolute* numbers of technically trained people rather than their relative numbers. The reality according to Freeman is that the USA is likely to lose its technological lead unless it takes extraordinary steps to reverse the present course of events. In the hi-tech sector, US pre-eminence is visibly under threat. The US share of world exports of hi-tech manufacturers fell from 30% in 1980 to 17% in 2000, and similarly its share of imports rose from 13 to 18% over the same period. To sum up, Freeman is basically suggesting that industrial revolutions in China and India represent gigantic supply-side shocks for many parts of the world economy, particularly the USA. These are likely to be extremely disruptive and harmful for these countries and regions, not just in the short run but also importantly in the long term.

Nevertheless, it must be emphasized that Freeman does not advocate protection as a way out of these difficulties. Although non-protectionist, Freeman's policy perspective is highly interventionist. He calls for resolute and determined government intervention, at the national level as well as at the international level, to manage the transition during which the new globalizers will catch up with the USA. He expects this transition to be long and protracted — it may take as much as 30–40 years. His examples of good transition include West European catch-up after World War II; the bad transitions include southern American states' integration after the civil war with the more industrialized north. These also include the East German integration with West Germany after the break-up of the Berlin Wall. Freeman argues against the current 'Washington Consensus' globalization that, in his view, is biased towards protecting the interests of capital. He writes eloquently:

> The international financial institutions may have to worry about instability of capital markets and crony corrupt capitalists, but they don't have to worry about capital more broadly: George Soros and his billionaire friends can take care of themselves. It is the average worker in the world who needs the protection of the international community. (Rocco C. and Marion S. Siciliano Forum, 2005, no page number)

Yet, as suggested below, while Freeman may be right in appealing for government action, he disregards the potential for international coordination of global demand and its impact on expanding the full employment frontier. This is because his focus is entirely on the US workers; he is not concerned at all with the desirability or otherwise of the DCs pursuing and completing their industrial revolutions.

## Supply-side shocks and the growth of demand

Professor Freeman's apprehensions about the impact of China's and India's integration on the North's workers are well argued and supported by careful analysis and evidence. His arguments therefore require careful consideration.

At a theoretical level, Professor Freeman's essential argument is that the supply side shock of doubling of the world's labour force will have a profound impact on labour markets in many countries. The size of the shock will make it disruptive. There is much in Freeman's analysis we agree with, but there are also parts with which we have difficulties. For reasons of space and to add to the debate, it is the latter that we highlight below.

Thus, one important shortcoming of Freeman's analysis, in our view, is that it provides very little explicit consideration of demand side factors. In an early contribution, Singh (1977) suggested that foreign competition and the balance of payments position of an economy can affect its growth and industrial development through three distinct but related channels: through the level and growth of demand; through the structure of demand; and, importantly, through investment. In considering these channels, R. S. Sayers's (1965) simple distinction between the complementary and competitive aspects of economic growth elsewhere is useful. The central point of Sayers's analysis is that:

> the expansion of the world economy, although it may raise the demand for a country's products, also creates alternative sources of supply, which may compete with them in any market, including its home market. So, from the point of view of a particular country, the development of the world economy may be characterised by a changing balance between 'complementarity' and 'competitiveness'. (Sayers, 1965, quoted in Singh, 1977, p. 117)

In the specific case of the integration of China and India with the world economy, economic growth in these two countries is on the whole likely to be more complementary than competitive with the US economy and that of many other countries. The essential point is that India and China, by virtue of their size and high growth rates, which they require for meeting their huge employment and other social needs, now constitute another growth pole of demand for the world economy. Together, these two countries accounted for about 20% of the increment in world production and world demand over the decade 1995–2005. Their demand side effects have already led to expansion in several countries, both developed and developing. There is evidence that in the recent period China's trade with Japan was helpful in preventing the Japanese economy from going into recession. As Overholt notes:

> Chinese demand provided the stimulus that lifted Japan out of recession [during the slowdown in world economic growth following the collapse of the technology bubble on the stock market]. It is difficult to overstate the risk the world economy faced from the Japanese situation, where mountainous debt created the risk of a domino-like collapse inside Japan and subsequent rippling collapses around the world. That risk seems to have passed, helped by a critical margin of stimulus from China. Few books are written about global depressions that never happened, but it is quite possible that China's globalisation saved us from beginning the new century with a drastic global economic squeeze. (2005, p. 9; parentheses added)

Developing countries in general have benefited from the demand stimulus for raw materials and commodities provided by fast economic growth in China and India leading also to faster economic growth elsewhere. Sustained growth in these two countries thus provides a stable source for the growth of world demand in general, with favourable effects on the DCs as well as developed countries.

The aggregate and sectoral demand effects of Chinese and Indian economic expansion manifest themselves in other significant ways too. For example, the production of cheap goods in India and China, particularly in the latter, helps reduce inflationary pressures in advanced countries, thereby allowing their economies to be run at higher levels of output and employment than they otherwise would. Unfortunately, there are few empirical studies that quantify the effects of this channel. The International Monetary Fund (2006) has recently explored the question of the effects of globalization on inflation. These effects are estimated to be in general quite small — a reduction in inflation of the order of 0.25%, although estimates rise to 1% or more for specific years and specific countries. These studies, however, are unable to measure the full extent of the effects of globalization on reducing the general level of prices, in large part because the real influence of globalization is in this instance not easily quantifiable and in part because the obsession of inflation-targeting in policy-making is not so openly admitted to allow proper counter-factual analysis. As Raghuram Rajan (2006, p. xi) notes:

> In my view, however, the true impact of globalisation has been in contributing to wage and price restraint at a time when central bankers were establishing their inflation-fighting credibility, thus allowing them to achieve targets and gain credibility without the need to tighten to politically difficult levels.

The favourable impact of Chinese and Indian economic growth on the US economy comes also through other related channels. For example, it is estimated that lower prices for basic goods as a result of trade with China, India and other developing countries has contributed significantly to the standard of living of low-paid American citizens. Preliminary estimates suggest that these lower prices help raise standards of living of poor Americans by about 5-10%. Similarly, Chinese purchases of US Treasury bonds have helped to finance US budget deficits without which the USA would have had higher interest rates, and hence slower growth. Although these may be regarded as short-term measures, they have nevertheless helped to keep up for several years the rate of growth of the US economy and hence of the world economy.

Fast growth of China and India thus benefits US workers through an increase in global demand. It also benefits them by keeping prices of manufactured products low. The negative effects of Chinese and Indian economic growth on the US economy lie elsewhere. The most important of the latter is the competition from the two countries for the world's scarce raw materials and commodities. If this was not properly addressed, the contribution of India and China in keeping global consumer price inflation tamed, averting contractionary monetary policies and allowing higher standards of living in ACs, would be greatly compromised. Furthermore, a growing Chinese and Indian demand for these products, including oil, would raise their world prices and thereby, other things being equal, disadvantage the US economy. These points will be developed further below

## Limitations of previous research

The above considerations do not show adequately, if at all, in the three generations (namely those covering the periods 1960–1980, 1980–2000 and 2000–2005) of conventional studies of the impact of globalization on US labour markets.[4] This is mainly because these are partial rather than general equilibrium studies. There is very little research of the latter kind that is available. There is, however, a recent contribution by Bailey and Lawrence (2004) that to some extent addresses this methodological problem. The two authors examine changes in employment between 2000 and 2003 in the US economy, a period that has been marked by a relatively short recession. The strong upturn following the recession did not, however, lead to much net job creation, and hence the emergence of 'jobless growth'. In the normal public discourse, these unfavourable labour market outcomes are blamed on globalization, including outsourcing of service jobs to India. The authors carried out their empirical analysis on a detailed individual industry basis. They use the following empirical model, as well as an input–output model of the US economy to address these questions.

$$e_i = w_{\mathrm{d}}(d - v) + w_{\mathrm{x}}(x - v) - w_{\mathrm{m}}(m - v)$$

where $e_i$ connotes percentage change in employment; and $w_{\mathrm{d}}$, $w_{\mathrm{x}}$ and $w_{\mathrm{m}}$ are the weights attached to domestic use, imports and exports, respectively. This equation is an *ex-post* identity, in which:

> percentage change in employment is equal to the weighted average of the percentage changes in the differences between the growth rate of labour productivity and value added due to domestic use, value added due to exports, and value added attributable to imports. (Bailey and Lawrence, 2004, p. 229 )

Using this framework, the authors conclude that of the 950 000 net manufacturing jobs lost by the year 2003, only 105 000 were due to trade and the remaining 845 000 due to reduced growth of domestic demand (see Sichel, 2004, p. 279).

Thus Bailey and Lawrence's paper suggests that the jobless growth in the US economy in the first half of this decade was not due to globalization as is commonly believed, but to other factors. It further indicates that imports from the Third World, including out-sourcing, had a negligible impact on US labour markets. Much the greater impact of globalization came from reduced US exports to other countries, which was mainly a result of the appreciation of the US dollar against other currencies. The other main reason for the jobless growth and unfavourable labour market outcomes such as job instability arose from insufficient expansion of aggregate demand in the US economy. Although Bailey and Lawrence's contribution represents a methodological advance over previous studies, even this does not yet provide a fully satisfactory understanding of the full implications of globalization for the US economy. Bailey and Lawrence assume that the rate of growth of productivity as well as the volume of global demand are exogenous variables, which many analysts would regard as being eminently endogenous.

## The dynamism of the US real economy

Although Professor Freeman has raised the right questions about the potential for disruption that doubling of the world labour force implies, he perhaps underestimates the capacity of the US economy to provide employment to those who would lose their jobs as a result of competition. As John Hicks suggests, although there is no guarantee that all those who have lost their jobs due to competition in the product markets will find jobs elsewhere, the probability is much higher that they will do so in a fast-growing, dynamic economy than in a stagnant, low-income economy. The USA, in view of what could be categorized as a Kaldorian-type interaction between demand and technology, is precisely the former kind of economy. This point was essential, although perhaps not sufficiently emphasized in the comprehensive research led by Harvard Professor D. Jorgenson (see Jorgenson *et al.*, 2005; Jorgenson, 1990, 2001).

Professor Freeman raises two other issues that require comment in the light of the discussion above. He is worried about the US economy being able to retain its technological lead in view of the much larger number of science and engineering graduates in developing countries. This apprehension also seems to be somewhat overdrawn. It is indeed true that India and China have large educated labour forces, but their capacity to innovate is hugely below that of the USA. This is because innovation does not just depend upon the ideas of science and engineering graduates, but also importantly on the scientific and technical infrastructure, on the country's technical culture, and on organizational capabilities of firms.

Further as Jorgenson and Vu rightly observe:

> Differences in per capita output levels (between countries) are mainly due to input per capita rather than productivity. This reflects the fact that technology is relatively easy to transfer from industrialized economies to developing economies, while mobilization of capital and labour inputs requires much more time and considerably greater effort. Outmoded techniques of production must give way to newer methods that incorporate the latest technologies, especially those that utilize information technology equipment and software. (2007, p. 140; parentheses added)

In these respects, the USA, and ACs more generally, are way ahead of India and China and will remain so for a long time. Baumol (2002) has convincingly argued that the US industrial structure of oligopolistic competition between giant firms is capitalism's built-in innovating machine. There is no reason to believe that this machine will become any less potent in the future, although it may also be the case that substantial government intervention may be required in this area to achieve the desired social goals. The economic historian William Lazonik (2007) suggests that the US Government is already taking important steps in this direction. Finally, Professor Freeman's point about investment is critical. However, the inherent dynamism of the US economy suggests that it will continue to be an attractive place both for domestic and foreign companies, particularly if the required government intervention is sustained over time.

## Preliminary assessment and the pending task of model simulations

Two major points of difference with Freeman have been emphasized. The first concerns his inadequate attention to the demand-side variables and to the interaction between the growth of demand and that of productivity. A related issue is whether the dynamism of the US real economy and its edge for innovation (and of advanced countries more generally) would actually be enhanced rather than weakened by fast growth in India and China.

To sum up, on the first point, a preliminary assessment of this paper is that there are significant forces at work both on the demand and the supply sides that suggest, notwithstanding the size of the two countries, the effects of China's and India's industrial revolutions on ACs in the future can arguably be accommodated just as well as those of Japan and Italy were in the past, during their periods of rapid industrialization in the 1950s and 1960s (see further Singh, 2005; UNCTAD, 1995). As elaborated in UNCTAD (1995) and Singh (2005), this accommodation occurred in the golden age, mainly because of faster OECD and world GDP growth. It will be recalled that between 1950 and 1973 real wages of the US workers rose at a rate of approximately 2% per annum. Thus, although the analysis so far indicates that Professor Freeman has perhaps been unduly pessimistic about the prospects of the US economy in response to Chinese and Indian industrial revolutions, he has nevertheless raised extremely important policy questions that deserve the attention of economists now and in the future. In the next section we will assess the impact of the fast growth of India and China on the global economy with the help of an empirical model.

The econometric model will also help us to understand the role of variables such as inflation and resource constraints, which have not so far received adequate attention in the analysis. However, the important point here is that the assessments above represent an intellectual evaluative exercise whose conclusions can only be regarded as preliminary. It is necessary to carry the analysis further because the issues involved are inherently complex and one needs to ensure that all the important inter-relationships between variables are taken into account and more precisely specified.

## A model to assess the global implications of fast growth in China and India

The model used below for the evaluation of our hypotheses and conjectures in previous sections is the Cambridge-Alphametrics Model (CAM, version 2), which draws its inspiration from a model that was influential in the UK during the 1970s and early 1980s and was associated with Francis Cripps and Wynne Godley.[5] It is described below in general terms.[6]

The CAM is essentially a demand-driven model but is subject to resource constraints. Each country or bloc is interacting with each other in a fully endogenous manner in such a way that there is neither a single 'driver' of the model nor a single 'closure'.[7] The nexus between each country or bloc with the rest is the current account. Thus, the current account reflects three simultaneous processes: domestic spending and net saving; trade and income flows; and financing. Version 2 of the CAM does not include financing explicitly, and therefore financial adjustments are imputed by empirically observable stock-flow regularities.

Explaining how the stock-flow regularity works is useful in order to introduce domestic spending, which, as noted, is one of the processes that connects each country with the rest via the current account.[8] Domestic spending adjusts to the anticipated income earned the current year and to the expected value of accumulated financial wealth, which in turn results from net savings in previous years. Thus, if spending in one year was above (below) what would otherwise be with the benefit of *a posteriori* information about incomes effectively earned or the real value of financial wealth, such would put a downward (upward) pressure on domestic demand in the future because net-saving was found to be insufficient (excessive) to maintain a stable relation between income and wealth.[9] Therefore, mistaken perceptions regarding incomes earned or the value of wealth are transmitted through the world economy, causing imbalances that may take some time to be resolved. At the very aggregate level of a country or a bloc, domestic expenditure is therefore influenced by previous years' income and by the current account, which is the net-saving variable for the economy as a whole.

Thus, the current account of blocs influences, and responds to, spending decisions that are primarily materialized through trade. Similarly, current account positions influence and are affected by international prices and exchange rates, whose variations influence domestic spending in turn. And finally, it is through the current account that changes in production are manifested. The latter observation is crucial in understanding how supply constraints emerge in the model and can, to an extent, be resolved. Let us take energy, but agricultural and extraction activities are similarly represented. The model captures the historic patterns of growth of supply and demand of energy in relation to the generation of global and regional (or country) output, the degree of specialization in manufactures, agriculture, and so forth; as well as with income and income growth, respectively. These relations, supply and demand, are also influenced by international prices and exchange rates. As income grows, for example, demand for energy (or any sector specified in the model: services, manufactures, agricultural and raw materials, energy) rises. This would push up prices, while the configuration of external positions among blocs or countries affect exchange rates as well (nominal and real). But as demand for energy and prices increase, so does the willingness (and expectation) to increase production. In turn, technological progress allows increases of production to catch up with increases of demand in ways that are historically observable (the model runs over a timeframe of nearly four decades).

While the 'technical progress function' in the model is not explicit, its performance is implied by the movements of prices, since at each cycle there is a price iteration that allows supply to match demand. The observable fact is that when global demand pressures rise at rates that are not historically matched by increases of production triggered by productivity, the price of energy rises, perhaps dramatically.[10] This signals a supply constraint. In this version of the model it is up to the modeller to determine whether the resulting pattern of international prices is unsustainable, essentially because such price fluctuations impose a distribution of world incomes in real terms that is untenable and/or call for unilateral policy intervention. The same notion of 'technical progress' is embedded in the price/production dynamics of other sectors as well, with the difference that for manufactures the variables that tend to change more effectively in response to demand pressures are the exchange rate and production itself, particularly in the event of strong policy intervention (evidences abound through history, not the least during war times, etc.).

In essence, 'full-employment' growth around historical trends is achieved in the CAM to the extent that the rise of income and demand is matched by technical progress at a rate that averts sustained price shocks. Thus, instead of adjusting the model results by suppressing the growth of production in some parts of the world to avoid unemployment somewhere else, as we suppose Freeman would do, we use the model to test the boundaries of technical progress by allowing domestic demand and production in each bloc and country to follow their inner dynamics. In brief, we do not adjust the model downwards and measure unemployment afterwards; we adjust the model upwards and measure how prices and world income distribution fare, and assess whether such an outcome is satisfactory to avert situations like crises or disrupting interventions.

The way the model simulations presented below work has some resemblance with real-life decision-making. We set out a target; for example, a rate of economic growth in a country or bloc, or even the world as a whole.

Growth is endogenous but we have the capacity to 'influence' such an outcome by imputing changes in variables that have been seen to change when growth takes place. Generally such could be government spending or taxation, private spending or investment, and so forth. Operationally, we use 'add-factors' in each endogenous equation of the model. The model outcome may in this way approach the target. But it may well be that the target is not achieved at all because other things like prices, or exchange rates, or demand in other sectors and countries affect real incomes, the value of wealth, and so forth, and either result on untenable price rises or cause perverse feedbacks. Such outcomes are induced by constraints imposed by the stylized patterns that reflect technical progress in each sector and country.

Through the process of construction of scenarios, the modeller may enjoy some room to increase the 'policy space'. Facing skyrocketing price rises of energy, for example, the model signals that production of energy at the pace determined *on the current given conditions* cannot increase at the rate required by the economic growth target and therefore growth has to be sacrificed. However, there remain two kinds of alternatives than simply accepting cutting down growth expectations (thus accepting either unemployment in the USA or growth below socially desirable rates in the developing world). Both sets of alternatives call for decisive policy action to overcome the mentioned given conditions, and, for the world as a whole, require policy coordination as well. One set of alternatives revolve around demand and the other about supply (of energy, in this example).

On energy demand, it ought to be observed that the pattern of demand captured by the model encompasses a variety of country experiences over time. However, energy resource-constrained countries, with some regularity advanced countries among them, have shown sustained periods of dramatic increases of energy efficiency per unit of output. Likewise, in practically every country different patterns of energy efficiency can be observed, with some periods yielding significantly better outcomes than others. Such increases beyond the pattern that determines current given conditions for the world as a whole are real. It seems legitimate to assume, in a model simulation, that improvements of a similar degree, even if not fully, could be achieved for the world as a whole. For that to happen it will be important to capture from the historical data (and subsequently replicate in the simulation) the factors that have probably triggered such improvements. On energy efficiency it seemed clear that capital deepening plus considerable injections of public-sector investment and research in technology were crucial.

Likewise, for energy supply, there are clear instances in some countries and periods where the production of energy has increased significantly and not because the discovery of new oil reservoirs, for example. In other words, there exist known cases of significant increases of non-fossil fuel energy production, like France, Brazil and other countries that increased production of either nuclear, biomass or electric energy in the aftermath of the oil crisis of the 1970s. Like in cases of improvements in energy efficiency, it can be traced that such success stories required injections of public investment above those of today standards. Moreover, as noted by the International Labour Organization (2008), efforts towards energy efficiency and renewable energy production can be prodigious generators of new jobs. Finally, as noted above, capital-endowed countries, as well as those with respectable advances in research, have a tremendous potential to grow by new investments geared to overcome natural resource constraints by greater efficiency and more sophisticated production systems.

In sum, the simulations with the CAM discussed below represent, first, a growth scenario constrained by supply bottlenecks in energy and food and raw materials expressed by staggering price changes. Such bottlenecks are deemed to kick off in a more dramatic way than the supply shock on employment presumed to emerge in Freeman's work. Yet an alternative scenario is presented that encompasses an international policy-coordinated effort of rescuing from the historic experience the success stories of the past that would allow developing countries embarked in fast growth to generate the global demand for goods, and the impetus for innovation that would maintain growth of employment in the north as well. While fast growth in India and China would require some sector diversification towards manufacturing, they could not avoid devoting more attention to production of food, raw materials and energy. Likewise, continuing 'full-employment' growth in the advanced countries could be achieved by complementing production across sectors to satisfy the growing global demand triggered by India and China, as well as intensifying efforts in areas that will prove to be essential in a world convergence scenario: new technologies towards efficiency of utilization of energy and raw materials, as well as towards increased production from renewable sources by dramatic improvements in new technologies.

## Assessing the model simulation results

Results from two simulations using the CAM are reported below. The first simulation assumes that current patterns continue without significant policy intervention ('business as usual'). The second simulation proposes socially desirable growth targets for China and India. China would grow at a long-term rate of 11% per annum (about the trend rate over the recent period) and India at 9% per annum; that is, the rate achieved during the past three years.[11] In the dynamics of the model, such growth rates are partly policy-driven. Increases in public investment and industrial policy cause a positive synergy with private-sector activity and contribute to a relative improvement in market shares for manufactures in the world market. For the world as a whole, manufacturing activity grows and thus in absolute terms manufacturing production in ACs also grows to partly accommodate the increased demand in China and India. None of these results prove to be disruptive, partly because of the saving/investment conditions and growth patterns from which these countries part, and partly because the policies in place help to alleviate resource constraints as explained further below.

The relevant features of the 'business as usual' scenario, which will yield average rates of growth of 5.5% in India and 8.5% in China, are as follows:

(a) Without policy intervention, the current patterns point to a continuation of global imbalances in which astronomic current account deficits in the USA will be matched by rapidly rising surpluses in other developed regions, with oil exporters showing the most dramatic rises. Exporters in primary commodities (like the Latin American region) will show surpluses as well, while China's surplus will start to decline as pressure on resources increase.

(b) These patterns are untenable. Firstly, for reasons that have started to emerge in the current financial crisis: credit-driven excesses of spending over income leads to the accumulation of unsustainable debts and thus are prone to crises, as noted earlier when discussing stock-flow regularities.[12] Secondly, the pressure on resources, particularly on energy but on primary products as well, is so great that, under current production and utilization patterns, prices will escalate (see Figure 3). This outcome will have severe terms of trade and inflation implications for all. First, the rapid rising of such prices relative to the price of manufactures will be a

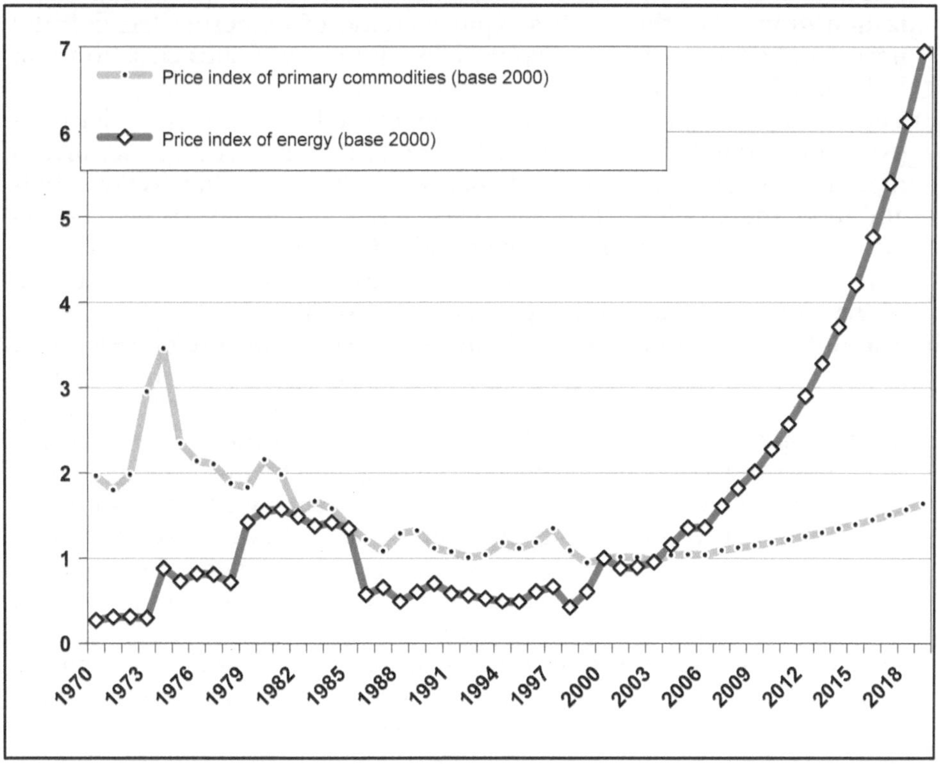


FIGURE 3. Estimated evolution of international prices of commodities and energy under a 'business as usual' scenario.

disincentive for countries in the developing world to industrialize. Second, such rises will hit severely the ACs, thus eroding the benefits of tamed world inflation that was argued above is a significant to avoid contractionary policies in ACs.

(c) In essence, even if the model simulation shows that the binding supply constraints emerge from natural resource scarcity under current production techniques, this result could be taken to be in a similar direction to Professor Freeman's hesitations about disruptions in labour markets caused by a continuing rapid growth of China and India.

Meanwhile, the alternative scenario is constructed on the premises exposed above; that is, China and India have high rates of growth justified on socially necessary objectives, while decisive concerted policy action is in place to match the growth of global demand with increased supply and efficiency of use of energy and food and raw materials to avoid a perverse effects of continuing global imbalances and skyrocketing international prices of energy and primary products. The scenario yields the following characteristics:

(d) China and India industrialize at a fast pace: China follows the pattern consolidated over the past decade, while India accelerates its industrialization drive. Together with a rapid increase of domestic demand, the impetus of exports of manufactures allow for growth rates close to 9% in India and 11% in China.

(e) The tremendous pressure on resources caused by such sustained rates over time requires these countries to increase public and private investment in primary commodity and energy sectors. Regarding raw materials and food, these policies manage to accelerate production as well as efficiency of use, replicating success periods of about five years in their past. On energy, the main effort by both countries is on efficiency use, but China will partially accelerate production as well.

(f) The rest of the world also contributes to alleviate pressure on resources. Most critically, major emerging economies that have a relevant weight in the global production of energy and primary resources will contribute significantly by improvements in efficiency of production. Improvements in energy production are assumed to be triggered by investments in non-fossil fuel sources.[13] Efficiency achievements are by no means outside historic periods of similar accomplishments and they are assumed to be supported by technology transfers and new investments in advanced countries. It is in these areas where developed countries find a prominent specialization and a space to preserve full employment.

(g) Thanks to the intensification of investments in these new areas and the exports of goods, services and technology that these imply, the USA experiences a slow reduction of its current account deficit.

(h) Moreover, the USA and other developed regions (Japan and other developed countries including Europe) will not be affected by significantly slower growth (their growth rates will be around 2.5%). The relatively more moderate growth in the USA throughout the initial years of this simulation results from a combination of reduced domestic absorption and real exchange rate depreciation that are both necessary to correct its external imbalance. Since such a depreciation turns out to be against all regions, the exchange rate appreciation of world regions drives the relatively moderate growth performance in those regions. This is one of the factors for the slowdown in ACs (exacerbated by the high impact of the international multiplier among these countries), but not the industrialization of India and China. Other developing regions will appear to be somehow, even if not significantly, affected. This is because global shifts in energy and primary resource production and demand do not allow such countries picking up rising terms of trade. Inevitably, while pressure on resources is resolved by greater efficiency, the scope for all developing countries to grow at fast pace relies on following more aggressive industrialization paths, perhaps similar to those postulated here for China and India. A model simulation of this kind is beyond the scope of this paper.

(i) The scenario improves measures of international income distribution as well as distribution of manufacturing exports, particularly to the extent that the most populated countries of the world sustain high growth rates by manufacturing. From this perspective, it is a win–win story.

We present plots to illustrate the outcomes of this scenario compared with the baseline. The first three sets (Figures 4–6) show the patterns of economic growth, the current account and the balance of manufactures. Taking together, these figures illustrate the main tenor of this paper; namely, sustained and acceptable growth patterns for all can be made compatible with smooth correction of global imbalances and a continuing industrialization of developing countries without 'taking away' from advanced economies. Worthy of notice is that the adjustment of the otherwise rising current account deficit of the USA requires only a partial and momentary slowdown in the USA. Meanwhile, surpluses in oil and commodity exporting countries will also shrink; and while these blocs will improve their balance of manufactures, such are not so strong as to fully substitute the growth observed in the 'business as usual' scenario.

Finally, the last set of plots (Figures 7 and 8) highlight the argument posed above about natural resource constraints and price escalations. In the alternative scenario the otherwise unsustainable rise in the price of energy is tamed. Meanwhile, there is an imperceptible rise in the price of primary products and food. Such patterns, in all respects sustainable, result from the additional efforts postulated in this scenario by which the fast-growing China and India are required to improve efficiency of use, while the characteristically net exporters of energy and raw materials manage to increase efficiency of production, aided in turn by technological investments in the advanced countries, which turns out to be a meaningful complementary source of revenues.

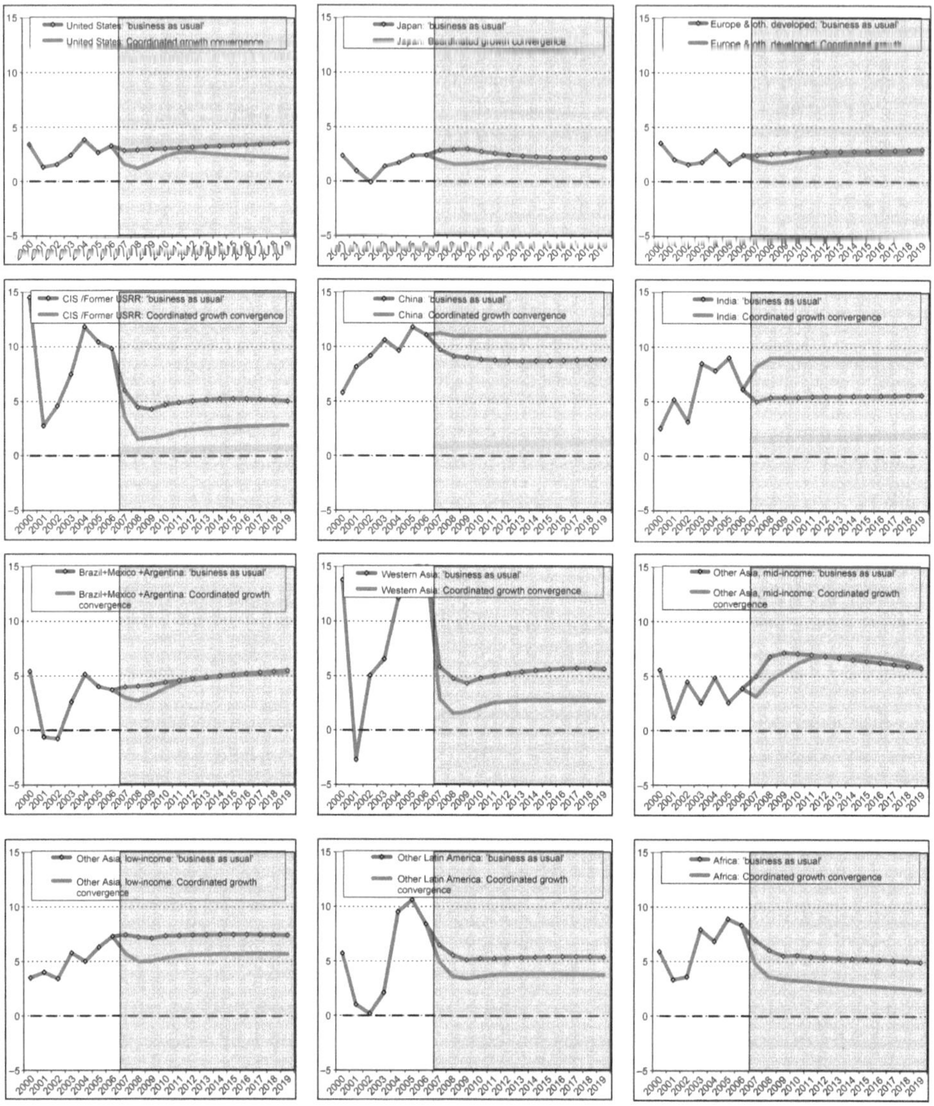


FIGURE 4. Annual percentage growth of income in all blocs: 'business as usual' and 'coordinated growth convergence' scenarios.

*Note*: Shadowed area indicates simulation period.

To sum up, a scenario based on a sustained and rapid industrialization in China and India requires postulating that India and China as well as other countries pursue strong programmes of achieving energy efficiency and make the necessary investments for more efficient production of primary products. By allowing ACs to benefit from technological transfers and improvements in their weaker external balances (manufacturing, energy or primary products), the postulated high growth rates for India

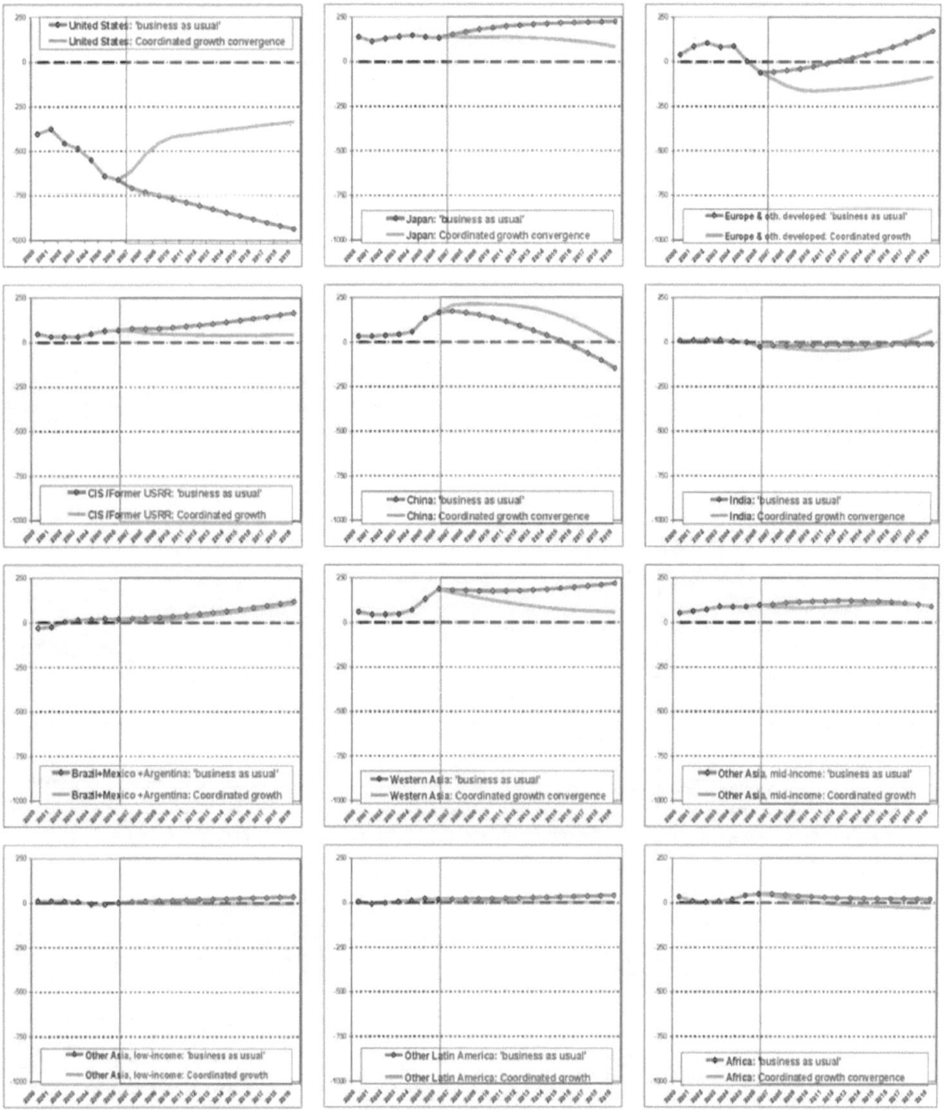


FIGURE 5. The current account: 'business as usual' and 'coordinated growth convergence' scenarios (billion US dollars).
*Note*: Area to right of vertical line indicates simulation period

and China can be made compatible with sustained G7 growth rates of about 2.5%. Thus, while Freeman is right in his apprehension about conflict between the interests of workers in the North and those in the South, this is for a different set of reasons and a possible resolution of such a conflict by concerted action could help to overcome such a conflict of interest.

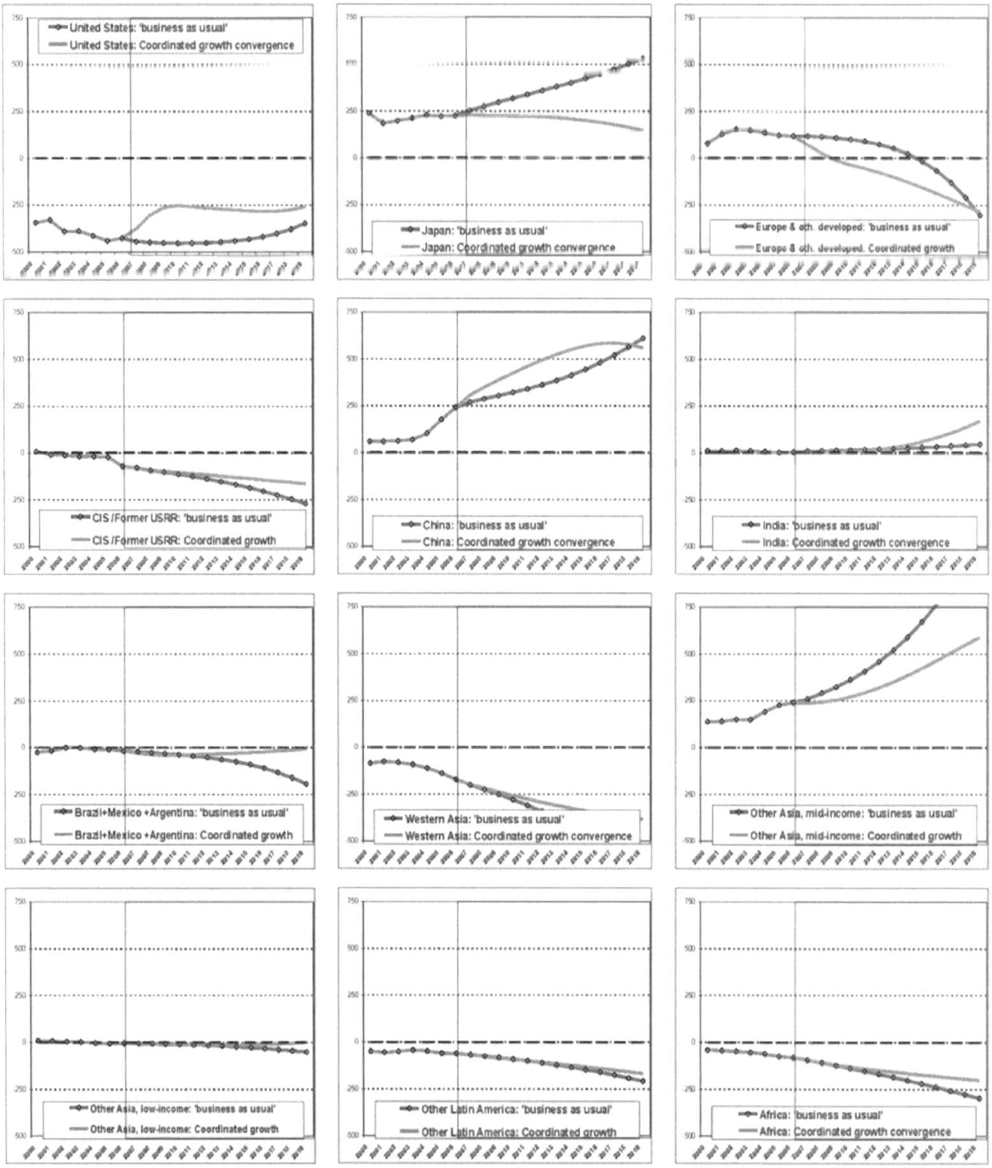


FIGURE 6. The balance of manufactures: 'business as usual' and 'coordinated growth convergence' scenarios (billion US dollars).

*Note*: Area to right of vertical line indicates simulation period

## Implications for North–South workers' solidarity of the current crisis and re-statement of our central conclusion

This paper has considered the effects of fast growth of India and China on the long-term growth of output and employment in the US economy up to 2007. It has not considered the current global financial crisis. While the sustained pace of economic growth based on increasing production capacity

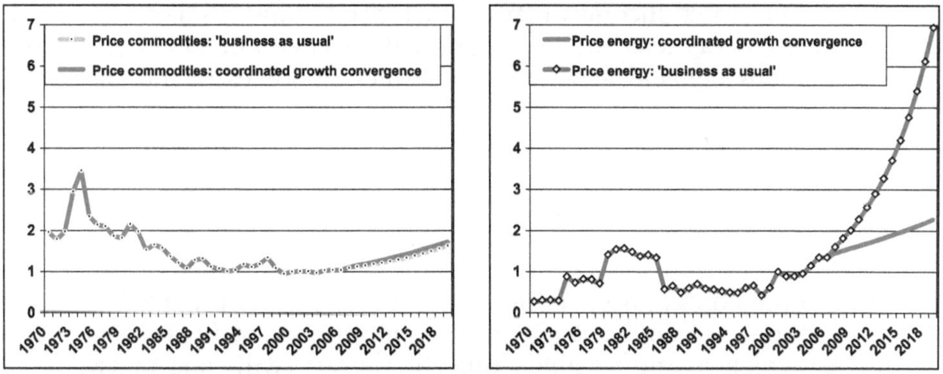


FIGURE 7. Price indices of commodities and energy: 'business as usual' and 'coordinated growth convergence' scenarios.

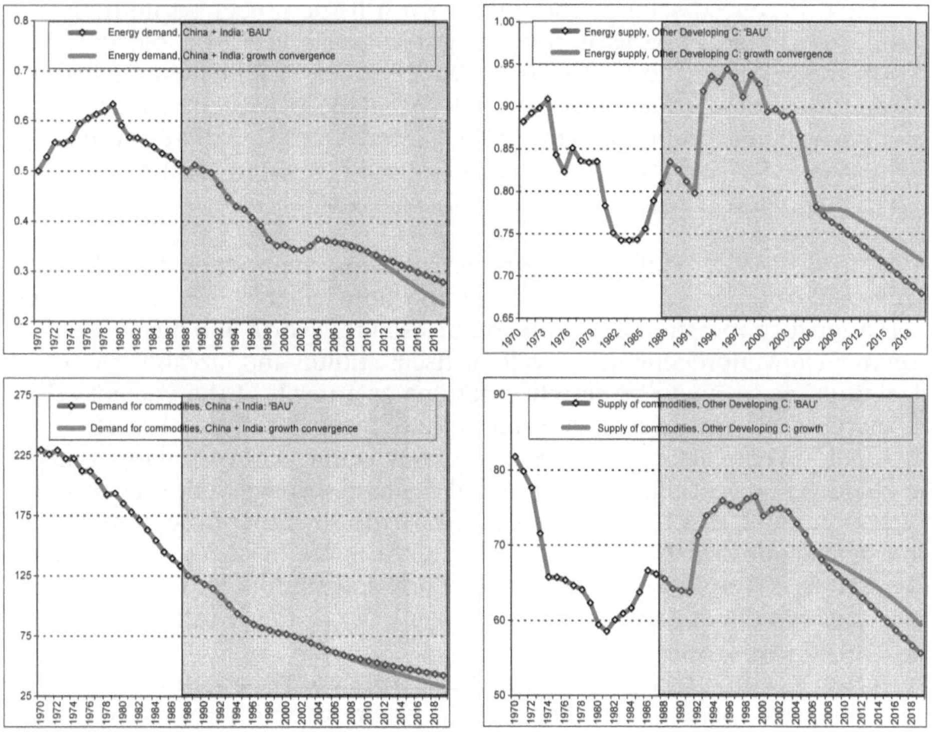


FIGURE 8. Improvements in production and use of energy and primary commodities: 'business as usual' and 'coordinated growth convergence' scenarios.

*Note*: Shadowed area indicates simulation period. Energy efficiency = tons of oil equivalent per dollar million of output. Primary resource efficiency = dollars at base year prices per $1000 of income.

and generation of real incomes that characterized countries like China and India in the past was real, such developments needed not to occur on the back of fictitious demand generated by financial bubbles in the advanced countries, especially the USA and the UK. An inherent global imbalance of debt-driven demand can, despite its dangerous accumulation, lead to increased world industrial production, but only for as long as such a precarious inertia does not come to an end when the potential for debt deflation and unemployment surges, as noted nearly 40 years ago by N. Kaldor:

> The continued excess of dollar outlays over receipts provided the rest of the world with a steady increase in international purchasing power which in turn enabled other countries (with one or two conspicuous exceptions!) to reap the benefit of continued and accelerating export-led growth. (1971, p. 61)
>
> [...] What went wrong? So long as countries preferred the benefits of fast growth and increasing competitiveness to the cost of part-financing the United States deficit (or what comes to the same thing, preferred selling more goods even if they received nothing more than bits of paper in return), and so long as a reasonable level of prosperity in the United States (in terms of employment levels and increases of real income) could be made consistent with the increasing uncompetitiveness of the United States [...] there was no reason why any major participant should wish to disturb this arrangement. (1971, p. 63)[14]

Our analysis is built on the premise that the mentioned global imbalances could not be sustained and that the only reliable way out required international cooperation between countries in the North and the South with agreement on unprecedented levels of fiscal stimuli and sizeable monetary relaxations, as seems to be slowly emerging as a result of the current crisis. It is therefore possible that, as a result of these measures, the real world economy could eventually experience a relatively stable recovery with some of the characteristics outlined in our global demand management scenario. But it is also possible that the damage caused by the severity of the crisis would leave many countries in both the North and the South in a truly impaired situation. Thus, severe and lasting demand-side constraints and the resulting mass unemployment may test workers' solidarity in the North and South as much as do supply-side constraints.

Yet our central conclusion could be re-instated. We postulate that India and China have socially necessary high growth rates, and so by extension do other developing countries not considered in this exercise. We resist the proposition that such is incompatible with the full employment growth rates in advanced countries. Our critique of such proposition may have an ethical connotation but is essentially based on theoretical and empirical findings. We find that even at current rates of growth there are impending conflicts over natural resources between India and China, on the one hand, and ACs on the other. Such conflicts seem to be more binding than the instability of labour markets enounced by Professor Freeman. We differ not only on what is the binding constraint, but also on what is the best way of resolving it. We conclude that, with technical progress and international cooperation to facilitate that the growth of demand is matched by more efficient use and production of energy and commodities, the problem is solvable. We are hopeful that international collective action on the lines currently being proposed by the world community around the 'G192' initiative could be taken to operational level.[15] Such a vision not only strives for full employment in the North but also seeks to ensure that China and India should complete their long delayed industrial revolution.

## Acknowledgments

We want to thank Francis Cripps for the production of the version of the model used for simulations, as well as for his useful comments. Comments by an anonymous referee helped to strengthen the argument in significant ways. The usual disclaimer applies.

## Notes

1 Integration is referred to as the process that is taking place under 'current globalization', which consists of free trade, free capital movements and domestic labour market flexibility (instead of free international movement of labour).

2 Many scholars would argue that these two countries should have had their industrial revolutions more than 100 years ago but they were thwarted in this endeavour by colonialism and imperialism.

3 For a recent review of this literature, see Singh (2007).

4 As noted earlier, this issue is discussed at some length in Singh (2007).

5 The model of the Cambridge Economic Policy Group. See also Cripps (1978, 1979) and Cripps *et al.* (1979, 2007). At the time of drafting this paper (early 2007), CAM version 2 was used. Subsequently version 3 was released in 2008, which adds more sophistication on the policy side. An experiment with such a version did not show significant differences with findings of version 2 in as far as the hypotheses of this paper are concerned.

6 A more elaborated exposition that lists the main model equations is available from the authors.

7 The straight-jacket of accounting consistency on the basis of which the model is constructed is preserved through model solutions, and thus all macro-economic variables, including exchange rates, are adjusted to comply with global identities by distributing the 'closures' in linear fashion (as in 'linear expenditure system functions').

8 For an exhaustive elaboration of this point in a fully specified macro-economic model, see Godley and Lavoie (2007). Godley and Cripps (1983) introduce this notion in an aggregate macro-economic setting.

9 The adjustment takes place over time with a regularity that is captured econometrically and is eventually represented by the introduction of lags in the expenditure function. The empirical determination of the lags incorporate by necessity the influence that financing has in allowing imbalances to persist to a certain degree.

10 An anonymous referee has correctly noted that the patterns of price escalations of energy are not the same as those of food and raw materials in the CAM simulations. This may well

reflect in part the fact that both kinds of products face different patterns of evolution of demand (e.g. 'Engel' curves), and in part the fact that embedded technical progress functions in the production of energy may face constraints that are either more difficult or take more time to resolve.

11 Fast economic growth in India and China is a social necessity to allow shifting hundred of millions of people from farms to industry. In India there is the additional compulsion of providing jobs for a growing labour force. The rise of the Indian growth rate to nearly 9% per annum during the past three years is internally sustainable as it is based on a trend increase in the country's saving and investment rates from about 25% to well above 35%.

12 Our simulations were run without hindsight knowledge of the current global recession. It is by now know that the crisis emerged towards the second half of 2007 as a consequence of sustained falls in house prices, which shook the subprime mortgage market, and turned severe in 2008 when the largest financial institutions in the USA and Europe started to be hit by failures in the markets for securities and other derivatives. While it is not the intention of this paper to explore the various theories and beliefs about the crisis, it is worth pointing out that both the process of financialization and deregulation of the global economy and the ensuing crisis that exploded in 2008 were not independent of the accumulation of unsustainable global imbalances captured earlier in the dynamics of the model and its core 'stock-flow' adjustment process.

13 According to the Intergovernmental Panel on Climate Change (2007) *Fourth Assessment Synthesis Report*, Section 4, significant improvements in energy production from non-fossil fuel sources can be achieved in the medium term, to the extent of actually reducing global carbon dioxide emissions even in a steadily growing economy.

14 The authors wish to thank Jane d'Arista who drew their attention to this article.

15 The United Nations Conference on the World Financial and Economic Crisis and its Impact on Development (New York, 24–26 June 2009) coded 'G192' to stress its more global and inclusive approach to international policy than the G20 or the G8.

## References


Bailey, M.N. and Lawrence, R.Z. (2004) 'What happened to the great US job machine? The role of trade and electronic offshoring', *Brookings Papers on Economic Activity*, 2, pp. 201–260.

Baumol, W. (2002) *The Free Market Innovation Machine: Analysing the Growth Miracle of Capitalism,* Princeton University Press, Princeton, N.J.

Cripps, F. (1978) 'Causes of growth and recession in world trade', *Cambridge Economic Policy Review.* Cambridge Economic Policy Group, March, University of Cambridge, Department of Applied Economics, pp. 37–43.

Cripps, F. (1979) 'Historical data and projections for world trade. Appendix A', *Cambridge Economic Policy Review.* Cambridge Economic Policy Group, April, University of Cambridge, Department of Applied Economics, pp. 45–55.

Cripps, F., Gudgin, G. and Rhodes, J. (1979) 'Technical manual of the CEPG model of world trade', *Cambridge Economic Policy Review. Cambridge Economic Policy Group,* June, University of Cambridge, Department of Applied Economics, Cambridge, pp. 1–70.

Cripps, F., Izurieta, A. and McKinley, T. (2007) 'Developing a global model for trade, finance and income distribution', *International Poverty Centre Technical Paper,* 1, pp. 1–27.

Dasgupta, S. and Singh, A. (2005) 'Will services be the new engine of economic growth in India?', *Development and Change Forum 2005,* 36(6).

Freeman, R.B. (1995) 'Are your wages set in Beijing?', *Journal of Economic Perspectives,* 9(3), pp. 15–32.

Freeman, R. B. (2005) 'What really ails Europe and America: the doubling of the global workforce', *The Globalist,* 3 June, [http://www.theglobalist.com/printStoryId.aspx?StoryId=4542], accessed 1 February 2010.

Godley, W. and Lavoie, M. (2007). *Monetary Economics: An Integrated Approach to Money, Income, Production and Wealth,* Palgrave MacMillan, New York.

Godley, W. and Cripps, F. (1983) *Macroeconomics,* Oxford University Press, Oxford.

Intergovernmental Panel on Climate Change (2007) *Climate Change 2007: Synthesis of the Fourth Assessment Report,* IPPC, Valencia.

International Labour Organization (2008) *Green Jobs. Facts and Figures,* [www.ilo.org/global/about_the_ilo/media_and_the_public_information/factsheets/lang-en/docName-WCMS_098484/index.htm].

International Monetary Fund (2006) *World Economic Outlook: Globalization and Inflation,* April, IMF, Washington, DC.

Jorgenson, D. (1990) 'Productivity and economic growth', in E. Berndt and J. Triplett (Eds), *Fifty Years of Economic Measurement: The Jubilee of the Conference on Research in Income and Wealth, Vol. 54,* Chicago, University of Chicago Press, 1990, pp. 19-118.

Jorgenson, D. (2001) 'Information technology and the U.S. economy', *American Economic Review,* 90(1), pp. 1-32.

Jorgenson, D. and Vu, K. (2007) 'Information Technology and the world growth resurgence', *German Economic Review,* 8(2), pp. 122-145.

Jorgenson, D.W., Ho, M.S. and Stiroh, K.J. (2005) 'The end of the boom', *Investors Chronicle,* 4 February, p. 39.

Kaldor, N. (1971) 'The dollar crisis', *The Times,* 6, 7 and 8 September . Reproduced in Kaldor, N. (1978) *Further Essays on Applied Economics,* Holmes & Meier Publishers, New York, pp. 60-73.

Kelkar, V. (2004) 'India: on the growth turnpike', *Mimeo: Narayanan Oration,* April, National Institute of Economics and Business, Australian National University.

Lazonik, William (2007) 'Corporate governance, innovative enterprise, and economic development, in Ha-Joon Chang (Ed.), *Institutional Change and Economic Development,* United Nations University, Tokyo, p. 115.

Martin, W.E. and Rowthorn, R. (2005) 'Accounting for stability', *CESinfo Economic Studies,* 51(4), pp. 649-696.

Overholt, W.H. (2005) 'China and globalisation', *RAND Corporation Testimony Series,* May.

Rajan, R. (2006) 'Foreword', in *World Economic Outlook: Globalization and Inflation,* April, International Monetary Fund, Washington, DC., pp. xi-xiii.

Sayers, R.S. (1965) *The Vicissitudes of an Expert Economy: Britain since 1880,* University of Sydney Press, Sydney.

Sen, A. and Himanshu (2004) 'Poverty and inequality in India', *Economic and Political Weekly,* 39(39), Special Article, September, pp. 4361-4375.

Sichel, Daniel E. (2004) 'Comment on Bailey and Lawrence (2004)', *Brookings Papers on Economic Activity,* 2.

Singh, A. (1977) 'UK industry and the world economy: a case of deindustrialization?', *Cambridge Journal of Economics,* 1(2), pp. 113-136.

Singh, A. (2005) 'Special and differential treatment, the multilateral trading system and economic development in the 21st century', in Kevin P. Gallagher (Ed.), *Putting Development First,* Zed Books, London, 2005, pp. 233-263.

Singh, A. (2007) 'Globalisation, industrial Revolutions in India and China and labour markets in advanced countries: implications for national and international economic policy', *Working Paper No. 81,* International Labour Office, Geneva.

Srinivasan, T.N. (2003) 'Commentary 2.1. on Singh, Nirvikar. The impact of international labour standards: a survey of economic theory', in B. Kaushik, H. Horn, L. Roman, and J. Shapiro (Eds), *International Labour Standards, History, theory and policy options,* Wiley-Blackwell, Oxford, pp. 182-186.

UNCTAD (1995) *Trade and Development Report,* United Nations, Geneva.

UNDP (2005) *Human Development Report 2005,* United Nations, New York.

# *The Crisis of Globalization as an Opportunity to Create a Fairer World*

ROB VOS
*Rob Vos is Director of the Development Policy and Analysis Division, the core economic research unit of the United Nations Department of Economic and Social Affairs, USA*

**Abstract** After having reviewed trends leading to greater international inequality, this article argues for a more stable international financial system allowing developing countries greater participation in international trade combined with full exploitation of their development potential. As emerging economies tap deeper into global supply chains, outsourcing of jobs will influence employment and there is need for a more transparent, coherent and balanced framework at the global level. Also a more balanced pattern of domestic demand will only be achieved with rising wages rather than through increased debt levels. Economies need continuously to increase their skill and knowledge base in order to successfully integrate themselves into the global production process. Active labour market policies (including skill development) should be strengthened to better prepare workers for the future job market. When temporary dislocation of workers cannot be avoided, appropriate social protection measures provide worker security. In all cases, the benefits that global production can bring should be properly weighted against the costs, and these costs can only be minimized through active involvement of all the major actors.

## Introduction

In 2008, an unprecedented although short-lived period of broad-based global economic growth came to an end. During 2002 and 2008, developing countries averaged about 5% of per-capita Gross Domestic Product (GDP) growth per year, outpacing by far welfare increases in developed countries. Also many of the poorest countries witnessed strong per-capita income growth (Figure 1), leading some observers to make the contradictory claims that globalization was effectively working to enhance living standards worldwide

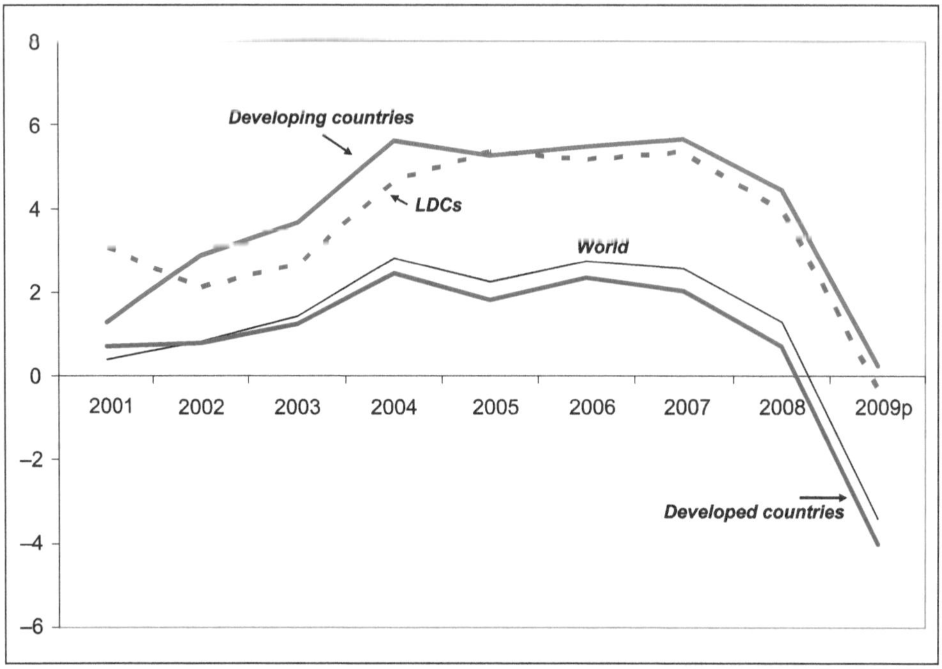


FIGURE 1. Growth of real GDP per capita by major country groups, 2001–2009.
*Note*: LDCs, least developed countries.
*Source*: United Nations Department of Economic and Social Affairs, database of World Economic Situation and Prospects 2009. Figures for 2009 are according to pessimistic forecast of 2009 World Economic Situation and Prospects (WESP) (see United Nations, 2009).

and that some kind of 'decoupling' was taking place, with strong endogenous growth in developing countries having become less sensitive to downturns in developed economies.[1]

As the world economy entered into its worst crisis since the Great Depression of the 1930s, both claims were proven utterly wrong. The present crisis emerged on the back of an intrinsically unsustainable global growth pattern. This pattern was characterized by strong consumer demand in the United States, funded by easy credit and booming house prices. Far-reaching financial deregulation facilitated a massive and unfettered expansion of new financial instruments, such as securitized sub-prime mortgage lending, sold on financial markets worldwide. This pattern of growth enabled strong export growth and booming commodity prices, benefiting many developing countries. Growing US deficits in this period were financed by increasing trade surpluses in China, Japan and other countries accumulating large foreign-exchange reserves and willing to buy dollar-denominated assets, and fuelling mounting global financial imbalances and indebtedness of financial institutions, businesses and households. In some countries, both developed and developing, domestic financial debt has risen fourfold or fivefold as a share of national income since the early 1980s. This rapid explosion in debt was made possible by the shift from a traditional 'buy-and-hold' banking model to a dynamic 'originate-to-sell' trading model (or 'securitization'). Leverage ratios of some institutions went up to as high as 30, well above the ceiling of 10 generally imposed on deposit banks. In the context of a highly integrated global economy without adequate regulation and global governance structures, this risky pattern of financial expansion implied that the breakdown in one part of the system thus would also lead to failure elsewhere. It is this systemic failure we are witnessing today. The de-leveraging now underway has brought down established financial institutions and has led to the rapid evaporation of global liquidity affecting the real economy in developed countries, and developing countries are being hit through collapsing global trade, plunging commodity prices and reversals of capital flows, thus falsifying the 'decoupling' hypothesis.

Until September 2008, all parties seemed to benefit from the boom, particularly major financial institutions in developed countries, despite repeated warnings, such as those highlighted in the United Nations' *World Economic Situation and Prospects* (WESP), that mounting household, public-sector and financial-sector indebtedness in the United States and elsewhere, and reflected in wide global financial imbalances, would not be sustainable over time (see United Nations, 2006a, 2007a, 2008a, 2009). The interconnectedness of excessive risk-taking in financial markets with the problem of the global imbalances, vast dollar reserve accumulation (especially in parts of the developing world), volatile commodity prices, and declining trends in productive investment explain why this crisis is systemic and worldwide.

This global growth pattern dictated by the US consumer, the Chinese businessman and the international financier has produced very uneven and unbalanced results. Some big developing countries, notably China, India and some other emerging market economies, have seen strong growth accelerations. Most recently, low-income countries also saw substantial average welfare improvements, epitomizing what might be seen as the 'rise of the rest' (Amsden, 2001). Yet, the longer term growth trend has been one of sharply rising levels of income inequality (Figure 2).[2] The more recent, more broadly shared global growth took place in a context of increasing macroeconomic disequilibria fuelled by an ever-widening role of finance. The process of 'financialization' greased the global growth engine alright, but merely to a point of overheating to reveal the systemic mechanical flaws of the engine itself. Can this engine be fixed or would the objective of a more inclusive and sustainable globalization process be better served by replacing the engine with a new one? The remainder of this paper discusses some key aspects of the process of financialization of worldwide trade and investment, and gives some hints at some of the ingredients (no blueprint) for global and national policies that could help steer the world towards a fairer and more sustainable pattern of growth.

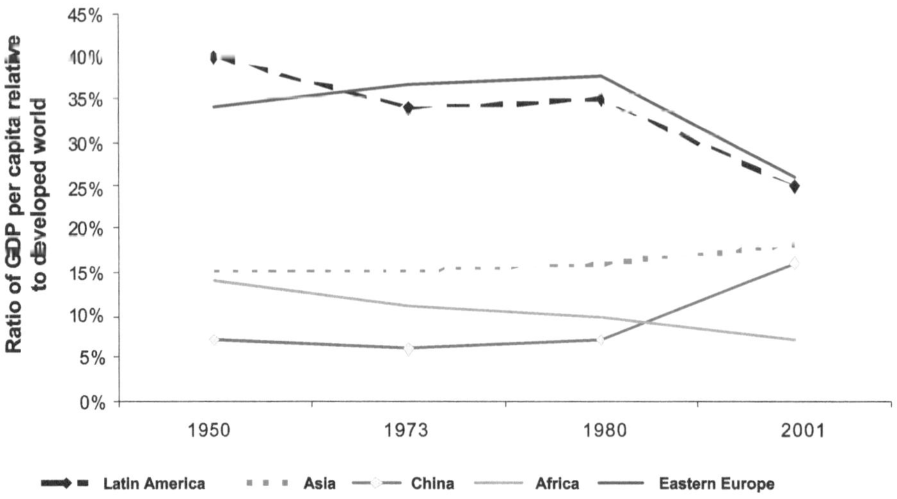


FIGURE 2. Rising global inequality and the rise of (some of) the rest.
*Source*: United Nations (2006a).

## The myth of the self-regulating market

The present crisis is also a crisis of the globalization paradigm advocating the virtues of fully liberalized commodity and financial markets. Indeed, the concept of the self-regulating market was the *idée fixe* of the late twentieth century. It was based on the belief that freeing markets would unleash the wealth creating forces of unrestricted competition and risk-taking, resulting in greater prosperity for all while achieving greater stability. A more flexible workforce, greater asset ownership and easier access to financial markets would help households respond better to market signals and smooth incomes as well as consumption over time. Greater economic and social security would naturally follow.

Pushing this idea was always a gamble. At least since Adam Smith, careful observers have understood that markets do not regulate themselves, but depend on an array of institutions, rules, regulations and norms that help moderate their more destructive impulses, mediate possible tensions and conflicts that normally arise and facilitate peaceful bargaining over how the gains and losses from risk-taking activities are distributed. The pioneers of the post-1945 mixed economy were persuaded by the experience of the inter-war years that unregulated markets were more prone to self-destruction than self-regulation. Idle tools, wasted wealth, wretchedness and, ultimately, political strife proved too high a price to pay for stable money and flexible markets. Their stated goal was to achieve full employment through active macro-economic management, public goods provided through a larger fiscal base and markets would become a more dependable source of wealth creation through an appropriate mixture of incentives and regulation. Moreover, given the close economic ties among countries, the new consensus would have an international dimension to ensure that trade and capital flows complemented these objectives.

Dismantling the checks and balances that emerged with this consensus has proceeded at an uneven pace among the advanced countries and has often been more enthusiastically embraced in the developing world and in transition economies, where 'shock therapies' promised rapid and positive effects. As part of a global trend, many of the stresses and burdens of unregulated financial and commodity markets have been unloaded on to individuals and households, and with diminished or only limited offsetting government responses. This has been described, with reference to the United States, as the 'great risk shift', but is also characteristic of shifting patterns in global trade and finance.

## Emergence of a debt-dependent trading system

Over the past 20 years, the volume of trade has grown on average by 9% per annum with particularly rapid growth in the period 2002–2007, averaging 14.5% per annum and faster still in developing countries. Four significant forces have helped shape the pattern of international trade in this period: the rise of export-orientated industrializing developing countries; the growth of intra-firm trade in global supply chains (itself made possible by new information and communication technologies and expanded capacity and skill in developing countries); rapid trade liberalization for goods and services, embodied in both multilateral and bilateral agreements; and the explosion of unregulated financial flows. These factors are often treated separately, but in a globalized world they need to be seen as closely interconnected.

At one end of the global supply chains are mostly low-income countries, which continue to be highly reliant on more traditional export sectors. Obtaining sustained gains from trade remains a challenge for these countries. In this sense, the contrast between East Asia and other regions is striking. The share of primary products, resource-based and low-technology manufacturing in the total exports of East Asia declined from 76% in 1980 to 35% in 2005. China alone reduced its share from 93% in 1985 to 44% in 2005. Other regions have been less successful in transforming the structure of their production for exports. South American countries still rely on primary products and simple manufactures (around 78% of exports in 2005, down from around 90% in 1983). In Africa, the concentration of exports in low value-added products is even greater (83% in 2005). Volatility in commodity prices strongly influences the business cycle in these countries. Strongly booming world market prices of primary products, especially from 2006, and their subsequent collapse from the start of the global financial crisis, have made this fate once again painfully clear. Figure 3 shows that long-term growth rates of countries at the lower end of the global value chain are well below those at the higher end and hence have been a source of perpetuating global inequality.

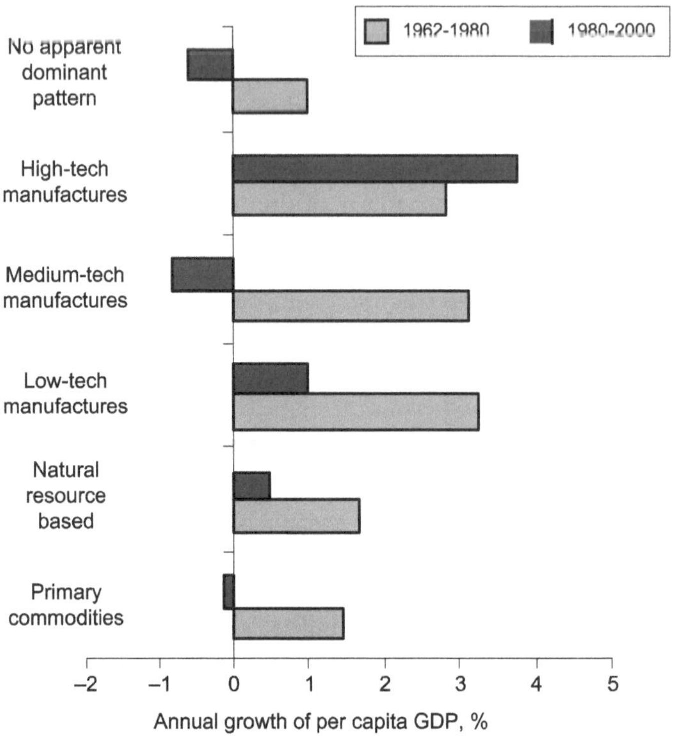


FIGURE 3. Trade specialization and long-term economic growth, 1962–2000.
*Source*: United Nations (2006b).

Creating more dynamic gains from trade also remains a challenge for many developing countries that did manage to diversify into exports of seemingly 'high-tech' manufactures. In many cases, however, this apparent switch to high-tech exports hides the fact that many countries are really engaged in mostly low-tech assembly activities rather than exporting the final good itself. In many cases, production takes place within enclaves, connected though trade and foreign direct investment flows to other parts of a corporate supply chain, but with only limited ties to the domestic economy.

The spread of intra-firm exchanges through global value chains explains much of the indicated growth of world trade, albeit with the final product still destined for a small number of markets, dominated by the United States. However, given that wages have, since the 1980s been largely stagnant in the United States and sluggish elsewhere, this growth of trade has coincided with rising levels of household debt and dwindling domestic savings in a number of large industrial economies along with ever-widening global imbalances (see United Nations, 2006a, 2007a, 2008a).

These shifting patterns of international trade have been closely associated with a new global business strategy adopted by many larger firms in the industrialized countries, which emphasizes a focus on 'core competence' and a greater attention to shareholder value (Millberg and Schöller, 2008). This focus has driven firms to break up the production process and take advantage of low-cost offshore production for all but the highest value added aspects of production. At the extreme this has created manufacturing firms that do no manufacturing at all, such as The Gap or Dell Computers. The focus on shareholder value has meant an increase in the use of profits for dividend payments, stock buybacks and mergers and acquisitions.

In this context, offshoring has served the new business model in two ways. First, it has led to cost reductions and thus increased mark-ups over cost, despite the fact that firms face stiff price competition in product markets. Figure 4 shows how since the 1970s the share of corporate profits in value added in most developed countries have risen to new highs in the most recent upward swing of the business cycle.

Second, by limiting the scope of the firm, and especially its domestic operations, offshoring has reduced investment needs, increasing its ability to return value to shareholders. This has supported a 'financialization of

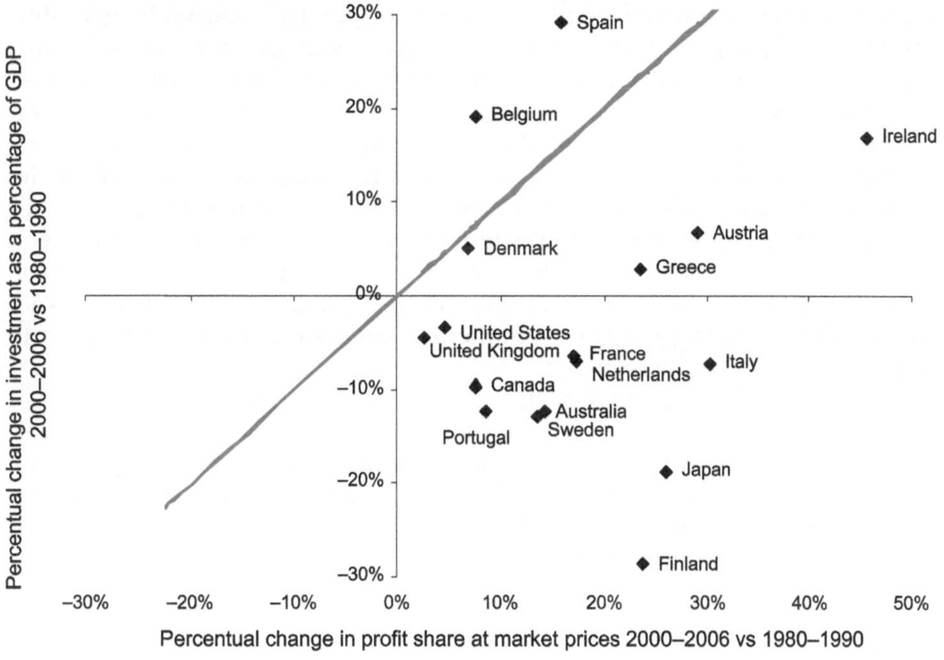


FIGURE 4. Profits and fixed investment in developed economies, 1980s versus 2000s.
*Source*: United Nations (2008b, figure II.8). Estimates are United Nations Department of Economic and Social Affairs' calculations based on AMECO (the annual macro-economic database) of the European Commission's Directorate General for Economic and Financial Affairs.
*Note:* The profit share is defined as 100% minus the wage share, where the wage share is defined as the compensation per employee as a percentage of GDP at market prices. Investment is defined as private sector gross fixed capital formation as a percentage of GDP at market prices.

non-financial corporations' in many industrialized countries, oftentimes at the expense of productive investment (as also shown in Figure 1), while imports from developing countries were steadily rising.

This interplay of financial and corporate dynamics has had far-reaching implications for the real economy, particularly in advanced countries. In many countries, the rise of the financial sector has coincided with the introduction of more flexible hiring practices and less secure employment conditions. Episodes of exceptionally rapid economic expansion driven by speculative financial flows have brought periods of growing prosperity, but have often ended very suddenly in recession or longer periods of slow growth. Moreover, losses of investment, employment and income incurred during recessions have not fully recovered when the economy turns up.

All of these factors together spell considerable income and job insecurity, even under conditions of relatively strong expansion. Also, in the majority of developed countries, growth of wages has not kept pace with labour productivity, resulting in greater income inequality.

Managing trade pressures are, however, not solely the problem of policy-makers in advanced countries. Indeed, the flip side of offshoring jobs by multinational companies is often low value-added and unstable assembly jobs in developing countries. Many of these countries have substantially increased the volume of their international trade over the past two decades, but not necessarily earning more from doing so, thanks to a combination of greater capital mobility, heightened competition in labour-intensive activities and flexible markets. All too often, such production still takes place in enclaves with the shallowest of linkages with the rest of the economy. This can leave them exposed to unexpected shocks if firms decide to run down or shift the activity. These problems are now exacerbated with the global economic recession, including the accelerated decline in world trade and sharp reversal in foreign direct investments that started in the last quarter of 2008.

Policy-makers have long sought ways to manage international trade in order to maximize the benefits and limit the costs. Success cases have never relied solely on trade liberalization. Offshoring in the advanced countries and trade shocks in the developing world point to a worrying shift in underlying macro-economic conditions and influence of global financial factors that has made success all the more difficult.

## Unleashing and crashing global finance

In parallel with shift trade patterns, the weight and influence of financial markets, financial actors and financial institutions has increased dramatically. This manifested itself in a massive accumulation of financial assets and by a seemingly 'deep diversification' of the financial system through a variety of institutional innovations and introduction of new, then labelled as 'exotic', financial institutions, especially through the derivatives markets. These developments fed growing levels of debt in the household, corporate and public sectors. In some countries, domestic financial debt as a share of GDP has risen fourfold or fivefold since the early 1980s. This process of 'financialization', in turn, helped to entrench a singular and narrow macro-economic policy focus on fighting inflationary threats.

In the decades following 1945, the business cycle was mainly driven by investment and export demand and was underpinned by strong wage growth that fed into high levels of consumer spending. This was not always a stable process. Levels of volatility were often quite high, and wages, profits and tax revenues would often outpace productivity growth, leading to inflationary pressures, current account deficits and rising indebtedness. These signalled to policy-makers that action needed to be taken, oftentimes ending in cyclical downturn.

This pattern changed fundamentally during the 1990s, as debt, leverage, collateral value and expected asset prices became dominant drivers of the cycle. This exacerbated an already strong pro-cyclical stance of market agents. This could lead to self-inflating bubbles driven by expectations of rising asset prices, and by and large detached from improved prospects of real income gains or losses or of the value of the underlying real assets. Intrinsic to financial market behaviour, lenders and investors would tend to underestimate risks in the upswing and overestimate these in the downturn. These attitudes were fortified by the financial innovations through the derivatives markets that promised security against downside risks. This led to ever stronger fluctuations in asset prices: strong asset inflation and extended financial booms in the upswing, and steep asset deflation and financial collapses during the downswing. This was already visible during the crises in emerging markets of the 1990s, and such factors now turned a broad-based boom into a worldwide bust.

Financial booms give rise to lop-sided investment patterns. These investments often involve little more than rearranging existing assets through leveraged buyouts, stock buybacks and mergers and acquisitions, or are in sectors susceptible to speculative influences, such as property markets. Unlike earlier cycles, these booms have delivered few benefits in terms of rising wages and employment. However, increased access of households to credits has meant that consumer spending can increase, even with stagnant incomes, as (rising) levels of indebtedness substitute for (falling) household savings. But as balance sheets adopt smaller margins of safety, the system becomes more and more fragile.

The shift from an income-constrained to an asset-backed economy has been supported by the liberalization of international capital markets. Indeed, the links between domestic financial markets and capital flows are much stronger in developing countries, many of which opened their capital accounts prematurely in the 1990s.

These flows have been strongly pro-cyclical. Their effects are often transmitted through public-sector accounts, especially through the effects of available financing on government spending and through the effects of interest rates on the public debt service. But the stronger effects typically run through private spending and balance sheets. During booms, private-sector deficits and borrowing tend to rise and risky balance sheets accumulate riding on perceived 'success', typically seen to be reflected in low-risk premia and spreads. Reversals in such perceptions lead to a cut off from external financing and provoke sudden increases in the cost of borrowing, inducing downward adjustment.

The shift towards export-led strategies in the developing world has actually accentuated this pattern in many countries. The growing influence of financial calculation has meant that commodity price volatility operates in an even more exaggerated pro-cyclical manner, which is further amplified by pro-cyclical policies among others, by expanding fiscal expenditures during the boom and reducing spending when prices are down. The latter is reinforced by the conditionality linked to international financial assistance during crises, which involves orthodox, pro-cyclical macro-economic stabilization policy packages.

These financial dynamics have far–reaching implications for the real economy. Episodes of exceptionally rapid economic expansion driven by financial bubbles can bring periods of growing prosperity, but they can end very suddenly - leading to deep recessions or even longer periods of stagnation. Vulnerability to a sharp reversal of flows varies, but in many emerging markets it is often triggered by factors beyond the control of recipient countries, including shifts in monetary policies or the bursting of a housing and financial bubble in a major developed economy.

The suggestion that the growth of cross-border financial flows would trigger a greatly improved investment climate is belied by the global trend of weaker capita formation since the 1990s (Figure 5) and the increased volatility of investment relative to that of output. This applies to both developed and developing countries (Figure 6).

With the exception of South Asia, and despite a recent world-wide recovery, this heightened volatility has resulted in average rates of capital formation still well below those enjoyed in the 1970s. Infrastructure investment and additional manufacturing capacity appear hardest hit, both critical to improving the resilience of countries against external shocks.

Moreover, losses of investment, employment and income incurred during recessions are not fully recovered when the economy turns up, pulling down the longer term average (Akyüz, 2008). The rise of the financial sector has, in many countries, also gone hand in hand with more flexible hiring practices. All this spells considerable income and job insecurity, even under conditions of relatively strong expansion. A clear sign of this has been the failure in the majority of advanced industrial countries for growth of labour compensation to keep pace with labour productivity, but the same trend is apparent in emerging markets as well. Oftentimes, rising levels of income inequality have been the flip side of this development.

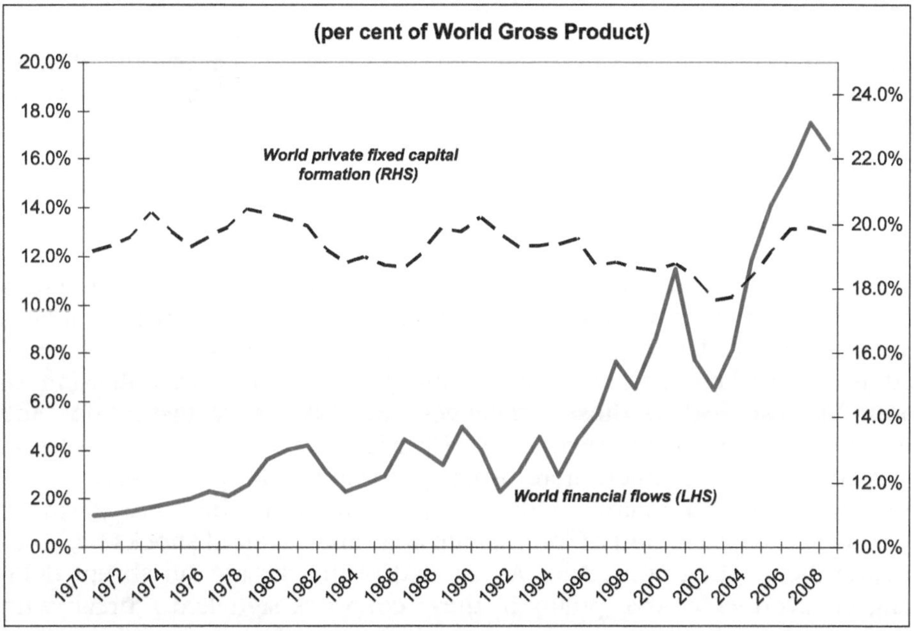


FIGURE 5. A not-so-healthy global investment climate.
*Source*: United Nations Department of Economic and Social Affairs database of World Economic Situation and Prospects (WESP).

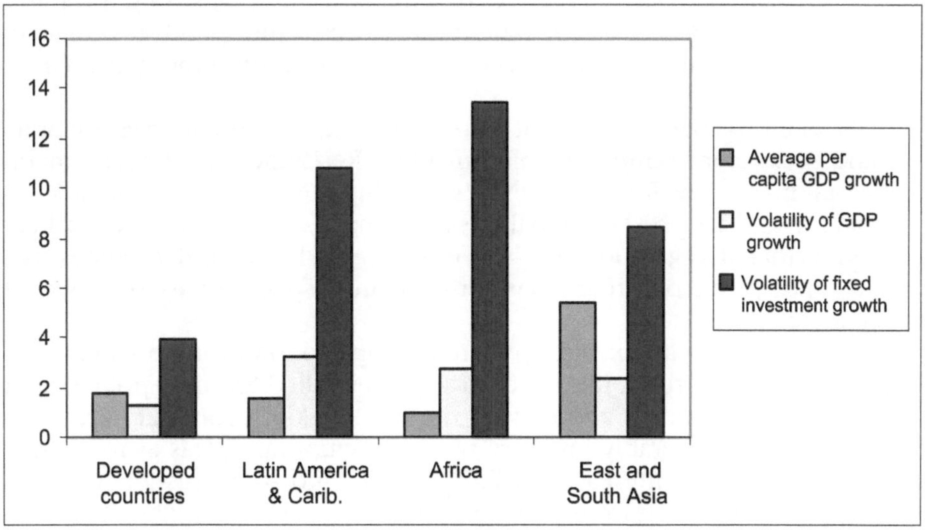


FIGURE 6. Volatility and growth, 1991-2006.
*Note*: Volatility is measure through the standard deviation of output and fixed investment growth, respectively.
*Source*: United Nations (2008b).

## Political economy

No social or economic order is secure if it fails to benefit the majority of those who live under it. This demands nothing less than what European political philosophers in the seventeenth and eighteenth centuries called a 'social contract': an implicit understanding among members of a community to cooperate for mutual benefit, along with formal rules and institutional mechanisms to help build trust, balance competing interests, manage disputes and provide a fair distribution of the rewards that are generated.

No single institutional blueprint prescribes what arrangement works best under particular historical and political circumstances. In the modern era, that contract has been forged around the challenges and risks generated by expanding markets and a more complex industrial division of labour. In response to those challenges and risks, new institutions and mechanisms for managing economic risk and extending social protection emerged, including a much more prominent role for the public sector. This period lasted until the early 1970s, when, beginning in the more advanced economies, a combination of internal tensions and external shocks began to threaten the existing consensus. At the end of the decade, an abrupt tightening of macro-economic policy in these countries signalled a break with past practice, and a willingness to rethink the social contract. Citizenship, cooperation and social protection slipped down the agenda and, in some cases, dropped off altogether; in their place, consumer choice, competition and risk-taking moved to centre-stage. The political checks and balances that had previously determined how markets could best serve the objectives of growth and stability were rolled back, leaving strong property rights, the rule of law and low transaction costs – the 'good governance' agenda – to guarantee the legitimate functioning of the emerging market order.

The trend has been somewhat restrained in advanced countries by practical and social constraints on policy-making. Resistance has proved much weaker in many developing countries, leaving them more vulnerable to downside risks. The present global crisis has made evident to policy-makers worldwide that deregulation and the erosion of checks and balances had gone too far, given rise to reconsidering many aspects of existing global arrangements.

Against the growing backdrop of increasing economic and political insecurity in inter-war Europe, John Maynard Keynes called for 'new policies and new instruments to adapt and control the workings of economic forces, so that they do not intolerably interfere with contemporary ideas as to what is fit and proper in the interests of social stability and social justice' (Keynes 1972 [1933], p. 306). Those words resonate just as strongly today. Responsibility for the choice and mix of policies to guarantee prosperity, stability and justice remains, of course, with national institutions and constituencies; but in an increasingly interdependent world and on a fragile planet, building a more secure home is a truly international endeavour.

## What is to be done?

In today's world of increased economic and political interdependence, achieving a broad-based, rapid and sustained growth in incomes and employment involves even more complex policy challenges than in the past. The complexities of global interdependence in trade and finance are but one dimension of these challenges. A rapidly ageing world population, the catastrophic threat of climate change, continued widespread poverty and social exclusion, as well as raging civil conflicts and wars in many parts of the world, are those putting heavy weight to the challenges ahead. The systemic nature of the present crisis has made overly clear that no benign solutions are likely to be found by relying on market forces. It would be a mistake, however, to let the pendulum swing back to the other extreme and put all our faith in state dirigisme to steer towards optimal solutions. The agenda, rather, should be one of making economic and social security and cohesion the basis for the unleashing of the creative impulses created by market forces, as much as through public–private partnerships. This will require strategic vision and leadership of governments and international organizations to give substance to a new social contract that strikes a balance between achieving greater (global) horizontal equity for present generation prosperity and peace, and intergenerational equity ensuring sustainable development for future (although ageing) world populations and overcoming the threat of climate change. In a world of great uncertainty, it is far from obvious how to strike such a balance, let alone what policies will work best.

The crisis of globalization and the huge global challenges ahead suggest the need for going back to the drawing board. New grand ideas are needed to reshape the global economy and to redefine the regulatory and multilateral frameworks to redraw the rules of the game and allow for a return of checks and balances in the system. Grand ideas may provide a guide, but there is no certainty any of those will work in practice and much experimenting with concrete policies may be needed to find a more sustainable global growth path.

### *A Global New Deal*

Grand schemes easily can end up in wishful thinking and no workable policy action. Yet the challenges of our time ask for big ideas that are global and address the links between core issues. Ahead of the present crisis, the United Nations' *World Economic and Social Survey 2008: Overcoming Economic Insecurity* called for a 'Global New Deal' (United Nations, 2008b). The 2008 food security crisis had led the World Bank to plead for a 'new deal' on global food policy. At the time, the Bank suggested that market forces through further agricultural trade liberalization, more compensatory financing and strengthened social safety nets should strike the right balance between the interests of food importers and exporters. However, this proposal underplayed some of the key elements that comprised President Roosevelt's original New Deal in response to the Great Depression, in particular the mechanisms that were created to expand and better manage markets, along with redistributional measures that aim to better distribute the burden of shocks. Just how far the redistribution agenda can be pushed to rebalance globalization and prevent a potentially damaging backlash is an open debate.

One possible complementary suggestion is to develop universal systems that would provide a minimum basic income in the form of a cash grant to all households. This picks up and extends the idea of a basic pension proposed in United Nations (2007b) and Vos *et al.* (2008) in response to the global population ageing challenge. Such measures are, of course, fraught with complications and difficulties. Yet, this idea has been pushed further in response to the crisis by the International Labour Organization in its proposal for a 'Global Jobs Pact' that sees that a sustainable and equitable recovery requires the pursuance of full-employment and universal social protection objectives (ILO, 2009).

Similarly, UN agencies have proposed a Global Green New Deal (United Nations Environmental Programme, 2009; United Nations Department of Economic and Social Affairs, 2009a) with the objective of pushing the world economy on a green, and thus more sustainable, growth path. Apart from new market incentives for households and businesses worldwide to allocate much more resources in energy efficiency, renewable energy and green products, this foremost will require massive public investment efforts to facilitate a transition towards carbon-free economic growth. Developing countries would need large-scale transfers of resources and access to relevant technologies to be able to both contribute to the greening of global growth and sustain sufficiently high growth rates to respond to the poverty challenge.

Until recently, such grand ideas would seem elusive and unrealistic. World leaders have shown willingness to think out of the box and have included resources for addressing climate change, providing additional social protection and overcoming crises in pension schemes in the massive fiscal stimulus packages for economic recovery. World leaders at the G20 Summit held in April 2009 also recognized the need for large amounts of additional resources needed for developing countries to overcome their immediate liquidity problems caused by the global financial crisis and engage in countercyclical responses that could be aligned with their long-term development needs. Probably, even the promised $1.1 trillion in additional resources will be far from sufficient (United Nations Department of Economic and Social Affairs, 2009b), as much as that it is far from clear how the aforementioned 'new deals' add up to a workable global strategy for sustainable growth. Yet, with further elaboration in more concrete directions, they could provide starting points that could evolve into new national and global social contracts that could live up to the challenges ahead.

### *Back to the multilateral drawing board*

Getting there will also require a return to the multilateral drawing board. The global economic crisis has already triggered a reconsideration of a range of existing multilateral arrangements. As in the crises of the 1930s that led to the Great Depression, the systemic causes of the present crisis are ultimately based on fundamental weaknesses in global economic governance, and overcoming these defects is the only genuine solution. These weaknesses underpin haphazard financial deregulation, the explosion of global imbalances and vulnerabilities, and inequities in balance of payments adjustments inherent to the present international reserve system. Much more fundamental changes are needed to reform the international financial system in order to provide better safeguards that can prevent it happening again, and to create a framework for global economic governance in line with twenty-first-century realities.

This will require a renewed Bretton Woods system for global financial stability. The multilateral arrangements designed at Bretton Woods in 1944 did not include a global regime for capital movements, given that capital mobility was expected to be limited. However, no such regime has emerged even after the breakdown of these arrangements, and despite the surge in private capital flows. In the aftermath of the Asian crisis, various codes and standards were established through international institutions - not just with respect to the financial sector, but also with regard to auditing and accounting, data collection, and so on. None of this helped prevent the present crisis. New rules of the game will need to be established.

A major challenge for the new multilateralism is to help both developed and developing countries, although especially the latter, mitigate the damaging effects of volatile capital flows and commodity prices, and provide counter-cyclical financing mechanisms to compensate for the inherently pro-cyclical movement of private capital flows. A number of options are available to dampen the pro-cyclicality of capital flows, provide counter-cyclical finance, and thus help create a better environment for sustainable growth. A first set of measures would include improved international financial regulation to stem capital flow volatility and provide advice in designing appropriate capital controls, including on a counter-cyclical basis.[3]

As new systems of regulation are being elaborated, immediate financing constraints should be addressed by enhancing available international liquidity and by reconsidering the terms of access to such resources, especially the access for developing countries to compensatory financing mechanisms to cope with external shocks. It is also important to end the tendency to impose pro-cyclical macro-economic conditionality at higher access levels. Improved multilateral surveillance will also need to take on board all possible international spillovers of national economic policies.

None of this will work well, however, if the democratic deficit that is undermining the credibility of the Bretton Woods institutions is repaired. The International Monetary Fund and the World Bank must be comprehensively reformed so that they can more adequately reflect changing economic weights in the world economy and be more responsive to current and future challenges and to strengthen the legitimacy and effectiveness of these institutions. Beyond the rebalancing of voting power in these institutions, it is important to introduce a fundamental revision of their functions and equip them with the necessary resources, such that they can effectively safeguard global financial stability, coordinate macro-economic policies and provide adequate long-term development financing.

Further, a new global reserve system must be created that no longer relies on the US dollar as the single major reserve currency. The dollar has not proven to be a stable store of value, a requisite for a stable reserve currency. Also global instability and deficiencies, the international financial institutions to address this instability have led many developing countries to accumulate a vast amount of reserves on their own. This build-up has contributed to the deflationary pressures to the world economy. A new system needs to be developed that allows for better pooling of reserves at the regional and international levels and that is not based on a single or even multiple national currencies, but which permits the emission of international liquidity (Special Drawing Rights (SDRs) or an equivalent thereof) so as to create a more stable global financial system.

The interest of developing countries in the stability of the international financial system is underpinned by the wish that it allows greater participation in international trade through a full exploitation of their development potential. Despite the general acceptance of the benefits of freer trade, the international division of labour is still heavily influenced by commercial policies that favour products and markets in which more advanced countries have a dominant position and a competitive edge. The recent collapse of the Doha trade talks should provide the breathing space for a much-needed assessment of the rules and norms governing international trade. In particular, high tariffs, tariff escalation, and subsidies in agriculture and fisheries are applied extensively to products that offer the greatest potential for export diversification in developing countries. The panorama of protectionism is no better for industrial products, including footwear, clothing and textiles, where many developing countries have competitive advantages. The trading system is also vulnerable to the increasingly volatile working of the international financial system, reversing the original intentions of the post-war multilateral architects and adversely effecting developing country prospects. A major concern is the destabilizing and deflationary feedbacks among trade and financial flows, which can create impediments to development, including through unstable and misaligned exchange rates and boom-bust cycles that lead to excessive expansion of investment, production and trade in particular sectors, which eventually come to an end with the collapse of the bubble, resulting in sharp declines in trade flows and prices.

Reforming the international financial system should be undertaken with the basic objective of easing the integration of developing countries into the international trading system. The interest of developing countries in the stability of the international financial system is that it allows greater participation in international trade to be combined with the full exploitation of their development potential.

It is also to be expected that the internationalization of production will continue, and that the *outsourcing* of jobs will influence employment outcomes as emerging economies tap deeper into global supply chains in attempts to create additional job opportunities for their workers. Indeed, there are reasons to expect this trend to become even more significant. Consequently, as labour markets become more integrated and ever more dependent on large and more footloose multinational enterprises, there may be a need for a 'more transparent, coherent and balanced framework' at the global level to address the employment dimensions of globalization.[4] Whether or not that materializes, a strategy of lifting all boats (and avoiding beggar-my-neighbour responses) requires a faster pace of investment in the advanced countries, including, in particular, public investment in infrastructure development and for managing the shift to low-carbon technologies consistent with commitments to mitigating the adverse impact of climate change.

Moreover, a more balanced pattern of domestic demand will only be achieved when rising wages (in line with productivity gains) rather than increased levels of debt provide a solid basis for expanding domestic market demand. The challenges ahead will also require economies to continuously increase their skill and knowledge base in order to successfully integrate themselves into the global production process; to ensure that the net effect of globalized production is not simply the displacement of workers; and to uphold core labour standards in order to ensure decent and productive work for all.

Active labour market policies (including skill development) should be strengthened to better prepare workers for the future job market. When temporary dislocation of workers cannot be avoided, appropriate social protection measures can be introduced to provide worker security. In all cases, the benefits that global production can bring should be properly weighted against the costs, and these costs can only be minimized through active involvement of all the major actors.

The responsibility for the choice and mix of policies required to guarantee prosperity, stability and justice, remains, of course, with national institutions and constituencies; but in an increasingly interdependent world and on a fragile planet, building a more secure home is a truly international undertaking.

## Notes

1 Both the International Monetary Fund and the World Bank, while recognizing trends towards rising global inequality, sustained the decoupling hypothesis until shortly before the present crisis (see, for example, International Monetary Fund 2007, 2008; World Bank 2008).

2 For further discussion of these trends, see United Nations (2006b, 2008b), Ocampo *et al.* (2008) and Ocampo and Vos (2008).

3 See United Nations (2005, ch. IV; 2008b, ch. II) and Ocampo and Vos (2008) for an elaboration of the principles for a fundamental reform of financial regulatory frameworks and their international coordination.

4 See discussion in World Commission on the Social Dimension of Globalization (2004).

## References


Akyüz, Yilmaz (2008) 'Financial instability and countercyclical policy', UN-DESA background paper to World Economic and Social Survey 2008, [http://www.un.org/esa/policy/wess/wess2008files/ws08backgroundpapers/akyuz_aug08.pdf], accessed 13 January 2010.

Amsden, Alice (2001) *The Rise of the Rest. Challenges to the West from Late-Industrializing Economies.* Oxford University Press, Oxford.

International Labour Organization (ILO) (2009) *The Financial and Economic Crisis: A Decent Work Response,* ILO, Geneva.

International Monetary Fund (2007) *World Economic Outlook: Spillovers and Cycles in the Global Economy,* April, IMF, Washington, DC.

International Monetary Fund (2008) *World Economic Outlook: Housing and the Business Cycle,* April, IMF, Washington DC.

Keynes, John Maynard [1933] (1972) *The Collected Writings of John Maynard Keynes, Volume X: Essays in Biography,* Macmillan for Royal Economics Society, London.

Milberg, William and Schöller, Deborah (2008) 'Globalization, offshoring and economic insecurity in advanced countries', UN-DESA background paper to World Economic and Social Survey 2008, [http://www.un.org/esa/policy/wess/wess2008files/ws08backgroundpapers/milberg_mar08.pdf], accessed 13 January 2010.

Ocampo, José Antonio and Vos, Rob (2008) *Uneven Economic Development,* Zed Books, London.

Ocampo, José Antonio, Jomo, K.S. and Vos, Rob (Eds) (2008) *Growth Divergences: Explaining Differences in Economic Performance,* Zed Books, London.

United Nations (2005) *World Economic and Social Survey 2005: Financing for Development,* United Nations, New York.

United Nations (2006a) *World Economic Situation and Prospects 2006,* United Nations, New York.

United Nations (2006b) *World Economic and Social Survey 2006: Diverging Growth and Development,* United Nations, New York.

United Nations (2007a) *World Economic Situation and Prospects 2007,* United Nations, New York.

United Nations (2007b) *World Economic and Social Survey 2007: Development in an Ageing World,* United Nations, New York.

United Nations (2008a) *World Economic Situation and Prospects 2008,* United Nations, New York.

United Nations (2008b) *World Economic and Social Survey 2008: Overcoming Economic Insecurity,* United Nations, New York.

United Nations (2009) *World Economic Situation and Prospects 2009,* New York: United Nations.

United Nations Department of Economic and Social Affairs (2009a) 'The global green new deal and sustainable development', *Policy Brief No. 12,* New York, UN-DESA, [http://www.un.org/esa/policy/policybriefs/policybrief12.pdf], accessed 13 January 2010.

United Nations Department of Economic and Social Affairs (2009b) 'The trillion dollar plan', *Policy Brief No. 13,* New York, UN-DESA, [http://www.un.org/esa/policy/policybriefs/policybrief13.pdf].

United Nations Environmental Programme (2009) 'Global green new deal', *Policy Brief,* March, Nairobi, UNEP, [http://www.unep.org/pdf/A_Global_Green_New_Deal_Policy_Brief.pdf], accessed 13 January 2010.

Vos, Rob, Ocampo, José Antonio and Cortez, Ana Luiza (2008) *Ageing and Development,* Zed Books, London.

World Bank (2008) *Global Economic Prospects 2008* The World Bank, Washington, DC.

World Commission on the Social Dimension of Globalization (2004) *A Fair Globalization,* ILO, Geneva.

# Index